GENDER, COLONIALISM AND EDUCATION

Woburn Education Series

General Series Editor: Professor Peter Gordon

ISSN 1462-2076

For over twenty years this series on the history, development and policy of education, under the distinguished editorship of Peter Gordon, has been evolving into a comprehensive and balanced survey of important trends in teaching and educational policy. The series is intended to reflect the changing nature of education in present-day society. The books are divided into four sections – educational policy studies, educational practice, the history of education and social history – and reflect the continuing interest in this area.

For a full series listing, please visit our website: www.woburnpress.com

History of Education

The Victorian School Manager: A Study in the Management of Education 1800–1902
Peter Gordon

Selection for Secondary Education *Peter Gordon*
The Study of Education: Inaugural Lectures
Volume I: Early and Modern   Volume III: The Changing Scene
Volume II: The Last Decade   Volume IV: End of an Era?
edited by Peter Cordon

History of Education: The Making of a Discipline
edited by Peter Cordon and Richard Szreter

Educating the Respectable: A Study of Fleet Road Board School, Hampstead, 1879–1903 *W. E. Marsden*

In History and in Education: Essays Presented to Peter Gordon
edited by Richard Aldrich

An Anglo-Welsh Teaching Dynasty: The Adams Family from the 1840s to the 1930s
W.E. Marsden

Dictionary of British Educationists *Richard Aldrich and Peter Gordon*

Biographical Dictionary of North American and European Educationists
Peter Gordon and Richard Aldrich

The Making of the Backward Pupil in Education in England, 1870–1914
Ian Copeland

Social History

The First Teenagers: The Lifestyle of Young Wage-earners in Interwar Britain
David Fowler

James Kay Shuttleworth: Journey of an Outsider *R. J. W. Selleck*

Targeting Schools: Drill, Militarism and Imperialism *Alan Penn*

The English Higher Grade Schools: A Lost Opportunity *Meriel Vlaeminke*

GENDER, COLONIALISM
AND EDUCATION
The Politics of Experience

edited by

JOYCE GOODMAN and
JANE MARTIN

WOBURN PRESS
LONDON • PORTLAND, OR

First published in 2002 in Great Britain by
FRANK CASS PUBLISHERS
Crown House, 47 Chase Side, Southgate
London N14 5BP

and in the United States of America by
FRANK CASS PUBLISHERS
c/o ISBS, 5824 N.E. Hassalo Street
Portland, Oregon, 97213–3644

Website: www.frankcass.com

Copyright © 2002 J. Goodman and J. Martin

British Library Cataloguing in Publication Data

ISBN 0-7130-0226-3 (cloth)
ISBN 0-7130-4046-7 (paper)
ISSN 1462-2076

Library of Congress Cataloging-in-Publication Data

A catalog record for this book is available from
the Library of Congress

Typeset by FiSH Books, London WC1
Printed in Great Britain by MPG Books Ltd., Bodmin, Cornwall

Contents

Illustrations

10. Raden Ajeng Kartini and her sister Roekmini in their schoolroom in the grounds of the official residence of the Regent of Jepara, June 1903.
    Source: Koninklijk Instituut voor Taal, -Land en Volkenkunde (KITLV), Leiden.
11. Miss Rose Gosling (headmistress 1906–34) and the girls of Bermuda High School.
    Source: Winifred Rogers Collection, Bermuda Archives.
12. The Korana's rock site. This site is still visible around Wentzeldam, and the Korana's rock art paintings can be seen all over the vicinity of Hartz River in Schweizer-Reneke.
    Source: Ziphora Moichela, private collection.

Acknowledgements

The photograph of 'Labour's Most Valuable Asset', published in the *Railway Review*, 16 August 1912, is reproduced with permission from the British Library. The images from the German cigarette cards are reproduced with permission from Geoffrey Giles' (private collection). The two photographs of Raden Anjeng Kartini are reproduced with permission from the Koninklijk Instituut voor Taal, -Land en Volkenkunde (KITLV), Leiden. The photograph of Miss Rose Gosling, Bermuda High School, is reproduced with permission from the Winifred Rogers Collection, Bermuda Archives. Joyce Goodman would particularly like to thank Kate Rousemaniere for alerting her to the photograph of Miss Gosling and for lending her the copy of the photograph she had obtained from Bermuda. She would also like to thank Margaret Hammer for granting access prior to publication of her entry on Annie Whitelaw for the *New Dictionary of National Biography* and Kay Morris Matthews for her enthusiasm, support and shared interest in the two-way traffic of highly educated women between England and Australasia. Jane Martin would particularly like to thank Jenifer Bridges-Adams and Christine Coates, librarian TUC Collections, for their help and encouragement with the on-going biographical project on Mary Bridges Adams.

Contributors

Nelleke Bakker teaches History of Education at the University of Gröningen, the Netherlands. Her main research interests are the history of childhood, of gender and education and of educational science in the Netherlands. She has published books and articles.

Joost Coté teaches Asian Studies and History at Deakin University, Melbourne, Australia. He writes on modernity and nationalism in the context of colonialism in South-east Asia. He has previously translated and edited two editions of the letters of Raden Ajeng Kartini.

Geoffrey Giles is a German historian, teaching at the University of Florida. During the academic year 2000–2001, he served as the Shapiro Senior Scholar-in-Residence at the United States Holocaust Memorial Museum, working on a manuscript about the persecution of homosexuals by the Nazis.

Joyce Goodman is Reader in History of Education at King Alfred's College, Winchester, where she co-ordinates research in the School of Education. She has recently published *Women, Educational Policy-Making and Administration in England: Authoritative Women since 1800*. She is co-director of a research project funded by the Spencer Foundation (USA) investigating Women and the Governance of Girls' Secondary Schools 1870–1997.

David Limond lectures in the Faculty of Education at Herefordshire College of Technology. He has published work on a variety of topics, including the influence of A. S. Neill on Scottish education, society and culture; teachers as conscientious objectors in the Second World War; and the relationship(s) between education and religion.

Jane Martin is a senior lecturer in Education Studies at the University of North London. She has published *Women and the Politics of Schooling in*

Victorian and Edwardian England (1999) and is presently writing a co-authored book on *Women and Education 1800–1980: Educational Reform and Personal Identities* (with Joyce Goodman).

Mark McBeth is the Director of the Writing Centre at the City College of New York, where he also teaches both undergraduate and graduate composition and rhetoric courses. He has recently been awarded his PhD, researching issues surrounding both British and American pedagogy. His published work includes articles about classroom practice, composition theory, queer theory and gay linguistics.

Ziphora Moichela is Professional Research Officer in the Office of the Dean of Research and Postgraduate Studies at Vista University, South Africa. She is currently engaged on a research project at Mamelodi Campus concerned with mentoring for women in research. Previously she lectured at Sebokeng Campus on educational philosophy, educational management, historical research methodology and special educational needs.

Christine Myers graduated with her PhD in History from the University of Strathclyde in 2000. Her thesis, entitled ' "Give her the apple and see what comes of it": University Co-education in Britain and America, c.1860–1940', traces the entrance of women into male higher education institutions, and focuses on the universities of Glasgow and Wisconsin. She is currently visiting lecturer at the University of Wisconsin-Whitewater.

Preface

The title chosen by the Editors, *Gender, Colonialism and Education: The Politics of Experience*, well illustrates the scope of this important book. As Joyce Goodman and Jane Martin point out, in recent years research has given us a better understanding of men's and women's lives as educators and the gendered, racialised and political nature of educational change. In the past, great attention was paid in the history of education to Western white women, just as historians of masculinities drew heavily on examples from the public school to make their points. The effects of colonial education on, for example, the formation of identity and the subsequent development of educational provision, are examined through case studies in the book.

Four aspects of the contributions are particularly valuable. First, the topics covered in these essays range widely: from studies of the National Association of Schoolmasters, the Workers' Educational Association movement and colonial pedagogy, to American women's university life in the nineteenth century, all of which have been chosen to illustrate the relationship between education and gender issues. Second, the various authors are able to draw on their close knowledge of a number of different countries, such as England, Scotland Germany, Indonesia, South Africa, the United States of America and the Netherlands, thus providing an international perspective. Third, the contributors make use of a wealth of sources, many of them hitherto little used. Finally, the several chapters show how ideals of manliness and femininity are located in informal contexts as well as formal ones. Some essays focus, for example, on the home or social aspects of public school life. On the other hand, a number of essays demonstrate the importance of establishing institutions organised and led by women to parallel male-dominated ones.

The Editors express the hope that this volume will contribute towards a revision of the history of education, which is beginning to integrate gender into its conceptual frameworks. I consider that this stimulating and thought-provoking book succeeds in this aim as well as providing a useful map for future researchers.

Professor Peter Gordon
Institute of Education
University of London

Foreword

This book is timely. For the past decade, glimpses of gender analysis within history of education have increasingly featured at national and international educational conferences. Within this genre, a new, exciting strand of ideas have emerged, ideas that go beyond mere addition of gender to traditional scholarship, but as applied to a range of issues central to an historical understanding of education within and between nations.

I write this two days after the acts of terrorism unleashed upon the United States (11 September 2001). As I watch the aftermath unfold it seems that while globalization in the economic and political sense is a reality that cannot be ignored, so too is the growing appreciation that people from across nations need to listen more to one another, to move from what are sometimes parochial positions to a space where exchanges of those positions are valued. This is the place from where cross-cultural and cross-national perspectives can be compared and contrasted. In so doing, surprise is often expressed as the realization dawns that educational experiences have many shared antecedents; that the various 'sites' of educational activity, both formal and informal, have impacted upon the real lives as lived by citizens, and particularly upon the choices women and men have made which affect the rest of their adult lives.

However, until now, there has been no collection that contributes in the way this one does to an international examination of the intersections of gender with a range of issues within education. Here are key works from ten authors covering seven countries, with challenges to traditional ways of thinking about history of education; not merely a looking back into the past but a raising of key issues central to current debates about education and gender equity.

Dr Kay Morris Matthews
Director, Women's Studies Academic Programme
Victoria University of Wellington

1

Introduction: 'Colonialism', 'Gender', 'Politics' and 'Experience': Challenging and Troubling Histories of Education

JOYCE GOODMAN AND JANE MARTIN

This collection grew out of a shared enterprise generated at the annual conference of the History of Education Society in 1999. The choice of *Breaking Boundaries: Gender, Politics and the Experience of Education* as conference title reflected current interest in questions of borders and boundaries. Much discussion of boundaries, borders and border crossings is occurring within post-colonial theory, particularly in relation to notions of diaspora and transnational methodologies. But questioning the permeability of boundaries has a longer genealogy. It stretches back to the feminist slogan of the 'personal is the political'[1] as well as forward to newer scholarship demonstrating ways in which gender boundaries around the public and private have historically been more variable than prescriptive literature suggests.[2] Postmodern approaches to knowledge and identity have also been premised upon the dissolution of binary categorisation and a recognition of the complexity and intertwining of multiple rather than unitary selves.[3]

Avtar Brah[4] and Gloria Anzaldua[5] demonstrate ways in which borders act as powerful metaphors for psychological, sexual, spiritual, cultural, class and racialised boundaries. According to Brah the concept of 'border' relates simultaneously to social relations and to subjectivity/identity. Brah defines borders as:

> Arbitrary dividing lines that are simultaneously social, cultural and psychic; territories to be patrolled against those whom they construct as outsiders, aliens, the Others; forms of demarcation where the very act of prohibition inscribes transgression; zones where fear of the Other is the fear of the self; places where claims to ownership – claims to 'mine', 'yours' and 'theirs' – are staked out, contested, defended and fought over.[6]

Brah notes that the metaphoric nature of borders calls attention to 'the geographical and/or psychic territories demarcated' as well as to 'the experience of those affected by the creation of border zones'. She argues that metaphors act as powerful inscriptions of political borders. Brah asks, 'How is a border regulated or policed? Who is kept out and why? What are the realities for those seen as undesirable border crossers?'

Brah's questions pose a challenge for historians of education; for education has served historically to regulate and police boundaries on the basis of class, gender, sexuality, age, dis/ability, 'race' and ethnicity.[7] Equally challenging is the implicit assumption of the conference title *Breaking Boundaries*: that borders can be contested and traversed, that boundaries can be broken, that change can and does occur. Approaches based on borders and boundaries move accounts away from linear narratives and away from the grand narratives of education's past. As Liz Stanley notes, in the 'borderlands' difference is often expressed neither as separation nor as silence, but as an interface in which some voices resound more than others:

> This interface is a frontier that sees the coming and going of peoples, the speaking and silencing of voices, the casting of gazes which look but do not necessarily see. Around this frontier are gathered the differences of 'race', ethnicity, sexuality, gender, class, age, dis/ability, and more: and it is this frontier which constitutes the cultural space in which 'difference' becomes the point at which fundamental epistemological disputes surface around seismic linguistic and ideational shifts. The frontier thereby provides 'the space between' for debate, contention and disagreement.[8]

Challenging traditional views often entails challenging the borders encircling disciplines themselves, which makes exploring the 'territory in between', 'the space of liminality' itself a borderland pursuit.[9] Sometimes it entails engaging with traditional 'stories' through traditional methods of the disciplines themselves. Some of the ways in which historians of education are developing analytical and methodological approaches informed by the challenges posed by notions of borders and boundaries are illustrated by the conference papers on women and education published in the special edition of *History of Education*.[10] This book continues and extends that debate.

The title of the book itself poses a challenge. 'Gender', 'colonialism', 'politics' and 'experience' are all highly contested terms. Each has its own

2

theoretical terrain and each its own history, troubled by and giving trouble to the others. Coming into use in the 1960s, the term gender was initially used to denote social and cultural aspects of analysis, in contrast to biological essentialism.[11] In this it drew on a tradition reaching back to Mary Wollstonecraft and beyond. Under the influence of Foucauldian scholarship, the meanings ascribed to the sex/gender distinction were historicised by writers like Joan Scott and Denise Riley,[12] while others, like Gayle Rubin, pointed to ways in which each society constructs its own sex/gender system.[13] Both sex and gender, argue David Glover and Cora Kaplan, are cultural categories, which refer to ways of writing about and understanding bodies and relationships, to ourselves and to others. Yet, as the title of Judith Butler's highly influential book *Gender Trouble* epitomises, this is far from straightforward.[14] For many the new millennium is a time of change, social transformation and uncertainty and profound personal disruption. Arguably what it means to be a man or woman has never been less distinct nor more fluid.[15] Glover and Kaplan caution against 'seizing too quickly upon a summary definition [of gender], seeking order and clarity where none is to be had'; for in their view 'gender' is:

> Now one of the busiest, most restless terms in the English language, a word that crops up everywhere, yet whose uses seem to be forever changing, always on the move, producing new and often surprising inflections of meaning...a much contested concept, as slippery as it is indispensable, but a site of unease rather than of agreement.[16]

The most recent troubling for gender has come from queer theory, with its aim of queering (in the sense of unsettling) assumptions and preconceptions about sexuality and gender and their relationships, particularly around notions of desire.[17] Developing out of a lesbian and gay re-working of the post-structuralist figuring of identity, queer theory challenges the notion of fixed identities, whether heterosexual or homosexual. 'Queer' is less an identity than a *critique* of identity itself.[18] Gender in this view is performative: what you do at particular times, rather than who you are - 'not a question of whether to *do* a gender performance but what form that performance will take'.[19] In Butler's terms, gender is 'performatively constituted by the very expressions that are said to be its results'.[20] Nevertheless, as Valerie Walkerdine argues, individuals do not take up *any* position in any discourse. Rather, 'the positions available to them exist *only* within certain limits'. According to

Walkerdine, these limits are material, though not 'directly *caused* by the materiality of the...body, but certainly by the limits within which that body can signify in current discursive practices'. In this sense it is not possible to take up an identity or position at will. For Walkerdine, this means that the contradictions and shifting relations of power necessitate the understanding of subjectivities, not a unique subjectivity.[21] Walkerdine's view also points to the situated nature of knowledge production; for as Kathleen Weiler argues, subjectivity and experience are closely inter-related with language and knowledge production:

> By knowledge, I refer to the debate about universal versus particular truth claims and the nature of historical evidence, the question of what exactly are our sources of understanding the past; by language the question of discourse and its relationship to experience as the source of our knowledge of the past; and by subjectivity, the question of essence and identity.[22]

By undermining the notion of a coherent identity, performative views of gender of necessity trouble the category of 'experience'. 'Experience' has played a key role in hermeneutics, particularly from Dilthey onwards.[23] In feminist writings, accounts of women's experience have been used to proclaim 'a relation, however, complex...between sociality and subjectivity, between language and consciousness, or between institutions and individuals'.[24] Kelly, Burton and Regan noted of some early feminist appropriations of 'experience':

> Whilst personal experience undoubtedly influences one's perspective and understanding, many current references to it are determinist and essentialist. Experience/identity is substituted for, or deemed to be equivalent to, politics, as if critical awareness and understanding are inscribed on a person through forms of oppression, with an implicit or explicit presumption that such awareness is inaccessible to those who have not 'lived' such experiences.[25]

One alternative is to retain the significance of experience but focus attention towards those instances when we recognise our place in the world. We may well recognise that what we call 'me' or 'I' differs in changing situations – and from day to day. Indeed, it is a sense of ourselves as constantly changing that Brah says is precisely what we see as concrete about ourselves – and which she terms a 'changing illusion'.[26]

From this perspective, rather than there being a fully constituted 'experiencing subject' to whom 'experiences happen', experience is the site of subject formation.[27] In Joan Scott's formulation: 'experience is at once always already an interpretation *and* is in need of interpretation'.[28] Penny Summerfield's *Reconstructing Womens' Wartime Lives* demonstrates just how fruitful an approach based on narrative analysis of the construction of subjectivity/identity can prove.[29]

Issues of subjectivity and the fluidity and 'fixing' of identities point to other ways in which new understandings of 'politics' are being developed. 'The established canons of political history have concentrated on political parties and the realm of the state. This has been exclusionary, both in terms of theory and practice. Developing new ways through which politics can be understood within civil society and alternative political structures often reverses common assumptions. This has been particularly evident in more recent scholarship on women's political action.[30] Rather than assuming that women exerted little political influence, newer scholarship looks closely at those places where women were (and are) most influential. It also explores polarities such as 'public' and 'private', patriarchy and matriarchy, sameness and 'difference', power and marginality. It is demonstrating that both individually and in their organisations, women from different social groups have used to advantage the territory in which they found themselves. Exclusion from national power structures produced imaginative responses as some dominant discources – like 'spiritual motherhood' or 'social maternalism' – were re-interpreted and reclaimed to provide a critical pathway into the political system, illustrating ways in which women *were* and still are active in their local communities, despite their absence from leadership positions. A gendered approach highlights the concentration of women on social and welfare issues as well as the enduring efficacy of their methods – grass-roots organisations and effective ways of networking – that introduced new and imaginative accounts of political activism. Yet, accounts of educational policy-making and administration based on state activity have often devalued and written out of politics many of women's educational activities, as well as the educational activities of marginalised groups.[31]

Approaches based on notions of the 'personal as the political', encompassing both public and private identities, have been seen as more able to capture women's political activity.[32] Identity politics, based on views of shared experience (and interests), have formed a central concern of both feminists and members of the men's movement, aiming to give a collective voice to women's/men's personal experiences of the constitution of being fe/male.[33] Performative views of gender, however, have undermined the notion of a coherent identity, in the process simultaneously providing a critique of the notion of politics and dissolving the basis on which forms of political action based on identity politics have stood. Identity politics has also been critiqued by black writers, who have pointed to the tendency for multiple oppressions within identity politics to be viewed as separate elements, added in a linear fashion. They have argued that the specificities of particular oppressions needed identifying and their interconnections with other oppressions understood as a way of building a politics of solidarity.[34]

Current post-colonial debate calling for attention to hybridity[35] and diaspora,[36] has widened this remit with the more recent deployment of transnational, rather than comparative, methodologies.[37] Historical relations between colony and metropole are no longer being viewed in terms of simple transmission from metropole to colony.[38] In the place of a series of discreet nation-states and colonies, 'empire is coming to be seen more as a framework structuring exchanges between metropole and colonies in a web of interactions that include relationships between colonies as well as so-called 'centre' and 'periphery'.[39] In this transnational revisioning,[40] spatial analyses of encounters have played an important role: for example, Gilroy's Black Atlantis,[41] Bhabha's 'third space',[42] Brah's 'diaspora space',[43] and Pratt's 'contact zones'.[44]

Some of the ways in which historians of education have engaged in these debates are reflected in this book, concerned as it is with political activism and the concept of 'experience' itself. In recent years, a growing body of research has both broadened our understanding of men's and women's lives as educators and the gendered, racialised and political nature of educational change. Female actors, coming in from the margins, are challenging the uneven recollection that constitutes the gendered dimension of traditional historical representation and cultural transmission. Historians of women's education are taking up the challenge posed by Mary Maynard and June Purvis in *New Frontiers in Women's Studies* to place Western women 'under analytical scrutiny' as they interacted in the past from a privileged position of 'whiteness' (and continue to interact in the present) with their non-Western counterparts.[45] Non-Western writers are providing counter-narratives of colonial education, pointing to the ambivalences of identity that colonial education engendered,[46] analysing ways in which they actively 'took' from colonial education, accommodated its demands and developed their own forms of educational provision.[47] Historians of masculinities are drawing attention to the central role of education – and particularly the public school – in the construction of gendered and sexualised identities in the education of men.[48] Historians are increasingly pointing to the homosocial and woman-centred cultures of schooling, alongside schooling's heterosexual imperative.[49] A variety of methodologies are being employed, from textual analysis, autobiography,[50] prosopography (collective biography)[51] and testimonial writing,[52] to more quantitative methods.[53] As a site of unease rather than of agreement, the troubling of gender within the history of education is proving highly productive.

The chapters in this book have been chosen to illustrate relations between education and masculinities as well as femininities and the ways in which postmodern, post-colonial, and feminist methodologies, and analysis within more traditional approaches to the history of education, all contain the potential to illuminate intersections of gender and education in a variety of ways. The book aims to illustrate how new ways of seeing, engaging with issues of identities, diversity and difference, might begin to re-narrate or nuance the history/histories of education. The volume explores the operation of gender in a variety of issues, sites of educational activity and countries. The issues explored include: citizenship; authority; colonialism and education; linkages between rationality and affect, desire and pedagogy; the construction of national identities; and the traversing of 'public' and 'private' identities by parents, educational reformers and teachers. The sites of educational activity cover informal education as well as more formal schooling, the educative activities of women's and labour organisations as well as issues of parenting in the home. The countries covered encompass different continents and include England, Scotland, Germany, Indonesia, South Africa, USA and the Netherlands. The diversity of approaches, issues and contexts form part of a project to illustrate the complexity of the intersection of gender with a range of issues that are central to our historical understanding of education. At the same time, a number of the key concerns, including citizenship, colonialism, identity and sexuality, go beyond the particular project itself and provide insights into the more general operation of gender in modern, modernising and postmodern societies.

The book is organised in three sections: 'Schooling Masculinities and Sexualities'; 'Gender, Politics and the Experience of Education'; and 'Gender, Colonialism and the Experience of Education'. The first section, 'Schooling Masculinities and Sexualities', illustrates some of the ways in which aspects of manliness, sexualised and gendered identities are constructed, represented and performed: through textbooks for parents, within the Cambridge colleges and informally through the collection of cigarette cards. The second section, 'Gender, Politics and the Experience of Education' examines issues that have traditionally been considered more overtly political: the rhetoric of the National Association of Schoolmasters, the activities of a female educator activist, and civic education on an early twentieth-century American university campus. Here, issues of class intersect with those of political action to demonstrate the highly gendered nature of (white) political identities and discourses. The last section, 'Gender, Colonialism and the Experience of Education', considers the relations between gender, identities and education in the political context of empire and colony. Transnational networks of highly educated women teachers, the complexity of gender differentiated, modern, 'native' elite identities and the re-working of colonial discourse in testimonial writing and history teaching are explored.

'Schooling Masculinities and Sexualities' opens with Nelleke Bakker's analysis of the shifts in the ways parenting roles in the Netherlands have been conceived and the consequences of religious beliefs for constructions of the fatherly role. Bakker uses child-rearing manuals and parents' magazines to clarify the relationship between gendered ideals of parenthood, religion, and educational styles. Mid-nineteenth-century Dutch child-rearing manuals addressed liberal Protestant bourgeois women as the best possible educators of the next generation of enlightened citizens of the nation. Half a century later the printed advice material – like its readership – had not only grown, but was differentiated according to religion as well. Family advice manuals were addressing either liberal Protestant, or orthodox Calvinist, or Roman Catholic middle-class parents. Moreover, these manuals were no longer directed at mothers only. The future of each of the new denominational sub-cultures within Dutch society depended just as much upon the performance of fathers. At least this is what family advisors wanted parents to believe. Bakker explores the role that Calvinism and Protestantism played in the dynamics of gendered expectations of parenthood. She asks whether orthodox Calvinism, which went through a revival at the end of the nineteenth century, was the main force behind a revaluation of the role of the father. Did orthodox Calvinists promote the strict educational style with which Calvinism is usually associated? If so, did Calvinists think women were too weak to take the lead in a modern version of biblical education? Did their liberal Protestant counterparts defend a gentler approach to the child as a woman's prerogative, as was the case with reformists and feminists in some European countries? And did they consider family upbringing a collective enterprise?

Mark McBeth's chapter moves to elite nineteenth-century English public school education. Shifts in economic markets and labour forces formed the background to the increasing entry of women, members of the working class, and colonial peoples into what was traditionally a wealthy Caucasian male educational world. Some educators thought that these new students would need to adapt to the established educational system, others thought they had no place in that system, while still others realised that the system itself would need to adjust. McBeth's study of Oscar Browning and William Johnson Cory demonstrates how these two men strove to create a more inclusive educational sphere at a point when education was reserved for the elite few, namely, white, wealthy males. Their educational activity occurred during the same periods as the Oscar Wilde trials, the medicalisation of sexuality, a heated dialogue about schooling and sexual activity, and an ongoing discourse of Hellenistic ideals in Victorian education. While working with students, the sexual practices of both men came under scrutiny. McBeth brings queer theory to examine the late nineteenth- and early twentieth-century context in which these men taught, and to speculate upon how their pedagogical practices and goals relate to their desires for people to learn. He argues that their particular stories exhibit a complex dynamic of education and desire, demonstrating moments when desire to learn interlinked with sexual desire. Although sexuality, desire, learning and pedagogy have been recognised as important factors of teaching since the dialogues of Plato, these men's historical moment offers a complex dynamic that perhaps affected educational ideals thereafter.

Geoffrey Giles' chapter moves to Germany and focuses on the period from the mid-nineteenth century to the Second World War. Giles illustrates the subtle messages of manliness transmitted through the sets of cigarette cards collected by millions of German families during this period. The value of sets of cigarette cards as a propaganda tool was realised by the National Socialists early on, though there is no evidence of direct Party intervention in the authorship of most sets. In exploring the broad concept of manliness used at the time, Giles examines several specific themes. Some historical sets looked back to the medieval period and emphasised knightly virtues. Related to this, and more common, were the many sets on military themes, particularly on the life of the soldier or sailor, which demonstrated particular manly virtues. Albums on Hindenburg held up the President as a model, highlighting his military career. Another important area was the political world of the Nazi Party. Sets celebrated as heroes those wounded in the course of Party activities (typically in fights with Communists), with politics deliberately cast in metaphors about battles and struggles. There were also parallels in the political sets of cigarette cards issued in communist East Germany in the

1950s. Giles concludes that though collecting cigarette cards was an informal hobby, the cards had as great an impact as school textbooks and Party handbooks, if not greater.

The chapter on the English National Association of Schoolmasters (NAS) by David Limond, which opens the second section, 'Gender, Politics and the Experience of Education', picks up on themes apparent in Geoffrey Giles' analysis of National Socialist conceptions of manliness. Limond explores the social, personal and ideological imperatives of the lives of quasi-fascistic NAS members from 1919–39, a period during which, he argues, the NAS 'enjoyed' a reputation amongst feminist women teachers and their pro-feminist male colleagues for mean-minded obstructionism and selfishness. As Limond notes, at its inception the NAS recruited from amongst returning service men, many of whom contributed to its journal the *New Schoolmaster* and drew on militaristic imagery to make their points. Limond argues that in its composition, the NAS brought together representatives of a long-standing strain of muscular socialism, combined these with a masculinist rhetoric influenced by military experiences (closely comparable to Mussolini's *Trincerocrasts* [Trenchocracy] and leavened this with professional (economic) and personal (intellectual) bitterness on the part of many members. In this it exhibited what might be called quasi-fascistic potential.

Active in the same period but with a very different agenda was the Welsh-born educator activist M Bridges Adams (1855–1939), profiled by Jane Martin. Bridges Adams was at the forefront of the struggle for democratic education in early twentieth-century Britain. She promoted the cause of class conscious education with a Marxist emphasis, in opposition to the liberal humanist provision of adult education sponsored by Albert Mansbridge and his supporters in the Workers' Educational Association (established in 1903). Martin traces Bridges Adams' early life and her career as an elected representative on the London School Board from 1897–1904, looks at her vision of education directed towards social change and then examines her involvement in the workers' education movement. This movement for independent working-class education emerged from the strike of militant worker-students at Ruskin Hall (later Ruskin College), Oxford, in 1908–9 as the result of curricular and disciplinary disputes. Underpinning the conflict was the question of the nature of the links with Oxford University – whether they should be closer or whether to establish a new educational structure definitely controlled by organised Labour. Bridges Adams contributed to this agitation through her propaganda, as a speaker and journalist. She was also heavily involved in the establishment of a Working Women's College and in agitation for the release of John Maclean, the best-known and most successful of the Marxist educationists.

Christine Myers shifts the focus to civic education at twentieth-century American state universities. At this point American state universities often felt a responsibility for producing well-rounded citizens of the nation, as well as providing a traditional education. At Wisconsin, the particular connection to the leader of the Progressive Party, Senator Robert LaFollette (who was himself a graduate of the institution) made the commitment to such a philosophy more impassioned than in other areas of the country. Myers uses the records of the Women's Self-Government Association, established in 1898 and still in existence in the 1950s, to trace the involvement of women in the civic component of higher education, which developed into a school of progressive thought known as the the 'Wisconsin Idea'. The philosophy of the 'Wisconsin Idea' was that the borders of the campus were not fixed and that the work of the institution should embrace the people of the city and state as well. In the 'Wisconsin Idea', not only were requirements placed on the women by the university to learn how to act as responsible members of society but also women students established their own standards of conduct in governing themselves and in interacting with their male counterparts as they made their way into larger society.

Joyce Goodman opens the final section, 'Gender, Colonialism and the Experience of Education', by exploring the links between diaspora, empire, gender, professional identities and professionalisation, demonstrated by the two-way traffic of highly educated women between England and the British colonies and dominions during the early twentieth century. Highly educated, highly mobile white women (head)teachers returning to teach in Britain were able to capitalise on their work in schools overseas, which was thought to provide them with a broad and searching experience of teaching. The Association of Headmistresses (AHM) developed formal links with imperial organisations and particularly with the Colonial Intelligence League, an emigration organisation for educated women which included six representatives of the AHM on the executive. Goodman explores the power relationships of the links forged by the AHM with headmistresses in Australia, New Zealand, Bermuda, Jamaica, Egypt, South Africa, India and China, as well as the opportunities for enhancing professional identities, which such relationships afforded. These links enabled the AHM to meet a demand from overseas associates for mistresses educated in England to be sent to overseas schools. They also fostered a two-way exchange of women teachers and headteachers between Britain and abroad. At a point when international questions about education were important, and educational travel was becoming increasingly common for women teachers and headmistresses, this two-way exchange impacted from periphery to metropole to the benefit of the professional identities of British headmistresses in England.

Joost Coté moves discussion to the early twentieth-century Dutch colony of Java. Coté draws on the extensive correspondence of Raden Ajeng Kartini, the Western-educated daughter of a Javanese aristocrat. Her correspondence provides the historian of colonial education with an extensive reflection on the nature of the colonial education experience. As well as illuminating aspects of colonial educational experience, it also shows how such education could be appropriated for counter-colonialist ends. Moreover, an examination of Kartini's own educational experience makes clear the objectives of Dutch colonial education to fashion a compliant and differentiated – and gendered – modern native elite. Coté asks, How did the colonial and nationalist political constructions of gender affect the educational experience on offer to Indonesian women and how do we distinguish Kartini's own educational and nationalist message to Indonesian women both historically and as a relevant contemporary document?

The final chapter from Ziphora Moichela is an example of testimonial writing.[54] Moichela illustrates the pedagogical implications of stories told by semi-rural women of Maamuse/Schweizer-Reneke and of her own story as an educational research and professional development colleague in South Africa. The life stories of the women of Maamuse/Schweizer-Reneke and her own account of her work with South African History teachers emerge as powerful tools to empower researchers, teachers, academics and students in harnessing oral testimonies as alternative sources of historical information. One of Moichela's aims is to correct perceptions of story-telling women as trivial. She sees women's stories serving as correctives to current epistemologies of History, particularly in schools in South Africa. She demonstrates how such historical sources can be used to redress the imbalances with regard to misrepresentations and distortions of apartheid history taught in South African schools. Moichela argues that such stories can also free students from the tyranny of written documents that are also regarded as the only legitimate sources of knowledge. The use of oral testimonies as alternatives can equip the learners with research skills that will enable them to reconstruct new versions of the past.

Several of the chapters can be seen as projects of recovery. The mother has tended to be the focus of scholarship on child-rearing literature, but Bakker highlights the role of fathers. By comparison to its arch-rival, the feminist National Union of Women Teachers, the NAS has received fairly limited attention from historians, as Limond notes. Martin's chapter is a project of recovery of women's involvement within left labour politics, but also one which shifts our understanding of the left and educational politics itself. Myers is part of a broader trend which is beginning to recognise the importance of social activity in the constitution of women's political identities. Goodman and Coté highlight the role of women within a project of empire that has, until more recently, been portrayed as a masculinist enterprise. Moichela demonstrates the importance of women's hitherto uncharted stories to the project of post-colonial histories.

Several chapters show how informal contexts were key sites in which ideals of manliness and femininity were constructed and in which desire operated and was regulated. Bakker, Giles and Coté focus on the home, McBeth on the informal sociable spaces of the otherwise spartan boys' public schools. Bakker and McBeth illustrate how the construction of gendered identities related to other powerful regulatory discourses in society; particularly those of religion, home and politics. When, as McBeth demonstrates, boundaries were thought to be overstepped, the regulatory mechanisms became more overt. As Limond demonstrates, institution-building has been a key form of advancement for men, enabling them to argue and organise to maintain entrenched privilege. Myers' and Goodman's focus on female organised and led institutions, upholds Linda Eisenmann's contention that institution-building also proved a key means through which women educator activists not only provided education to women (through both informal and formal means) but also supported women's career needs.[48]

The collection illustrates just how diverse gendered ideals and identities have been, how they have shifted over time and how they have been crossed by class and ethnicities. Martin demonstrates the commitment of Bridges Adams to education for the working class, while Goodman's highly educated women were firmly middle-class. McBeth shows the complexities of sexualised identities. Coté demonstrates the simultaneous construction of the self within competing discourses of nation and colony, while Goodman points to the contradiction of white settler identities, simultaneously colonised and coloniser. Both Coté, Goodman and Moichela illustrate the possibilities that such contradictions engendered for education, for politics broadly conceived and for experience.

The book shows the diverse ways in which education has often played a central role in demarcating social, cultural and psychic borders. These have historically constructed social relations and subjectivities/identities that are not only gendered but also simultaneously psychological, sexual, classed and

13

racialised. The chapters also demonstrate how through education, the boundaries that have been constructed and the subjectivities/identities that have been constituted have also been subject to contestation and change in 'the territory in between'. The chapters illustrate the challenges for historians of education in elucidating and unravelling the degree to which the overall development of education has been a gendered process. We hope that this volume will contribute to a revision of history of education, which is learning to integrate gender into its conceptual frameworks.[55] As the contributors to this book illustrate, this is not just a question of academic interest. Rather, it is a political project in itself.

ENDNOTES

1. See G. Weiner, *Feminisms and Education* (Milton Keynes: Open University Press).
2. A. Vickery, 'Golden age to separate spheres: a review of the categories and chronology of English women's history,' *Historical Journal*, 36, 2, pp. 384–414.
3. B. Smart, *Postmodernity* (London: Routledge).
4. A. Brah, *Cartographies of Diaspora: Contesting Identities* (London: Routledge) p. 198.
5. G. Anzaldua, *Borderlands/L Frontera: the New Mestiza* (San Fransciso: Spinsters/Aunt Lute).
6. Brah, *Cartographies*, p. 198.
7. M. Hickman, *Religion, Class and Identity: the State, the Catholic Church and the Education of the Irish in Britain* (Aldershot: Avebury); M. Hickman, 'Constructing the nation, segregating the Irish: the education of Irish Catholics in nineteenth century Britain', *Aspects of Education*, 54 , pp. 33–54; J. Goodman, 'Undermining or Building up the Nation? Elizabeth Hamilton (1758–1816), national identities and an authoritative role for women educationists', in G. McCulloch and R. Lowe (eds), *Education and National Identity, History of Education, Special Edition*, 28, 3, pp. 279–97; S. Humphries and P. Gordon, *Forbidden Britain: Our Secret Past 1900–1960* (London: BBC Books); H. Hendrick, *Images of Youth: Age, Class and the Male Youth Problem, 1880–1920* (Oxford: Clarendon); L. Mahood, *Policing Gender, Class and Family: Britain 1850–1940* (London: UCL Press); L. A. Jackson, *Child Sexual Abuse in Victorian England* (London: Routledge).
8. L. Stanley, 'Introduction: on academic borders, territories, tribes and knowledges', in L. Stanley (ed.), *Knowing Feminisms* (London: Sage).
9. L. Abrams and K. Hunt, 'Borders and frontiers in women's history', *Women's History Review*, 9, 2, pp. 191–200.

10. J. Goodman and J. Martin (eds), *Breaking Boundaries: Gender, Politics and the Experience of Education, History of Education, Special Edition*, 29, 5. The dialogue engendered by the special edition continued at the 2000 annual conference, *Reforming Lives? Progressivism, Leadership and Educational Change*. Linda Eisenmann's opening plenary, 'Reflections of an historical lexicographer: lives, leadership and educational change for American women', responded to issues raised by the editorial, *History of Education* 30, 5, (2001), pp. 385–8.
11. D. Glover and C. Kaplan, *Genders* (London: Routledge), p. xix.
12. J. W. Scott, *Gender and the Politics of History* (New York: Columbia University Press); D. Riley, *Am I That Name? Feminism and the Category of 'Women' in History* (London: Macmillan).
13. G. Rubin, 'The traffic in women: notes on the "political economy" of sex', in R. R. Reiter (ed.), *Towards an Anthropology of Women* (New York: Monthly Review Press); G. Rubin, 'Thinking sex: notes for a radical theory of the politics of sexuality', in H. Abelove, M. A. Barale and D. Halperin (eds), *The Lesbian and Gay Studies Reader* (New York: Routledge).
14. J. Butler, *Gender Trouble: Feminism and the Subversion of Identity* (New York: Routledge).
15. There is an interesting parallel in Showalter's argument that at the end of the nineteenth century male artists feared a coming apocalypse and the death of familiar structures, while women writers had less to lose as old cultural forms disappeared and much to hope for in the birth of a new century. E. Showalter, *Daughters of Decadence: Women Writers of the Fin-de-Siècle* (London: Virago), p. xviii. See also S. Ledger and S. McCracken (eds), *Cultural Politics at the Fin-de-Siècle* (Cambridge: Cambridge University Press), introduction.
16. Glover and Kaplan, *Genders*, p. xi.
17. D. Altman, 'On Global Queering', *Australian Humanities Review*, July (1996). http://www.lamp.ac.uk/ahr/archive/Issue-July-1996/altman.html, downloaded 18 January 2001.
18. A. Jagose, 'Queer theory', *Australian Humanities Review*, December (1996). http://www.lamp.ac.uk/ahr/archive/Issue-Dec-1996/jagose.html, downloaded 18 January 2001
19. 'Judith Butler', http://www.theory.organisation.uk/ctr-butl.htm, downloaded 18 January 2001.
20. J. Butler, *Gender Trouble*, p. 25.
21. V. Walkerdine, *Schoolgirl Fictions* (London: Verso), p.14.
22. K. Weiler and S. Middleton (eds), *Telling Women's Lives: Narrative Enquiries in the History of Women's Education* (Milton Keynes: Open University Press), p. 44.
23. L. Marcus, *Auto/biographical Discourses: Theory, Criticism and*

Practice (Manchester: Manchester University Press), p. 136.

24. T. De Lauretis (ed.), *Feminist Studies/Critical Studies* (Bloomington: Indiana University Press), p. 5.

25. L. Kelly, S. Burton and L. Regan, 'Researching women's lives or studying women's oppression? Reflections on what constitutes feminist research', in M. Maynard and J. Purvis (eds), *Researching Women's Lives from a Feminist Perspective* (London: Taylor and Francis), pp. 29–30.

26. Brah, *Cartographies*, p. 116.

27. Brah says the result is that 'identity then is an enigma which, by its very nature defies a precise definition', ibid., p. 20.

28. J. W. Scott, 'Experience' in J. W. Scott (ed.), *Feminists Theorise the Political* (London: Routledge,), p. 37.

29. P. Summerfield, *Reconstructing Women's Wartime Lives: Discourse and Subjectivity in Oral Histories of the Second World War* (Manchester: Manchester University Press).

30. A good example of the more recent scholarship is: K. Gleadle and S. Richardson (eds), *Women in British Politics, 1760–1918: the Power of the Petticoat* (London: Macmillan).

31. J. Goodman and S. Harrop, '"Within marked boundaries": women and the making of educational policy since 1800', in J. Goodman and S. Harrop (eds), *Women, Educational Policy-Making and Administration in England: Authoritative Women Since 1800* (London: Routledge), p. 3.

32. J. Martin, *Women and the Politics of Schooling in Victorian and Edwardian England* (London: Leicester University Press), p. 11.

33. M. Wetherall and C. Griffin, 'Feminist psychology and the study of men and masculinity, part 1 – assumptions and perspectives', *Feminism and Psychology*, 1, 3, pp. 361–91.

34. Brah, *Cartographies*, p. 108.

35. R. J. G. Young, *Colonial Desire: Hybridity in Theory, Culture and Race* (London: Routledge), p. 26.

36. S. Hall, 'Cultural identity and diaspora', in J. Rutherford (ed.), *Identity, Community, Culture, Difference* (London: Lawrence and Wishart), p. 235.

37. K. Kaplan and I. Grewal, 'Transnational feminist cultural studies: beyond the marxism/poststructuralism/feminism divides', *positions*, Fall (1994), pp. 430–45.

38. A.L. Stoler, 'Carnal knowledge and imperial power: gender, race and morality in colonial Asia', in J. Wallach Scott (ed.), *Feminism and History* (Oxford: Oxford University Press), p. 210; A.L. Stoler and F. Cooper, 'Between metropole and colony: rethinking a research agenda', in A.L. Stoler and F. Cooper (eds), *Tensions of Empire: Colonial Cultures in a Bourgeois World* (Berkeley: University of California Press); L. Mani, *Contentious Traditions: The Debate on*

Sati in Colonial India (Berkeley: University of California Press), p. 3;
I. Grewal, *Home and Harem: Nation, Gender, Empire and the Cultures
of Travel* (Leicester: Leicester University Press), p. 9; M.L. Pratt,
Imperial Eyes: Travel Writing and Transculturation (London:
Routledge), p. 5.

39. L.A.E. Nym Mayhall, P. Levine and I.C. Fletcher, 'Introduction', in
E.C. Fletcher, L.A.E. Nym Mayhall and P. Levine (eds), *Women's
Suffrage in the British Empire: Citizenship, Nation and Race* (London:
Routledge, 2000), pp. xiii, xvi.

40. Grewal, *Home and Harem*, p. 18; C. Kaplan and I. Grewal,
'Transnational feminist cultural studies', pp. 430–45.

41. P. Gilroy, 'Route work: the Black Atlantic and the politics of exile', in
Chambers and Curti (eds), *The Post-Colonial Question*, p. 22.

42. H. Bhabha, 'The Third Space: interview with Homi Bhabha', in
Rutherford (ed.), *Identity*, p. 211.

43. Brah, *Cartographies*, p. 208.

44. Pratt, *Imperial Eyes*, p. 6.

45 M. Maynard and J. Purvis (eds), *New Frontiers in Women's Studies:
Knowledge, Identity and Nationalism* (London: UCL Press), pp. 1–11,
25; see for example, R. Watts, 'Breaking the boundaries of Victorian
imperialism or extending a reformed "paternalism"? Mary Carpenter
and India', *History of Education*, 19, 5, pp. 443–56.

46. M. Kosambi, 'A window in the prison house: women's education and
the politics of social reform in nineteenth-century Western India',
History of Education, 29, 5, pp. 429–43.

47. K. Morris Matthews and K. Jenkins, 'Whose country is it anyway? The
construction of a new identity through schooling for Maori in
Aotearoa/New Zealand', *History of Education*, 28, 3, p. 349.

48. S. Humphries and P. Gordon, *A Man's World: from Boyhood to Manhood
1900–1960* (London: BBC Books); C. Heward, *Making a Man of Him:
Parents and their Sons' Education at an English Public School,
1929–1950* (London; Routledge); J. A. Mangan and J. Walvin,
*Manliness and Morality – Middle Class Masculinity in Britain and
America 1800–1940* (Manchester: Manchester University Press); J. A.
Mangan, *The Games Ethic and Imperialism – Aspects of the Diffusion of
an Idea* (Harmondsworth: Viking, 1985); J. Mangan (ed.) *The Cultural
Bond: Sport, Empire and Society* (London: Cass); J. Springhall, *Youth,
Empire and Society – British Youth Movements 1883–1940* (London:
Croom Helm); M. Roper and J. Tosh (eds), *Manful Assertions:
Masculinities in Britain Since 1800* (London: Routledge).

49. M. Vicinus, *Independent Women – Work and Community for Single
Women 1850–1920* (London: Virago); E. Edwards, 'Women principals,
1900–1960: gender and power', *History of Education*, 29, 5, pp. 405-15;
E. Edwards, *Women in Teacher Training Colleges, 1900–1960: A*

Culture of Femininity (London: Routledge).
50. M. Blair, J. Holland and S. Sheldon (eds), *Identity and Diversity – Gender and the Experience of Education: A Reader* (Clevedon: Multilingual Matters/The Open University Press); M. Erben (ed.), *Biography and Education: A Reader* (London: Falmer, 1998); P. Munro, *Subject to Fiction: Women Teachers' Life History Narratives and the Cultural Politics of Resistance* (Milton Keynes: Open University Press); Weiler and Middleton, *Telling Women's Lives*.
51. P. Cunningham, 'Innovators, networks and structures, towards a prosopography of progressivism', in J. Goodman and J. Martin (eds), *Reforming Lives? Progressivism, Leadership and Educational Change, History of Education*, 30, 5, pp. 433–52.
52. K. Casey, *I Answer with my Life: Life Histories of Women Teachers Working for Social Change* (London: Routledge).
53. G. Weiner, 'Harriet Martineau and her contemporaries: past studies and methodological questions on historical surveys of women', in *History of Education*, 29, 5, pp. 389–404.
54. For testimonial writing, see: K. Casey, *I Answer with my Life*.
55. Eisenmann, 'Creating a framework for interpreting US women's educational history: lessons from historical lexicography'. *History of Education*, 30, 5, pp. 453–70.

REFERENCES

Abrams, L. and Hunt, K. 'Borders and frontiers in women's history', *Women's History Review*, 9, 2 (2000), pp. 191–200.
Altman, D. 'On Global Queering', *Australian Humanities Review*, July 1996, http://www.lamp.ac.uk/ahr/archive/Issue-July-1996/altman.html downloaded 18 January 2001.
Anon, 'Judith Butler', http://www.theory.organisation.uk/ctr-butl.htm, downloaded 18 January 2001.
Anzaldua, G. *Borderlands/L Frontera: the New Mestiza* (San Fransciso: Spinsters/Aunt Lute, 1987).
Bhabha, H. 'The Third Space: Interview with Homi Bhabha', in J. Rutherford (ed.), *Identity, Community, Culture, Difference* (London: Lawrence and Wishart, 1990), pp. 207–21.
Blair, M., Holland, J. and Sheldon, S. (eds) *Identity and Diversity – Gender and the Experience of Education: A Reader*, (Clevedon: Multilingual Matters/The Open University Press, 1995).
Brah, A. *Cartographies of Diaspora: Contesting Identities*, (London: Routledge, 1996).
Butler, J. *Gender Trouble: Feminism and the Subversion of Identity*, (New York: Routledge, 1990).

Casey, K. *I Answer with my Life: Life Histories of Women Teachers Working for Social Change* (London: Routledge, 1993).

Cunningham, P. 'Innovators, networks and structures, towards a prosopography of progressivism', in J. Goodman and J. Martin (eds) *Reforming Lives? Progressivism, Leadership and Educational Change, History of Education*, 30, 5 (2001), forthcoming.

De Lauretis, T. (ed.) *Feminist Studies/Critical Studies* (Bloomington: Indiana University Press, 1986).

Edwards, E. 'Women principals, 1900–1960: gender and power', *History of Education*, 29, 5 (2000), pp. 405–15.

— *Women in Teacher Training Colleges, 1900–1960: A Culture of Femininity* (London: Routledge, 2001).

Eisenmann, L. 'Creating a framework for interpreting US women's educational history: lessons from historical lexicography', in J. Martin and J. Goodman (eds) *Reforming Lives? Progressivism, Leadership and Educational Change, History of Education* 30, 5 (2001), pp. 453–70.

Erben, M. (ed.) *Biography and Education: A Reader* (London: Falmer, 1998).

Gilroy, P. 'Route work: the Black Atlantic and the politics of exile', in I. Chambers and L. Curtin (eds), *The Post-Colonial Question: Common Sides, Divided Horizons* (London: Routledge, 1996), pp. 17–29.

Gleadle, K. and Richardson, S. (eds) *Women in British Politics, 1760–1918: The Power of the Petticoat* (London: Macmillan, 2000).

Glover, D. and Kaplan, C. *Genders*, (London: Routledge, 2000).

Goodman, J. 'Undermining or building up the nation? Elizabeth Hamilton (1758–1816), national identities and an authoritative role for women educationists', in G. McCulloch and R. Lowe (eds) *Education and National Identity, History of Education, Special Edition*, 28, 3 (1999) pp. 279–97.

— and Harrop, S. '"Within marked boundaries": women and the making of educational policy since 1800', in J. Goodman and S. Harrop (eds) *Women, Educational Policy-Making and Administration in England: Authoritative Women Since 1800* (London: Routledge, 2000), pp. 1–13.

— and Martin, J. (eds) *Breaking Boundaries: Gender Politics and the Experience of Education, History of Education, Special Edition*, 29, 5 (2000).

Grewal, I. *Home and Harem: Nation, Gender, Empire and the Cultures of Travel* (Leicester: Leicester University Press, 1996).

Hall, S. 'Cultural identity and diaspora', in J. Rutherford (ed.) *Identity, Community, Culture, Difference* (London: Lawrence and Wishart).

Hendrick, H. *Images of Youth: Age, Class and the Male Youth Problem, 1880–1920* (Oxford: Clarendon, 1990).

Heward, C. *Making a Man of Him: Parents and their Sons' Education at an English Public School, 1929–1950* (London: Routledge, 1988).

19

Hickman, M. *Religion, Class and Identity: the State, the Catholic Church and the Education of the Irish in Britain* (Aldershot: Avebury, 1995).

— 'Constructing the nation, segregating the Irish: the education of Irish Catholics in nineteenth-century Britain', *Aspects of Education*, 54 (1997), pp. 33–54.

Humphries, S. and Gordon, P. *A Man's World: from Boyhood to Manhood 1900–1960* (London: BBC Books, 1996).

— and — *Forbidden Britain: Our Secret Past 1900–1960* (London: BBC Books, 1994).

Jackson, L. A. *Child Sexual Abuse in Victorian England* (London: Routledge, 2000).

Jagose, A. 'Queer theory', *Australian Humanities Review*, December (1996), http://www.lamp.ac.uk/ahr/archive/Issue-Dec-1996/jagose.html, downloaded 18 January 2001.

Kaplan, C. and Grewal, I. 'Transnational feminist cultural studies: beyond the marxism/poststructuralism/feminism divides', *positions*, Fall (1994), pp. 430–45.

Kelly, L., Burton, S. and Regan, L. 'Researching women's lives or studying women's oppression? Reflections on what constitutes feminist research', in M. Maynard and J. Purvis (eds) *Researching Women's Lives from a Feminist Perspective* (London: Taylor and Francis, 1994.) pp. 27–48.

Kosambi, M. 'A window in the prison house: women's education and the politics of social reform in nineteenth-century Western India', *History of Education*, 29, 5 (2000), pp. 429–43.

Ledger, S. and McCracken, S. (eds) *Cultural Politics at the Fin-de-Siècle* (Cambridge: Cambridge University Press, 1995).

Mahood, L. *Policing Gender, Class and Family: Britain 1850–1940* (London: UCL Press, 1995).

Mangan, J. A. *The Games Ethic and Imperialism – Aspects of the Diffusion of an Idea* (Harmondsworth: Viking, 1985).

Mangan, J. A. and Walvin, J. *Manliness and Morality – Middle Class Masculinity in Britain and America 1800–1940* (Manchester: Manchester University Press, 1987).

Mangan, J. (ed.) *The Cultural Bond: Sport, Empire and Society* (London: Cass, 1992).

Mani, L. *Contentious Traditions: The Debate on Sati in Colonial India* (Berkeley: University of California Press, 1998).

Marcus, L. *Auto/biographical Discourses: Theory, Criticism and Practice* (Manchester: Manchester University Press, 1994).

Martin, J. *Women and the Politics of Schooling in Victorian and Edwardian England* (London: Leicester University Press, 1999).

Mayall, L. A. E. Nym, Levine, P. and Fletcher, I. C. 'Introduction', in T. C. Fletcher, L. A. E. Nym Mayall and P. Levine (eds), *Women's Suffrage in the British Empire: Citizenship, Nation and Race* (London: Routledge, 2000).

Maynard, M. and Purvis, J. (eds) *New Frontiers in Women's Studies: Knowledge, Identity and Nationalism* (London: UCL Press, 1996).

Morris Matthews, K. and Jenkins, K. 'Whose country is it anyway? The construction of a new identity through schooling for Maori in Aotearoa/New Zealand', *History of Education*, 28, 3 (1999), pp. 339–50.

Munro, P. *Subject to Fiction: Women Teachers' Life History Narratives and the Cultural Politics of Resistance* (Milton Keynes: Open University Press, 1999).

Pratt, M. *Imperial Eyes: Travel Writing and Transculturation* (London: Routledge, 1992).

Riley, D. *Am I That Name? Feminism and the Category of 'Women' in History* (London: Macmillan, 1988).

Roper, J. and Tosh, J. (eds) *Manful Assertions: Masculinities in Britain Since 1800* (London: Routledge, 1991).

Rubin, G. 'The traffic in women: notes on the "political economy" of sex', in R. R. Reiter (ed.) *Towards an Anthropology of Women* (New York: Monthly Review Press 1975).

Rubin, G. 'Thinking sex: notes for a radical theory of the politics of sexuality', in H. Abelove, M. A. Barale and D. Halperin, (eds) *The Lesbian and Gay Studies Reader* (New York: Routledge, 1993).

Scott, J. W. *Gender and the Politics of History* (New York: Columbia University Press, 1988).

— 'Experience', in J. W. Scott (ed.) *Feminist Theorise the Political*, (London: Routledge, 1992).

Showalter, E. *Daughters of Decadence: Women Writers of the Fin-de-Siècle* (London: Virago, 1993).

Smart, B. *Postmodernity* (London: Routledge, 1993).

Springhall, J. *Youth, Empire and Society – British Youth Movements 1883–1940* (London: Croom Helm, 1977).

Stanley, L. 'Introduction: on academic borders, territories, tribes and knowledges', in L. Stanley (ed.), *Knowing Feminisms* (London: Sage, 1997).

Stoler, A.L. 'Carnal knowledge and imperial power: gender, race and morality in colonial Asia', in I. Wallach Scott (ed.), *Feminisms and History* (Oxford: Oxford University Press, 1977), pp. 207–66.

Stoler, A.L. and Cooper, F. 'Between metropole and colony: re-thinking a research agenda', in A.L. Stoler and F. Cooper (eds), *Tensions of Empire: Colonial Cultures in a Bourgeois World* (Berkeley: University of California Press, 1977), pp. 1–58.

Summerfield, P. *Reconstructing Women's Wartime Lives: Discourse and Subjectivity in Oral Histories of the Second World War* (Manchester:

Manchester University Press, 1999).

Vicinus, M. *Independent Women – Work and Community for Single Women 1850–1920* (London: Virago, 1985).

Vickery, A. 'Golden age to separate spheres: a review of the categories and chronology of English women's history', *Historical Journal*, 36, 2 (1993), pp. 384–414.

Walkerdine, V. *Schoolgirl Fictions* (London: Verso, 1990).

Watts, R. 'Breaking the boundaries of Victorian imperialism or extending a reformed 'paternalism'? Mary Carpenter and India', *History of Education*, 19, 5 (2000), pp. 443–56.

Weiler, K. and Middleton, S. (eds) *Telling Women's Lives: Narrative Enquiries in the History of Women's Education* (Milton Keynes: Open University Press, 1999).

Weiner, G. *Feminisms and Education* (Milton Keynes: Open University Press, 1994).

— 'Harriet Martineau and her contemporaries: past studies and methodological questions on historical surveys of women', in *History of Education*, 29, 5 (2000), pp. 389–404.

Wetherall M. and Griffin, C. 'Feminist psychology and the study of men and masculinity, part 1 – assumptions and perspectives', *Feminism and Psychology*, 1, 3 (1992), pp. 361–91.

Young, R. J. G. *Colonial Desire: Hybridity in Theory, Culture and Race* (London: Routledge, 1995).

SECTION 1

SCHOOLING MASCULINITIES AND SEXUALITIES

2

A Head and a Heart: Calvinism and Gendered Ideals of Parenthood in Dutch Child-rearing Literature c.1845–1920

NELLEKE BAKKER

In 1845 in the Netherlands, an enlightened medical doctor, the liberal Calvinist Gerard Allebé (1810–92), published a child-rearing manual, which became so popular among the liberal bourgeoisie that it was still being reprinted more than 60 years later. Childcare, according to the physician, was a woman's task, for which nature had endowed her with a special talent. The book appeared shortly after the Dutch translation of a famous German treatise on family upbringing, Johann Paul Richter's *Levana*. Richter (1763–1825), the novelist son of a Lutheran clergyman and admirer of Rousseau (after whom he called himself Jean Paul), was a representative of the literary movement which contributed to the so-called romantic polarisation of the sexes.[1] His *Levana* (1807) is often mentioned as a prime example of this tendency.[2] The *Levana* does, indeed, stress women's predisposition for home-making and child-rearing and it emphasises natural differences between the sexes; but it does not exclude men from family duties. Compared with his contemporary, Johann Heinrich Pestalozzi, Jean Paul Richter gave the father a much more important role: he was to be the legislator, the mother the executive. The two parents had to work together and even share roles because their 'natural' talents complemented each other.[3] This division of labour reminds us not so much of Jean-Jacques Rousseau but of the Puritan tradition of collective parental responsibility with the father in control.[4]

In spite of the 'christianisation' of the original text at certain points 'to make it fit' Dutch educational *mentalité*, Jean Paul Richter's treatise was not appreciated by the reading public until after 1900, when it was valued for its respectful view of the child. In 1919, the editor of a popular introduction to the *Levana*, a Dutch Reformed minister, recognised it as 'a piece of true Christian knowledge'.[5] In the meantime Dutch society had gone through processes of political and economic modernisation. These changed a liberal, elitist and economically backward state into a modern, democratic and industrial nation. National integration and the political participation of the masses were realised through a process of differentiation along the lines of religion rather than class, the so-called 'pillarisation' (*verzuiling*) of Dutch society. Pillarisation implied that each denomination created its own political, social and cultural community. Not only political parties and trade unions, but also schooling and youth clubs were organised along religious lines. Pillarisation was stimulated by a revival of religious orthodoxy, particularly from the 1880s. One consequence was the relatively strong cultural impact of the churches and their doctrines. Both orthodox Neo-Calvinist dissenters and Roman Catholic revivalists considered family life crucial to the continuation of their sub-cultures within the predominantly liberal Calvinist nation.[6] In the Netherlands, therefore, ideals of parenting were strongly connected with religion.

For Protestants the father was always an important figure.[7] Historians particularly mention Puritans, the English counterparts of the orthodox Dutch Calvinists, as supporters of rigid fatherly authority.[8] This suggests the hypothesis that one consequence of late nineteenth-century Protestant revivalism was the replacement of the romantic idealisation of motherhood, which manifested itself in the Netherlands from the end of the eighteenth century, by a period of belief in the rule of the father a century later. If this is true, developments in the Netherlands ran counter to those in the wider Anglo-Saxon world. Around 1900 in Britain and the United States a new orientation to the child and its condition, partly inspired by the Child Study Movement, cleared the ground for the 'century of the child' and its corollary, the 'renaissance of motherhood'. In particular, this implied the rise of the new ideal of the 'scientific' mother, well-informed through expert knowledge about child development and hygiene.[10] The Netherlands, in contrast, may have seen a reappraisal of the patriarchal father precisely at the point when historians of fatherhood would have expected a further decrease of interest in the male contribution to family life. Historians of fatherhood argue that as a consequence of industrialisation, fathers turned into largely absent figures without any responsibility for what happened inside the home.[11] Because industrialisation manifested itself in the Low Countries only at the very end of the nineteenth century,[12] it is not particularly likely that economic developments can explain the trajectories of the Dutch concern for gendered parenthood. As a result, recent interpretations of renewed interest in and recognition of fathering from the 1920s, especially in the

United States, in terms of a reaction to the reality of absent and uninvolved 'industrial' fatherhood,[13] are not particularly helpful in shedding light on the Dutch case.

In Dutch historiography, the years between the publication of the translation of the *Levana* (1844) and its recognition as part of the Protestant educational tradition (1919) are known, in spite of the advancing pillarisation, as the liberal era.[14] This refers both to politics and to the prevailing intellectual climate. The liberal era is to be understood in comparison with the post-First World War era, when denominational groups began to dominate Dutch society and culture. Child-rearing manuals during the liberal era and parents' magazines after the turn of the century both stressed the autonomy of the individual. Parents were addressed as free and responsible citizens, capable of raising their children according to instructions from experts. Children, in turn, were depicted as incomplete individuals, whose lack of morality made them the natural subjects of education. Not surprisingly, during this period, advice to parents was meant for the bourgeoisie, the model citizens of liberal anthropology. Beginning in the 1880s and then only gradually, the middle classes became part of the experts' audience. Moreover, the advice was differentiated according to religion, with orthodox Calvinists and Roman Catholics beginning to publish their own blueprints for ideal family upbringing. Furthermore, and of particular note, manuals were no longer meant for mothers only.[15]

This chapter focuses on the role of religion, especially Calvinism, in the dynamics of gendered ideals of parenthood. As moral education was considered the most important dimension of family upbringing, the main focus of the chapter is directed at this aspect of the parent–child relationship. It tells the story of a predominantly Calvinist country, in which religion continued to play an important social and cultural role until the 1970s. Was orthodox Calvinism the main force behind the apparent revaluation of the role of the father? Did religious fundamentalists promote the kind of patriarchal fatherhood with which they are usually associated? Did they consider women incompetent for a new version of biblical education? What kind of idealisation of motherhood did they have to confront? Did their counterparts, liberal Calvinists, defend a gentler approach to the child as a woman's prerogative, like educational reformers and feminists in other countries? And if they considered family upbringing a collective enterprise, which role was to be played by the father and which by the mother? To answer these questions the chapter examines the most widely read child-rearing manuals and the most important parents' magazine published between 1845 and 1920. First, I consider versions of the nineteenth-century idealisation of motherhood; second, I discuss key texts written by both liberals and orthodox Calvinists representing the turn-of-the-century revaluation of the role of the father; I then examine the last phase of the debate on the qualities of men and women as home educators, as well as the conditions that determined the waning of public interest in the topic. Finally, I evaluate the role of Calvinism in the dynamics of gendered ideals of parenthood.

REASON AND FEELING

Doctor Allebé's best-selling handbook (1845) on childcare was part of a larger campaign, which propagated hygiene in both the public and the private sphere. The 'enlightened' hygienists believed that happiness and prosperity were rooted in virtue. As domesticity and hygiene were considered preconditions for a virtuous life, the family was supposed to lay the foundation for virtue. While the results of this campaign were slow to appear in the public sphere, the publishing directed at the liberal bourgeoisie bore fruit immediately. Allebé's manual, *De Ontwikkeling van het Kind* (The Development of the Child, 1845),[16] discussed the physical and mental development of the young child. The doctor believed in the interrelatedness of body and mind. In his view, a harmonious development of the two ought to be the goal of family upbringing.

As a child of the Enlightenment, Allebé stressed the necessity of an upbringing based on reason. He argued that when a mother was guided by nature and reason instead of blind love, her child would grow up to be of use to the not as yet very prosperous Dutch society. Reason dictated that she respected the natural development of the child. Like Rousseau, he feared precocity and advised against any formal instruction particularly during the first seven years. He believed that the mind developed itself and that what the young child needed most was freedom to play and discover. The body, however, needed more than freedom to move and fresh air. In the spirit of John Locke, Allebé stressed the necessity of physical hardening. 'Civilised' mothers, he complained, were terribly deficient in this respect. Allebé echoed the Genevan Albertine Necker de Saussure's view that whether or not the child grew up to be virtuous was decided during early childhood. Consequently, moral education was to begin immediately, with good example as the major force. When a mother showed herself to be loving, kind, cheerful and conscientious her child would imitate her. In the third edition of *De Ontwikkeling* (1865) Allebé added habit training, and order and regularity grew more important. These changes were inspired by Friedrich Fröbel's work, with which the Doctor had recently become acquainted.[17]

According to Allebé, child-rearing was the exclusive right of the mother. Nannies, servants and other 'uncivilised' women were to keep their distance. As mother, the bourgeois woman could contribute tremendously to the (passionately desired) economic recovery of the state: 'Mothers! Prize and use the matchless power, given to you, because you are mothers! Leading the early years of the new generation means commanding the future of the nation.'[18] Through the domestic sphere women's influence would prove profitable to all society. According to him, women had a finer sense, a purer love, and a natural tendency for self-sacrifice, while men were often egoistic. However, women's educational talent had a weak side: women tended to indulge and spoil the child. Children needed the opposite approach, especially hardening, if they were to become brave and energetic citizens. The mother needed, therefore, to control herself. In effect, the Doctor's advice aimed to defend the 'civilised' woman from her 'natural' tendency to let feeling prevail over reason.

THE POWER OF MOTHERLY LOVE

The idea that women could make use of their special educational talents was elaborated by one of the earliest Dutch feminists, Elise van Calcar-Schiotling (1822–1904), a pedagogue and novelist. Since her youth she had been inspired by the romantic religious revival movement, the *Réveil*. Success as a writer gave her the courage to become the first Dutch woman to lecture publicly; Fröebel's educational ideals were the topic. In a six-volume series, *Onze Ontwikkeling* (Our Development, 1861–62),[19] she stated her principles for the education of young children at home and in the Kindergarten, based on Fröbel's ideas. She agreed with Fröbel that civil society was too demanding to the mind. The heart should be the basis of morality, not the head. Like Allebé, she insisted on moral education, to prevent degeneration of the instincts. Her central concept, the 'power of the first impressions', related to early upbringing and to the decisive influence of the mother. The first impression would mould the child's character.

In *Onze ontwikkeling* van Calcar explained that motherhood had to be transformed into a 'science' and that child rearing was the essence of the female existence: 'It is her part and her purpose to raise children... thou art educators, because thou art women.'[20] She equated femininity with the qualities of the good mother: love, patience and self-sacrifice. She excluded the male, portraying him as the reverse: fathers were clumsy dopes, who undermined the mother's achievements. Only the mother was capable of the moral improvement of the child's soul. The mother's talent for self-control made her the natural example of restrained instinct. Servants, like men, were unable to live up to van Calcar's standards. 'Hired nurses', she pointed out, were by nature inane, loveless, uncivilised and indolent.

Although the series was meant for all female educators, including infant school teachers and governesses, it was only the mother who was put on a pedestal. Van Calcar described motherly love as 'an infinite power', capable of confronting the immense 'power of the first impressions'. Presented as a supernatural force, her love made a mother do the right things intuitively. This moral superiority of mothering women was also present as a theme in van Calcar's novels. Her novels exemplified the extension of femininity from the private into the public sphere by introducing 'motherly love' as a professional qualification for social work. Her heroines showed themselves superior in virtue and piety towards sinners and in front of the poor they appeared more affectionate than was possible for any male philanthropist. Her writings read like a hymn of praise to domestic happiness, pivoted around morally superior females. At the turn of the century these ideas were warmly embraced by Dutch feminists, a majority of whom emphasised gender differences rather than equality. The concept of superior motherhood was used to claim access for women to schooling, professions and, finally, suffrage.[21] In old age, however, van Calcar lost her interest in society. What is even more striking, she lost her optimism about the power of education and began to stress the necessity of parental authority. Disappointed in modernity, especially with the rational and egalitarian society of the turn of the century, she wanted the middle-class mother to turn her home into a castle, strong enough to resist the spirit of materialism.[22]

MORAL AUTHORITY VERSUS WARMTH

Critique of the growing power of rationality in the rapidly modernising society of late nineteenth-century Netherlands was also prominent in the blueprints of family life designed by clergymen. This is exemplified by the work of P. H. Ritter (1851–1912), a modernist theologian and philosopher, who left the pulpit but not the Dutch Reformed Church. He became very influential among parent advisors and the public at large. Basing his ideas on Immanuel Kant's ethics, he introduced the concept of moral autonomy as the prime purpose of all education. His treatises can be seen as expressions of the dominant liberal principles. Ritter focused on the individual, whose moral improvement would serve the interest of society. Just as Doctor Allebé had provided the mid-nineteenth-century liberal bourgeoisie with a convenient educational theory, Ritter's ideal served the next generation of liberals. His writings continued to be popular until well into the 1920s.

In his *Paedagogische Fragmenten* (Educational Fragments, 1887),[23] Ritter emphasised the primacy of morality, to which all questions of individual and collective life could be reduced. In his view, the level of individual morality determined man's worth. As a result, Ritter feared a one-sided emphasis on intellectual instruction, explaining that personality disclosed itself much more in emotion than in rationality. Ritter believed in the possibility of character training. Stimulating the opposite good qualities could compensate a child's bad qualities. His educational optimism is also revealed in the educational style he advocated: gentle but not indulgent, steady but not severe, and primarily tender. Only tenderness would open up a child's heart, he claimed. In spite of a growing belief in the power of hereditary predisposition, Ritter set the trend towards a general confidence among liberal Calvinists in the possibilities of character formation. Although at the time considerable numbers of liberals and social democrats were embracing Darwinism as a social theory, in the Netherlands it proved to be relatively unsuccessful as an antidote against educational optimism.[24] While the intellectual or physical performance of a child might be limited by hereditary disposition, as far as morality was concerned educationalists were unwilling to accept restraints on their influence. Their attitude explains why the Anglo-Saxon Child Study Movement, which was strongly influenced by evolutionary theory,[25] did not gain much popularity among Dutch family advisors.[26]

Ritter not only broke with the relatively one-sided appreciation of children's obedience, he also departed from the nineteenth-century doctrine of separate spheres.[27] In the Netherlands he was the first liberal author since the Enlightenment to give fathers a task within the intimacy of the family. He intended his manual to be read by both parents, each of whom should set the correct example. As parents were themselves the source of morality, their personalities were extremely important. In conformity with the Protestant tradition, but carefully avoiding the idea of the man as head of the family, Ritter conceived of the father as the founda-tion of family life: he embodied the principle, the mother worked out the details. In effect, Ritter invited the bourgeois father to participate in the training of a child's emotional life. He assured the bourgeois father that his moral authority surpassed the mother's, while she radiated the warmth, without which a child's innermost feelings could not be reached. Her loving care made a child trust her/his surroundings. However, when adulthood approached, the father had to teach the rules of society: '...the real world is not at all like the small world of the family'.[28] The father's moral authority and mother's warmth were supposed to be complementary.

A whole generation of child-rearing manuals, especially those written by progressive educators, breathed Ritter's spirit of trust and optimism and his ideal of shared parenting. Of these books only the one published by Ietje Kooistra (1861–1923), *Zedelijke Opvoeding* (Moral Education, 1894),[29] became a best-seller. Until the early 1920s, her book was a popular present for newly wed couples and it was even respected (although not recommended for reading) by orthodox Calvinist and Roman Catholic educational authorities. Kooistra was the first woman to be appointed in a pedagogical 'top job' in the Netherlands; in 1896, she became the director of the only teacher training college for girls set up by the state. Compared with Ritter, she was even more optimistic about the successful outcome of moral upbringing. Indeed, she told parents, 'the child becomes what you believe it to be'.[30] Her concept of child-rearing was extremely positive. More explicitly than other advisors at the turn of the century, she claimed that preventing trouble was better than redressing bad behaviour. She advised a style of upbringing that combined mild severity – especially firmness, righteousness and consistency – with a gentle approach, based on love, understanding and confidence between parents and children.

Kooistra claimed that friendly authority would teach children a whole range of Christian and civil virtues, from love for the truth to modesty, all of which were considered indispensable for happiness and successful participation in society. Kooistra and other liberal teachers explained that the family offered the best chances; for the school lacked personal contact and trust. However, as the family turned into the foremost socialising institution, it could not be considered private at the same time. In a sense, the doctrine of 'separate spheres' was traded for a dogma of 'united spheres'. Correspondingly, family upbringing became too important to leave to women. The words these teachers used to convince middle-class fathers of the importance of child rearing resembled the ones used many decades earlier to convince bourgeois women of the importance of their commitment to motherhood: 'the future of the fatherland rests in your hands'.[31]

PATRIARCHAL FATHERHOOD

Although relatively strong among educationalists, fear of rationality was not so much a peculiarity of Dutch liberalism at the turn of the century, but rather the catchword of the revival of confessionalism. The reawakening of religious fervour among orthodox Calvinist dissenters from the 1880s even went under the banner of 'anti-revolutionism', suggesting that nothing had done more harm to Dutch culture and society than the Enlightenment. Neo-Calvinists used all the typically modern ways of organising themselves. Their political leader, the theologist Abraham Kuyper (1837–1920), was an extremely gifted speaker and an astute politician. In the 1880s, even before they had established a church of their own, the Neo-Calvinists set up a political party and a university, the Free University. The beginning of pillarisation is often traced to the establishment of these separate Neo-Calvinist cultural and political institutions, largely the initiative of Kuyper, who was a zealous and uncompromising leader

Kuyper himself published a manual about parents' duty to raise their children according to the right principles: *Antirevolutionair óók in uw Huisgezin* (Anti-Revolutionary even at Home, 1880). This pamphlet was later attached to the official party's programme.[32] The author departed from both the strict Calvinist tradition of authority 'out of love' as the central element in the parent–child relationship[33] and from the nineteenth-century romantic orientation toward the child. Children owed their parents unconditional obedience, according to Kuyper. Love he considered a 'false ground' for parent–child interaction. The relationship he painted between husband and wife was clearly patriarchal: they related to each other like state versus parliament. The former embodied authority and justice, the latter controlled this authority, softened it if necessary and acted as spokeswoman of 'the rights of her people'.[34] The ideal wife was slavish to her husband, underwent all his wrongs patiently, but fought like a lioness for the interests of her children.

Other Neo-Calvinists, who wrote on family life during the reawakening of Calvinism, relied mainly on the Bible. They referred to parents as 'God's stewards' or 'God's educational instruments'. These orthodox ministers viewed children born with original sin and bearing 'the germs of all evil'. As a result, education had to be strict, directed at exorcising sin. Like 'guardian angels of God' parents had to defend their poor little sinners and prepare 'the acre of the child's heart' for 'the life-seed of God's spirit'. These ministers insisted that the parent–child relationship was a reflection of God's relation with humanity. Thus, a child learning to obey its parents was also learning to obey God. Authority and discipline, especially punishment, 'out of love' were the central means. According to the strict Calvinist tradition that was now revived, the father was firmly in command, the mother only his assistant. She was warned not to be too weak and to discipline her child herself when her husband was out earning the family's bread.[35]

It was only at the end of the 1920s that this orthodox Calvinist upbringing 'in the fear of The Lord' was replaced by an ideal that came close to liberal educational thinking.[36] During the first two decades of the twentieth century Herman Bavinck (1854–1921), Kuyper's successor as the intellectual leader of the Neo-Calvinists and as the Free University Professor of Theology, paved the way for mainstream Neo-Calvinism to shake off its old obsession with punishment and discipline. Bavinck was well acquainted with modern psychological and pedagogical theory and considered it his task to introduce the rank and file of his religious community to this body of knowledge. As a result he also wrote textbooks and parents' manuals. Only the Bible equalled his authority among his flock.[37]

According to Bavinck the family was of divine origin and, consequently, the model for society and the source of moral life. When a family lived under the authority of God's Word, it was nothing less than the 'school of life'.[38] Bavinck and other Neo-Calvinist child-rearing experts called fighting against the child's innate wickedness the foremost parental duty. In order to do so God had invested his 'stewards' with an absolute authority. Parents could maintain His justice only by demanding strict obedience. Spanking was a fair punishment and it was a Christian's obligation not to refrain from administering it. However, Bavinck and others pointed out that sensible educators used this means only in the worst cases. Authority, he explained, had to be practised 'in the Lord', which meant 'with wisdom and in the spirit of love'.[39]

Both parents were to practice the ideal Neo-Calvinist upbringing. They should act unanimously and never undermine each other's authority. However, they were no equals. The man was the head of the family, the woman only his God-ordained 'helping mate'. The father was invested with earthly power over all members of the family. As it was the mother who spent most of the time with the children, the father ought to admonish her to apply fixed rules. This warning was normally accompanied by a negative appreciation of the female contribution. Because authority and punishment were fundamental to Neo-Calvinist educational theory, the mother was portrayed as constrained by deficiencies: a lack of calmness and consistency, and particularly an inclination towards indulgence.

Some Neo-Calvinists did see a positive role for the mother. Their ideal was a flowing together of 'male' strength, seriousness, steadiness and severity with 'female' tenderness. Some called the mother the 'centre' or 'bearer' of the family. Proposals for a gender specific division of labour often related to religious education; for example, the man as 'priest', preceding in prayer and reading from the Scriptures, with the woman setting the example through personal prayer and piety.[40] Bavinck, however, had a clear, worldly view of the contribution of each parent: if the man was the head, then the woman was the heart of the family. Both were needed, he stated in the spirit of his liberal fellow believers.[41]

OBJECTIONS AGAINST IGNORING FATHERS

At the beginning of the twentieth century liberal child-rearing literature developed into a broad and varied phenomenon. The number of published manuals grew and, for the first time, periodicals on family upbringing began to appear. In addition, with the establishment of the parents' magazine *Het Kind* (The Child, 1900),[42] something resembling a national community discussing child rearing began to exist. Jan Gunning (1859–1951), editor-in-chief of *Het Kind* was the first Dutch academic pedagogue, a classicist and principal of a classical gymnasium. Like him, the majority of the authors and readers of *Het Kind* were liberals and members of the Dutch Reformed Church. Gunning's editorial policy was liberal to the extent that social democrats and orthodox Calvinists also contributed to the journal. Even some Roman Catholic pedagogues, who still lacked a theory of family upbringing of their own, read the journal. Gunning's personality and opinions were largely responsible for this co-operation. Politically he was a rather conservative liberal, which may account for his aversion to Dutch pillarising tendencies. At the same time, as a result of his own upbringing, he was deeply religious.[43] Therefore, it is not surprising that for Gunning moral and religious upbringing were inextricably linked.

In *Het Kind* family upbringing was discussed both theoretically and practically. Gunning put a clear stamp on the former; the latter was delegated to a multitude of experienced bourgeois mothers. But, whenever someone expressed an opinion that differed from his own, Gunning as editor added his comment, with the result that his view of child rearing prevailed. His ideas were not original. Rather eclectically he brought together apparently conflicting principles and created his own amalgam. He connected Rousseau's respect for the natural development of the child with Calvinist belief in original sin; enlightened trust in education with orthodox distrust in the child's disposition towards moral goodness;

35

reformist belief in learning by doing with an admonition to intervene; Ritter's belief in the good example with a strict Calvinist emphasis on obedience and discipline; a romantic belief in the educational force of a good atmosphere with the ethical belief that moral autonomy could be reached only after struggle; and finally the romantic idea that the child's heart could be reached only through emotion with the enlightened conviction that parents, especially mothers, should not let themselves be guided by feelings only. Like Kooistra and other liberals, Gunning propagated an educational style that traversed the middle road between authority and freedom. True severity was 'tender, because she was the fruit of true love', he stated.[44]

The more practical contributions to the magazine equated 'parents' with mothers. Many articles were inspired by the feminist concept of the naturally talented female educator: she was mild, patient, empathic and self-effacing. However, there were no signs of disqualification for the father, simply silence about his role. It was this disregard to which Gunning objected. Again he seems to have been inspired by an awkward synthesis. In the spirit of both the Enlightenment and the revived strict Calvinist tradition he disqualified mothers as educators: the woman's nature was whimsical, capricious and it lacked willpower; therefore it needed male guidance. Like Allebé, he warned against women's intuition and overprotectiveness. Gunning did not know 'a more solid family-cement' than the father, who 'preceded daily in reading from the Bible and in collective prayer'.[45]

The opposite opinion, that women possessed a greater educational talent, was still deeply rooted and widely accepted among liberals, especially those who sympathised with feminists emphasizing gender differences. This conviction inspired Gunning to repeat his objections to the lack of attention being given to fathers. Subscribing to the general view that rearing infants was a woman's task, he expected fathers to take a larger part in rearing school-aged children, especially boys. He called it 'a regrettable, if not criminal neglect of duty' when fathers left the whole task to women. Because women spent most of the time with the children, men were more capable of drawing the outlines. In his opinion, the father was responsible for 'the spiritual tonometer'.[46]

In spite of his great authority, Gunning did not succeed in moulding the educational *mentalité* after his ideal. On the contrary, a sudden upsurge of interest in gender-specificity was caused by the appearance of *Psychologie der Vrouwen* (Psychology of Women, 1910), an example of the new branch of academic psychology, which focused on differences between groups of people, witten by the well-known Dutch psychologist and philosopher Gerard Heymans (1857–1930).[47] Heymans' conclusion that the woman was superior in emotion was used by many feminists as proof of women's greater talent for child rearing. For them, woman's smaller egoism and stronger intuition was now scientifically confirmed. Even Kooistra, who was not particularly feminist, paid tribute to motherly love and female intuition as superior educational forces in her later work.[48] Consequently, around 1920, a rather vague consensus existed among child-rearing experts, in which it was claimed that family upbringing was best served by a combination of 'male', objective reason and 'female', subjective feeling.[49]

Apart from some Neo-Calvinists who continued to emphasise the importance of active fatherhood, during the inter-war era gender-specificity was no longer a theme among child-rearing experts. Parents were now addressed as a unit. The only exception was childcare during early childhood. This continued to be a 'female' domain. During the following stages of development some contribution to child-rearing was expected of the father, although it was not specified. The disappearance of interest in gender-specific parenting can be related to the twin processes of professionalisation and medicalisation, the early signs of which began to manifest themselves during the 1920s. 'Real' professionals, like psychologists and especially psychiatrists, replaced moral experts like teachers and clergymen, as parents' advisors. This, in turn, was a result of the fact that family upbringing was no longer conceived of primarily as moral education. Particular attention was now given to the emotional development of the child. As a consequence, parents, both fathers and mothers, were no longer seen as the source of morality for their children; they had to content themselves with a humbler role as managers of the emotional parent–child relationship.[50]

CONCLUSION

Surveying key texts in Dutch child-rearing literature during the liberal era illustrates that Calvinism was an important but not the only determinant of gendered ideals of parenthood. At first, the concept of child rearing as a woman's prerogative dominated the advice literature. As the example of Doctor Allebé shows, this did not appear to be incompatible with the enlightened liberal Calvinism of the mid-nineteenth century. The romantic concept of 'superior motherhood', as propagated by Elise van Calcar, was limited mainly to Dutch feminists. From the 1880s the ideal of family upbringing as a collective parental enterprise was shared by a majority of parental advisors. Only orthodox Calvinists, like Kuyper and Bavinck, propagated the rule of the father. The general revaluation of the role of the father, however, was not limited to supporters of a strictly biblical education. As the examples of Ritter and especially Gunning indicate, liberal Calvinists showed the same interest in fathers as co-educators.

As liberals, Ritter and Gunning assigned moral authority to the father, but deliberately avoided the idea of the man as head of the family. The mother was expected to give warmth, create intimacy, and be responsible for the details of the child's daily life. Significantly, compared with the earlier romantic emphasis on the power of motherly love, women lost moral authority to their new co-educators. As parents continued to be *the* source of morality for their children, this happened to be their most important role. References to the father were invariably positive from the 1880s: the father was capable of drawing the outlines, he was by nature steady, and consequently he knew enough about the 'real' world to teach its rules. The mother, on the other hand, was often referred to in a negative sense: she had an inclination towards indulgence and for spoiling her 'little darlings'. In other words, she needed a man to correct her faults. At the end of the period covered by this chapter, a common opinion among all Calvinists was that family upbringing was best served by a combination of 'male' reason and 'female' feeling: a head and a heart.

Those authors who tended to a positive view of the role of the father and a negative view of the role of the mother stressed authority as an educational means. In the revived orthodox Calvinist tradition the father was firmly in command. The mother was only his assistant. She was warned not to be too weak and to discipline her child herself when her husband was out earning the family's bread. The man was expected to control and guide his wife's authority and to admonish her to apply fixed rules. Because authority and discipline were fundamental in the Neo-Calvinist educational theory, the mother's 'deficiencies' were exaggerated to the extreme. At least in the case of Dutch Calvinism, the relationship between religion and gendered ideals of parenthood was closely linked with educational style.

The more parents were advised to handle their children gently, the more positive became the appreciation of the female contribution. When romanticism asked for a tender approach to the child, then the mother was appreciated for her highly valued 'female' qualities. When, on the other hand, Calvinist orthodoxy renewed the call for discipline, fathers were warned not to neglect their duty and were exhorted to compensate for the mother's weakness with their power. Liberal Calvinist experts generally recommended the golden mean between authority and freedom, between strictness and a gentle approach. Therefore, it is no surprise that from the 1880s the ideal of child rearing as a collective enterprise with both parents equally responsible, was pre-eminent among all Calvinists, not only the orthodox. Jean Paul's *Levana* would have fitted only too well within this educational *mentalité*. Readers of the 1919 introduction probably understood the meaning of the title much better than the 1844 audience possibly could: for *Levana* was the goddess invoked by Roman mothers, when they put a new-born child at the feet of its procreator, lest she give him the heart of a father.

END NOTES

1. K. Hausen, 'Die Polarisierung der "Geschlechtskaraktere". Eine Spiegelung der Dissoziation von Erwerbs- und Familienleben', in W. Conze (ed.), *Sozialgeschichte der Familie in der Neuzeit Europas* (Stuttgart: Klett), pp. 363–93.
2. J. Albisetti, *Schooling German Girls and Women. Secondary and Higher Education in the Nineteenth Century* (Princeton NJ: Princeton University Press), p. 6; D. Gaus, 'Bildende Geselligkeit. Untersuchungen geselliger Vergesellschaftung am Beispiel der Berliner Salons um 1800', *Jahrbuch für Historische Bildungsforschung*, 4, pp. 165–208.
3. Jean Paul [Richter], *Levana oder Erziehlehre*. Besorgt von K.G. Fischer (Paderborn: Schöningh).
4. M. Todd, *Christian Humanism and the Puritan Social Order* (Cambridge: Cambridge University Press); L. F. Groenendijk, *De Nadere Reformatie van het Gezin. De Visie van Petrus Wittewrongel op de Christelijke Huishouding* (Dordrecht: Van den Tol).
5. J. P. [Richter], *Levana. Wenken voor de Opvoeding van Kinderen voor Oouders en Jonggehuwden* (Amsterdam: Portielje); C.W. Coolsma, *Jean Paul's Levana* (Gröningen/Den Haag: Wolters).
6. A. Lijphart, *The Politics of Accommodation. Pluralism and Democracy in the Netherlands* (Berkeley: University of California Press); S. Stuurman, *Verzuiling, Kapitalisme en Patriarchaat. Aspecten van de Ontwikkeling van de Moderne Staat in Nederland* (Nijmegen: SUN).
7. P. Greven, *The Protestant Temperament. Patterns of Child-Rearing, Religious Experience, and the Self in Early America* (New York: Knopf); S. Ozment, *When Fathers Ruled. Family Life in Reformation Europe* (Cambridge, MA/London: Harvard University Press); S.

Ozment, *The Bürgemeister's Daughter. Scandal in a Sixteenth-century German Town* (New York: St Martin's Press).

8. Greven, *Protestant Temperament*; P. Greven, *Spare the Child. The Religious Roots of Punishment and the Psychological Impact of Physical Abuse* (New York: Vintage Books); Groenendijk, *De Nadere Reformatie*.

9. E. Wolff, *Proeve over de Oopvoeding, aan de Nederlandsche Moeders* (Meppel/Amsterdam: Boom). See also E. Badinter, *L'amour en plus. Histoire de l'amour maternel (XVIIe–XXe siècle)* (Paris: Flammarion).

10. J. Grant, *Raising Baby by the Book: The Education of American Mothers* (New Haven/London: Yale University Press), pp. 113–36; R. D. Apple, 'Constructing mothers: scientific motherhood in the nineteenth and twentieth centuries', *Social History of Medicine*, 8, pp. 161–78; C. Hardyment, *Dream Babies. Child Care from Locke to Spock* (Oxford: Oxford University Press), pp. 87–155.

11. J. Demos, *Past, Present and Personal. The Family and the Life Course in American History* (Oxford: Oxford University Press), pp. 41–67; P. N. Stearns, 'Fatherhood in historical perspective: the role of social change', in F. W. Bozett and S. M. H. Hanson (eds), *Fatherhood and Families in Cultural Context* (New York: Springer), pp. 28–52.

12. J. A. de Jonge, *De industrialisatie van Nederland tussen 1850 en 1914* (Nijmegen: SUN).

13. R. LaRossa, *The Modernization of Fatherhood. A Social and Political History* (Chicago/London: University of Chicago Press).

14. S. Stuurman, *Wacht op onze Daden. Het Liberalisme en de Vernieuwing van de Nederlandse Staat* (Amsterdam: Amsterdam University Press).

15. N. Bakker, *Kind en Karakter. Nederlandse Pedagogen over Opvoeding in het Gezin, 1845–1925* (Amsterdam: Het Spinhuis).

16. G. A. N. Allebé, *De Ontwikkeling van het Kind naar Ligchaam en Geest. Eene Handleiding voor Moeders bij de eerste Opvoeding* (Amsterdam: Mosmans). The book was last reprinted in 1908.

17. Bakker, *Kind en Karakter*, pp. 11–20.

18. Allebé, *De Ontwikkeling*, pp. 299–300.

19. E. van Calcar, *Onze Ontwikkeling of de Magt der eerste indrukken* (Amsterdam: Van Gelder) 6 vols. This series was last reprinted in 1898.

20. Ibid. I, p. 5.

21. A. van Drenth and F. de Haan, *The Rise of Caring Power. Elizabeth*

Fry and Josephine Butler in Britain and the Netherlands (Amsterdam: Amsterdam University Press); P. de Vries, *Kuisheid voor Mannen, Vrijheid voor Vrouwen. De Reglementering en Bestrijding van Prostitutie in Nederland, 1850–1911* (Amsterdam: Het Spinhuis); U. Jansz, *Denken over Sekse. De Eerste Feministische Golf* (Amsterdam: Sara/Van Gennep).

22. E. van Calcar, *Het Jonge Leven. Hoe het te Kweeken en te Beschermen. Een Boek voor Ouders en Oopvoeders* ('s-Gravenhage: IJkema). See Bakker, *Kind en Karakter*, pp. 32–5

23. P. H. Ritter, *Paedagogische Fragmenten* (Utrecht: Beijers), pp. 37–41. This work was last reprinted in 1924.

24. I. N. Bulhof, 'The Netherlands', in T. F. Glick (ed.), *A Comparative Analysis of the Reception of Darwinism* (Austin: University of Texas), pp. 269–306; P. de Rooy, *Darwin en de Strijd langs vaste Lijnen* (Nijmegen: SUN); E. Mulder, 'Patterns, principles, and profession: the early decades of educational science in the Netherlands', *Paedagogica Historica. International Journal of the History of Education*, Special Series III, pp. 231–46.

25. M. Depaepe, *Zum Wohl des Kindes? Pädologie, Pädagogische Psychologie und Experimentelle Pädagogik in Europa und den U.S.A., 1890–1940* (Weinheim/Leuven: Deutscher Studien Verlag/Leuven University Press).

26. Bakker, *Kind en Karakter*, pp. 92–6.

27. This concept was developed by: N. Cott, *The Bonds of Womanhood. 'Woman's Sphere' in New England, 1780–1835* (New Haven/London: Yale University Press).

28. Ritter, *Paedagogische Fragmenten*, p. 97.

29. I. Kooistra, *Zedelijke Opvoeding* (Groningen: Wolters). This manual was last reprinted in 1919.

30. Kooistra, *Zedelijke Opvoeding*, p. 104.

31. H. Douma, *Opvoeding in het Huisgezin* (Loosdrecht: Van Haselen), p. 8.

32. A. Kuyper, *Antirevolutionair óók in uw Huisgezin* (Amsterdam: Kruyt).

33. B. Kruithof, 'Continuïteit in opvoedingsadviezen in Protestants Nederland van de 17e tot de 19e eeuw', *Amsterdams Sociologisch Tijdschrift*, 9, pp. 476–92.

34. Kuyper, *Antirevolutionair*, pp. 45–8.

35. Bakker, *Kind en Karakter*, p. 49.

36. N. Bakker, 'Opvoeden met de harde hand? Een historisch-kritische beschouwing van de neo-calvinistische opvoedingsmentaliteit

1880–1930', in G. Biesta, B. Levering and I. Weijers (eds), *Thema's uit de Wijsgerige en Historische Pedagogiek* (Utrecht: SWP), pp. 79–85.

37. Bakker, *Kind en Karakter*, pp. 177–9.
38. H. Bavinck, *Het Christelijk Huisgezin* (Kampen: Kok), p. 140.
39. H. Bavinck, *Bijbelsche en Religieuze Psychologie* (Kampen: Kok), p. 217.
40. Bakker, *Kind en Karakter*, pp. 188–9.
41. Bavinck, *Het Christelijk Huisgezin*, p. 124.
42. *Het Kind. Veertiendaagsch Blad voor Ouders en Opvoeders* 3 (1902) – 27 (1926), first published under the title *Maatschappelijk Werk, Afdeeling B* 1 (1900) – 2 (1901).
43. E. Mulder, *Beginsel en Beroep. Pedagogiek aan de Universiteit in Nederland 1900–1940* (Amsterdam: University of Amsterdam), pp. 26–38.
44. J. H. Gunning Wzn., 'De rechten van het kind', *Het Kind*, 6, pp. 66–8, 73–5, 81–3, 91–3, 101–2, especially 92.
45. J. H. Gunning Wzn., 'Iets over godsdienstonderwijs', *Het Kind*, 5, pp. 58–9, especially 59.
46. Ibid.
47. G. Heymans, *Psychologie der Vrouwen* (Amsterdam: Maatschappij voor Goede en Goedkoope Lectuur).
48. Kooistra, *Opvoeder en Kind. Paedagogische Voordrachten en Schetsen* (Amsterdam: Van Kampen); I. Kooistra, *Onze Groote Kinderen* (Amsterdam: Van Kampen), 2 vols.
49. Bakker, *Kind en Karakter*, pp. 148–51.
50. N. Bakker, 'Child-rearing literature and the reception of Individual Psychology in the Netherlands, 1930–1950: the case of a Calvinist pedagogue', *Paedagogica Historica. International Journal of the History of Education*, Special Series III, pp. 583–602; N. Bakker, 'Health and the medicalization of advice to parents in the Netherlands, ca. 1890–1950', in M. Gijswijt and H. Marland (eds), *Cultures of Child Health*, (Amsterdam/Atlanta: Rodopi).

REFERENCES

Allebé, G. A. N. *De Ontwikkeling van het Kind naar Ligchaam en Geest. Eene Handleiding voor Moeders bij de Eerste Opvoeding* (Amsterdam: Mosmans, 1845).
Albisetti, J. C. *Schooling German Girls and Women. Secondary and*

Higher Education in the Nineteenth Century (Princeton NJ: Princeton University Press, 1988).

Apple, R. D. 'Constructing mothers: scientific motherhood in the nineteenth and twentieth centuries', *Social History of Medicine*, 8 (1995), pp. 161–78.

Badinter, E. *L'amour en plus. Histoire de l'amour maternel (XVIIe–XXe siècle)* (Paris: Flammarion, 1980).

Bakker, N. *Kind en Karakter. Nederlandse Pedagogen over Opvoeding in het Gezin, 1845–1925* (Amsterdam: Het Spinhuis, 1995).

— 'Child-rearing literature and the reception of individual psychology in the Netherlands, 1930–1950: The Case of a Calvinist Pedagogue', *Paedagogica Historica. International Journal of the History of Education*, Special Series III (1998), pp. 583-602.

— 'Opvoeden met de harde hand? Een historisch-kritische beschouwing van de neo-calvinistische opvoedingsmentaliteit 1880–1930', in G. Biesta, B. Levering and I. Weijers (eds), *Thema's uit de wijsgerige en historische pedagogiek* (Utrecht: SWP, 1998), pp. 79–85.

— 'Health and the medicalization of advice to parents in the Netherlands, ca. 1890–1950', in M. Gijswijt and H. Marland (eds), *Cultures of Child Health* (Amsterdam/Atlanta: Rodopi, forthcoming).

Bavinck, H. Het *Christelijk Huisgezin* (Kampen: Kok, 1908).

— *Bijbelsche en Religieuze Psychologie* (Kampen: Kok, 1920).

Bulhof, I. N. 'The Netherlands', in T. F. Glick (ed.), *A Comparative Analysis of the Reception of Darwinism* (Austin, TX: University of Texas, 1974), pp. 269–306.

Calcar, E. van *Onze ontwikkeling of de magt der eerste indrukken* (Amsterdam: Van Gelder, 1861–62), 6 vols.

— *Het jonge leven. Hoe het te kweeken en te beschermen. Een boek voor ouders en opvoeders* ('s-Gravenhage: Ljkema, [1905]).

Coolsma, C. W. *Jean Paul's Levana* (Gröningen/Den Haag: Wolters, 1919).

Cott, N. *The Bonds of Womanhood. 'Woman's Sphere' in New England, 1780–1835* (New Haven/London: Yale University Press, 1977).

Demos, J. *Past, Present and Personal. The Family and the Life Course in American History* (Oxford: Oxford University Press, 1986).

Depaepe, M. *Zum Wohl des Kindes? Pädologie, Pädagogische Psychologie und Experimentelle Pädagogik in Europa und den U.S.A., 1890–1940* (Weinheim/Leuven: Deutscher Studien Verlag/Leuven University Press, 1993).

Douma, H. *Opvoeding in het Huisgezin* (Loosdrecht: Van Haselen, 1891), 8.

Drenth, A. van and de Haan, F. *The Rise of Caring Power. Elizabeth Fry and Josephine Butler in Britain and the Netherlands* (Amsterdam: Amsterdam University Press, 1999).

Gaus, D. 'Bildende Geselligkeit. Untersuchungen geselliger Vergesellschaftung am Beispiel der Berliner Salons um 1800', *Jahrbuch für Historische Bildungsforschung*, 4 (1998), pp. 165–208.

Grant , J. *Raising Baby by the Book: The Education of American Mothers* (New Haven/London: Yale University Press, 1998).

Greven, P. *The Protestant Temperament. Patterns of Child-rearing, Religious Experience, and the Self in Early America* (New York: Knopf, 1977).

— *Spare the Child. The Religious Roots of Punishment and the Psychological Impact of Physical Abuse* (New York: Vintage Books, 1992).

Groenendijk, L. F. *De Nadere Reformatie van het Gezin. De Visie van Petrus Wittewrongel op de Christelijke Huishouding* (Dordrecht: Van den Tol, 1984).

Gunning J. H. Wzn., 'De rechten van het kind', *Het Kind*, 6 (1905), pp. 66–8, 73–5, 81–3, 91–3, 101–2.

— 'Iets over godsdienstonderwijs', *Het Kind*, 5 (1904), pp. 58–9.

Hardyment, C. *Dream Babies. Child Care from Locke to Spock* (Oxford: Oxford University Press, 1984).

Hausen, K. 'Die Polarisierung der "Geschlechtskaraktere". Eine Spiegelung der Dissoziation von Erwerbs- und Familienleben', in W. Conze (ed.), *Sozialgeschichte der Familie in der Neuzeit Europas* (Stuttgart: Klett, 1976), pp. 363–93.

Heymans, G. *Psychologie der Vrouwen* (Amsterdam: Maatschappij voor Goede en Goedkoope Lectuur, 1911) orig. edited in German in 1910.

Jansz, U. *Denken over Sekse. De Eerste Feministische Golf* (Amsterdam: Sara/Van Gennep, 1990).

Jonge, J. A. de *De Industrialisatie van Nederland tussen 1850 en 1914* (Nijmegen: SUN, 1976).

Kind, Het. Veertiendaagsch Blad voor Ouders en Opvoeders 3 (1902) – 27 (1926), first published under the title *Maatschappelijk Werk, Afdeeling B* 1 (1900) – 2 (1901).

Kooistra, I. *Zedelijke Opvoeding* (Groningen: Wolters, 1894).

— *Opvoeder en Kind. Paedagogische Voordrachten en Schetsen* (Amsterdam: Van Kampen, 1916).

— *Onze Groote Kinderen* (Amsterdam: Van Kampen, 1918–19), 2 vols.

Kruithof, B. 'Continuïteit in opvoedingsadviezen in protestants Nederland van de 17e tot de 19e eeuw', *Amsterdams Sociologisch Tijdschrift*, 9 (1982), pp. 476–92.

Kuyper, A. *Antirevolutionair óók in uw Huisgezin* (Amsterdam: Kruyt, 1880).

LaRossa, R. *The Modernization of Fatherhood. A Social and Political History* (Chicago/London: University of Chicago Press, 1997).

Lijphart, A. *The Politics of Accommodation. Pluralism and Democracy in the Netherlands* (Berkeley: University of California Press, 1968).

Mulder, E. *Beginsel en Beroep. Pedagogiek aan de Universiteit in Nederland 1900–1940* (Amsterdam: University of Amsterdam, 1989).

— 'Patterns, principles, and profession: the early decades of educational science in the Netherlands', *Paedagogica Historica. International Journal of the History of Education*, Special Series III (1998), pp. 231–46.

Ozment, S. *When Fathers Ruled. Family Life in Reformation Europe* (Cambridge, MA/London: Harvard University Press, 1983).

— *The Bürgemeister's Daughter. Scandal in a Sixteenth-century German Town* (New York: St. Martin's Press, 1996).

[Richter], J. P. *Levana. Wenken voor de Opvoeding van Kinderen voor Ouders en Jonggehuwden* (Amsterdam: Portielje, 1844);

— *Levana oder Erziehlehre*. Besorgt von K.G. Fischer (Paderborn: Schöningh, 1963).

Ritter, P. H. *Paedagogische Fragmenten* (Utrecht: Beijers, 1888, 2nd edn).

Rooy, P. de *Darwin en de Strijd langs Vaste Lijnen* (Nijmegen: SUN, 1987).

Stearns, P. N. 'Fatherhood in historical perspective: the role of social change', in F. W. Bozett and S. M. H. Hanson (eds), *Fatherhood and Families in Cultural Context* (New York: Springer, 1991), pp. 28–52.

Stuurman, S. *Verzuiling, Kapitalisme en Patriarchaat. Aspecten van de Ontwikkeling van de Moderne Staat in Nederland* (Nijmegen: SUN, 1983).

— *Wacht op onze Daden. Het Liberalisme en de Vernieuwing van de Nederlandse Staat* (Amsterdam: Amsterdam University Press, 1992).

Todd, M. *Christian Humanism and the Puritan Social Order* (Cambridge: Cambridge University Press, 1987).

Vries, P. de *Kuisheid voor Mannen, Vrijheid voor Vrouwen. De Reglementering en Bestrijding van Prostitutie in Nederland, 1850–1911* (Amsterdam: Het Spinhuis, 1997).

Wolff, E. *Proeve over de Opvoeding, aan de Nederlandsche Moeders* (Meppel/Amsterdam: Boom, 1977), 1st edn. 1779.

3

The Pleasure of Learning and the Tightrope of Desire: Teacher–Student Relationships and Victorian Pedagogy

MARK MCBETH

And when I may no longer live,
They'll say, who know the truth,
He gave whate'er he had to give
To freedom and to youth .
—William Johnson Cory[1]

In the late nineteenth century, on the vast green lawns of King's College, Cambridge, students strolled rehearsing Latin and Greek translations while their gowned professors headed to lectures. Athletes strained their muscles in sculling races or in cricket matches, while aesthetes pondered over the poetry of Tennyson, the sermons of Thomas Arnold, the art criticism of John Ruskin, or the essays of John Stuart Mill. This was a regimented world where clothing and comportment signified one's position in the college and one's interests in the world. The sportsman wore his athleticism as the art lover wore his aestheticism, while tutors of the classics, mathematics and modern foreign languages competed in a shifting hierarchy of curricular importance. People understood their prescribed positions because roles were rule-bound by centuries of tradition and, for the most part, members adhered to these conventions. Into this landscape pedalled Oscar Browning on his tricycle, a short, rotund man waving jovially to the passers-by. Browning, on one summer excursion, had joined one of his students on a cycling tour on which they retraced a Napoleonic trek through the Alps on their way to Venice. 'From Trevico it was a short run to Mestre, where I put my tricycle in a gondola and was rowed to Venice...' remarked Browning in his memoirs.[2] I imagine his student smiling at the edge of the water, watching the gondolier balance the roly-poly, huffing-puffing Browning and his three-

46

wheeled bike on the slender, shaky vessel. Browning, or O. B. as he was known in the college, boasted, 'I was certainly the first Englishman who crossed the Alps on a tricycle.'[3] How this student, as well as his peers at Cambridge, must have enjoyed this eccentric tutor, who was always either in an uphill struggle or rocking the boat.

Browning had been involved in the privileged, upper echelons of British educational circles for years. In January 1851, aged fourteen, he went to Eton and, by the age of nineteen, had completed his scholarship there with no great failures and no great successes. Following a longstanding tradition between Eton and King's College, he was offered a place at Cambridge.[4] Browning's four years at King's were more successful than his years at Eton. He became President of the Cambridge Union and was invited to be a member of the intellectual enclave of the 'Apostles'. He blossomed as a scholar, meeting like minds who became his life-long friends, and who were, like himself, committed educationalists. Notably, Browning's initial biography (1927) by his nephew, H. E. Wortham, was first entitled simply *Oscar Browning*, but the 1956 edition was renamed *Victorian Eton and Cambridge – Being the Life and Times of Oscar Browning*; his educational narrative not only chronicles his own life but, also, presents a portrait of changing Victorian British education overall.

Wortham wrote about his uncle's mind-set as a developing educator: 'O. B. discovered that he was no Whig, but a Liberal, even a Radical, that his political creed could rest securely on the writings of John Stuart Mill, and that his life must be devoted to the cause of humanity.'[5] O. B's radicalism would manifest itself in his pedagogical approaches. Browning took to heart J. S. Mill's insistence that educational critics should not attack the students, but 'denounce the wretched methods of teaching'. Mill wisely continued, 'Let us try [to see] what conscientious and intelligent training can do, before we presume to decide what cannot be done.'[6] In the educational process, Mill focused upon and dignifies pedagogy – 'conscientious and intelligent teaching' – and he saw that the greatest difficulty in this process is the 'teaching of teachers'.[7] Browning devoted a lifetime to perfecting his own pedagogical abilities, preparing others in the methods of conveying knowledge, and turning this work into a viable scholastic discourse.

Industrialisation, and the accompanying technology was altering people's daily lives: workers left home to find employment, people travelled further and more frequently with growing availability of train transport, and mechanisation changed the types of labour undertaken, and the experience and know-how needed to earn a living. Previously, the majority of England's population remained uneducated – with at most functional literacy and numeracy – because they did not *need* learning to survive. However, with the advent of industrialisation, the knowledge and know-how required for daily living was refashioned. The Industrial Revolution uprooted century-old traditions and radically changed people's thinking.[8] This burgeoning work force would need to keep accounts, read machinery manuals, manage workers and negotiate business deals, all of which demanded literacy and numeracy skills. Consequently, schools were being called upon to respond to this economic force. Educators needed to revaluate the curricula they would offer and reconsider the types of students they would serve; the conventional classical lessons no longer sufficed, nor would the new student population be so accustomed to the expectations of the academy. Education was crucial in preparing this labour force for this shift from a pastoral and agrarian way of living to an industrial and mechanised lifestyle.

Eventually, the labour pressures of industry and economy would trickle down to the classroom where students would learn new technologies and workaday strategies. Traditional subjects would not be ignored, but they would need to serve a new purpose for students. Teachers as well would need to be informed in order to properly instruct. Browning recognised how these industrial implications affected the British cultural and educational forum. In his Introduction to the *History of Educational Theories*, Browning questioned how nineteenth-century educators would revise their definition of the 'perfectly educated man':

> The perfectly educated man may find no place for himself in the economy of things... Consider the new industries of the last fifty years [1838–88], what necessities have been created by railways and telegraphs. The skill of a pointsman, an engine-driver, or a telegraphist requires qualities of knowledge which probably did not exist before the present century. They have been produced by no school, taught by no master. As Persius says, the belly was their teacher, the necessity of making a livelihood formed them into the moulds. So, then, we have this antagonism between the individual and the world... What are we to do?[9]

In this passage to teachers, Browning asked them to reconsider the value of education, and how technology had altered it. His introduction went on to address how effective pedagogy could negotiate the conflict between the world and the individual. He knew that innovative teaching would help students make meaning of their rapidly changing lives, and offer them some agency in their decision-making processes. However, if education was to help in this transformation, it would need to be thoughtfully planned and executed.

In the 1860s, the British public school came under close scrutiny by the media and the government. According to Christopher Hollis in his Eton history, various critiques were written in serious magazines about the imperfections of public school curricula and how they were not preparing students for the rising industrial exigency. The State reinforced the monitoring of schools as it invested the first grants of public money in the education of the people; public inquiries were launched.[10] Among the 'press' coverage were critiques of the quality of learning at Eton College. The critics severely doubted the education it offered, the textbooks it used, and the manner of instruction it followed.[11] This criticism would escalate until a Royal Commission headed by Lord Clarendon was appointed to examine public school education. The Clarendon Commission reported in 1864 that boys who entered schools were 'ill-prepared'. '[T]he Commission recommended entry examinations which were then not usual. The lag caused by this poor start affected the curricula throughout the schools, and ensured that the universities had to undertake much groundwork which "rightly" was the schools' responsibility. This in turn affected university "standards".'[12] The Clarendon Report resounds like an all too familiar response to educational problems covered in contemporary British and American news media. Historically, governments have found limited solutions when educational problems arise, opting for quick-fix rhetoric of 'standards' and 'testing', rather than considering *how* students can be more efficiently and creatively taught.

One of the reasons Victorian public education was responding so poorly to these new cultural needs was because, previously, public schools existed to train boys to become gentlemen. Curricula did not include the sciences, mathematics and modern languages (crucial elements in competitive international trade). Public school education was not a preparation for managerial labour in industry, but rather, a public status symbol. For the upper-class male, his ability to cite the classics in their original tongues confirmed his predisposed place in the upper echelon of society; however, the skill was not very useful when settling business issues. Many early manufacturers, who were not considered gentlemen but who had gained wealth, wanted their sons to acquire a public education which would allow them to sustain their businesses while simultaneously crossing the magical class-line.[13] Increasingly, this crossover was going to happen as a result of financial gain rather than by dint of bloodlines. The British aristocracy may have cared little about its

49

inadequate education, but the rising middle class, who needed education to fulfil new industrial positions and class mobility aspirations, needed quality learning. Middle-class parents were not willing to risk their children's prosperity on a second-class education. The educational investigations would question public schools' content and method in the light of the changing financial and labour contexts.

Beyond the era's polemics of curricula and standards, living conditions were also difficult at public schools. Throughout the middle decades of the nineteenth century, the public schools, such as Eton, had gained an unsavoury reputation for harsh living conditions – conditions Oscar Browning experienced when he entered the school in 1851. Of O.B's early school days, Wortham recorded:

> His earliest years at Eton were the most unhappy. He was delicate, small, ill-fitted for the life in College ... the Collegers [scholarship boys, Browning being among them] were badly fed and their accommodations were exceedingly rough. The only apparatus for washing consisted of a number of enamelled basins in a trough, at each end of which was a cold-water tap. The windows in the room were broken. The towels were deliberately drenched by the first-comers ... At 7:30 they went into school, cold and unwashed ... It is not surprising that O. B. (then known as Bosque) used to get up from the table as hungry as when he sat down and, as he tells us, in a much worse temper.[14]

Generally in this scenario, tutors and lecturers gave little support to their charges, and left them to their own scholastic and emotional devices. Having suffered this hands-off approach, Browning compared the old student–teacher relationship to one he found more conducive to learning: 'Nothing can be more removed from the *camaraderie* which is now common with excellent results between the younger masters at many public schools and their pupils, and the stiffness and distance which was thought essential to the usefulness of even the youngest schoolmaster fifty years ago.'[15] In an 1890 article reviewing the contributions of Dr Matthew Arnold, Browning commended the renowned Rugby educator for having 'known every boy in the school, his appearance, his habits, and his companions. This intimate acquaintance with separate characters has been the source of much that makes modern education superior to that which preceded it.'[16]

Browning's experiences as a student remained with him throughout his life and informed how he reflected upon acts of teaching. He decided no student of his should be subjected to learning as an unpleasurable experience. He did not want them to react as he had in his journal of 1854, 'Bah, I hate Eton.'[17] Browning understood that the experience of school, books and lessons should not be hated but, instead, be nurtured and enjoyed through the love of learning. As a teacher, he felt accountable for this nurturing.

Perhaps one saving grace in the young Browning's Eton education was the presence of his tutor William Johnson Cory – at that time known only as William Johnson. In a letter of 1918, as an octogenarian, Oscar Browning recollected, 'I went to Eton in 1851 at the age of fourteen and I was in the division of William Johnson, who was also my tutor, in my opinion the greatest genius who ever gave himself to the education of boys.'[18] Cory's presence must have offered a needed refuge of compassion within the hardships that Eton imposed, or as Browning called the accommodations Cory offered, 'the paradise of my tutor's pupil room'.[19] In *King's College, A Short History*, Christopher Morris writes, '[Cory] was an inspiring teacher, perhaps the most inspiring Eton ever had.'[20] Richard Ollard, in his *An English Education*, agrees: 'No one did more to transform [Eton] than William Johnson Cory. In his life and in his writing, Cory gives the most lucid, the most articulate expression to the ideas and standards for which, rightly or wrongly, Eton has been admired.'[21] Within the limitations of this article, it is sufficient to say that William Cory contributed to Browning's and other tutors' perspectives about teaching, making a lasting impression upon his colleagues' pedagogy. In his *Hints to Eton Teachers*, he offered sage advice to his colleagues about teacher–student interaction. He wrote, 'And this brings me to the question, how far a teacher can be, and ought to be, intimate with all whom he teaches . . . I think a tutor had better start from the wish to be known to his pupils, than from the wish to know them.'[22] His *Hints* further suggested specific classroom practice, such as how to command discipline without punishment and how to engage students in their work. Paradoxically, for a teacher who was so dedicated to student success, Cory was eventually fired from Eton. Although it is never substantiated, Cory's eventual dismissal from Eton was the result of an 'indiscreet letter' (read sexually provocative) to a student that was intercepted by his father and reported to the Headmaster.[23] Another version of his dismissal, however, claims that what Cory did was frankly criticise another tutor in support of the student, and the act was deemed inappropriate.[24] Whichever version may be correct, William Johnson was expelled from Eton, and his name erased from all his books in the Eton library. His removal foregrounded an institutional opinion regarding teachers' roles, and forecast what would later happen to Oscar Browning.

As noted, Browning revered Cory throughout his life, and is said to have 'hand[ed] on Johnson's [pedagogical] torch to many later generations of Kingsmen'.[25] Browning was not only Cory's student, but later became his colleague when he returned to Eton as a tutor and housemaster. The younger master attributed his educational ideas to his senior colleague: 'In those days [when arriving at Eton as a tutor], I was a violent reformer, made so, partly by the influence of William Johnson [Cory], and partly by the radicalism of Cambridge, in which I had lived.'[26] Both men were influenced by the dissidents emerging out of Oxbridge, who challenged established mores about education and related social issues. These were Oxbridge men who, although schooled in the traditional curricula of the classics, felt that this knowledge should be revaluated and used to serve cultural and social reform.

For many of these social reformers, ancient Greek ideals were the optimal model of society if filtered through Christian beliefs. The classics, they believed, could instill a sense of honour, a devotion to one's country, and the moral efficacy needed to be a qualified leader.[27] However, other unspoken issues remained resonant in these ancient studies. In *An English Education*, Ollard discusses Victorian curricula and the conflict between Christian and Hellenic ideals, which gave, in his words, 'a peculiar tang to the education in schools and colleges such as Eton'.[28] The 'tang' to which Ollard refers is again the blatant same-sex male desire present in ancient texts such as the *Symposium* or *Phaedrus*. The rub, therefore, between Victorian Christian ideals and Hellenic texts was this male–male passion found in the major literature studies of the nineteenth century. Impacted by their rigorous Hellenistic scholarship, Oxbridge men placed great value in male companionship, a passionate and, allegedly, celibate fraternity. By no means overt, their writing propagated a close, yet 'chaste', binding between men that was thought to act as a muse to intellectual endeavours. Homosexuality, thus, was a veiled, yet palpable, issue of the strongly homosocial world of Victorian British public school education.[29]

In most critical studies about Victorian Hellenism, the issue of homosexuality is either condemned or dismissed as an inconvenient evil. Richard Jenkyns maintains in *The Victorians and Ancient Greece*, 'The truth is that the Greeks were used or abused to suit the convenience of the moment. For the most part, however, the Hellenic tone was employed to becloud emotions whose nature would otherwise be too glaringly plain.'[30] In addition, Ollard in his Eton history reports an extensive testimonial by a former Etonian informant, who confirmed but downplayed the homosexual desire at public schools. Ollard concludes, recommending that we should 'not make a fuss about things that don't in the end matter.'[31] I think it does matter, but for reasons the majority of Victorian scholars and commentators choose to ignore. What educational historians, such as Jenkyns and Ollard, do not recognise is how this is part of the pedagogy. When we ignore the positive results of what they deem unspeakable – the unspoken presence of desire in learning – we dismiss an important part of the pedagogical story. The twentieth-century educational theorist Max van Manen asserts, 'To be human is to be concerned with meaning, to desire meaning... Without desire there is no real motivated question.'[32] Without acknowledging the desire of learning and its potentials, it is impossible to envisage how students will enjoy learning and, subsequently, gain the confidence in their pursuits to make meaning.

Victorian classical studies and their desirous implications influenced Browning's classroom practice. He advocated a classroom which took desire and pleasure into account. In the context of the pleasurable learning environment and how it is created, it is important to remember the squalid living conditions in which Browning lived as a boy at Eton. In contrast to these conditions, Browning provided genteel living for his young boarders and even those not under his direct care at Eton. Father O. R. Vassal-Phillips testified to O. B.'s hospitality:

> I was not one of O. B.'s pupils, but from the time that I was a small boy he was very kind to me, and evidently took an interest in the growth of my mind. When I was sixteen he took me with him to Florence and Rome one winter holiday... O. B. used to talk to me about everything and I became the depository of certain most intimate secrets. No doubt in many ways it must have been very bad for me, but in others it was excellent... On our return home O. B. gave me two things, a free invitation... to breakfast with himself, his mother, and his sister whenever I pleased, and the run of his library.[33]

Browning treated his students with adult seriousness. He conversed with them as peers and respected their ideas, facilitating their growth with resources (books, music, art) to cultivate their young minds. Even when he entertained the celebrities of his day, students were not excluded, as Wortham describes:

> Life in Browning's house was a pleasant combination of high thinking and good living. Artists and men of letters, actors and musicians, Ruskin and Solomon, George Eliot and Water Pater, [the

list continues] were more or less frequent visitors and brought with them the atmosphere of the intelligent and civilized society to which Oscar Browning liked to think that he belonged in spite of his being a schoolmaster. Theatricals used to be given by the boys in the dining-room, which was so arranged that it could be turned into a theatre for the occasion. Concerts were held periodically on Saturdays at which professionals from London performed chamber music.[34]

'In spite of his being a schoolmaster', Browning did not find academia and glamour mutually exclusive entities. He sought the company of Victorian Britain's cultural leaders and intellectuals, and introduced his young charges to them to still further their development.

Although this generous living furnished for his boys made him a popular housemaster among his students and their parents, it annoyed his fellow dons who felt obliged to match the benchmark he set. Browning had a waiting list of students wanting to enter his house, and a reservation list of young boys who hoped to attend Eton one day. If other housemasters were to make their residences appealing to incoming parents and students, they would need to rise to the occasion. Browning was setting 'standards' of institutional demeanour and, consequently, putting his colleagues to the 'test'. Hornby, Browning's Headmaster, disapproved of Browning's musical and theatrical activities, considering them a waste of time.[35] He condoned the manly pursuits of Athleticism, a popular trend at the time, and Browning's soirées were in direct resistance to this public school prescription. The growing cult of athletics was a means to 'toughen upon the boys into men', and was a way to keep them occupied and free of vice. In *Eton Renewed*, Tim Card comments:

> The worries about homosexuality were doubtless behind other changes at Eton which were made by Hornby and which were generally regarded as evidence of philistinism. Theatricals were stopped; games took on an increasing importance. Whether athletes are any less liable to adolescent homosexuality seems doubtful, to put it mildly, but that view was widely accepted at the time.[36]

In other words, athletics allegedly curbed the boys' desires, but not only their potential sexual desires but, likewise, their desires about what and how to learn. Athletics were used to limit the boys' perceptions, restricting their involvement in the 'less manly' study of the arts. Hornby responded angrily to O. B.'s subversive extracurricular functions:

> You are the greatest shuffler I have ever met. You shuffle in
> everything you do... You neglect your work. Why don't you read
> Madvig's Latin Grammar? You lecture ladies; you examine here
> and there; you give musical parties on Saturday evenings. Why
> don't you stick to your work?[37]

Is it not odd that a Headmaster of a public school denounced such
intellectual and acculturating activities for students? Hornby accused
Browning of shirking his duties, because he was not using conventional
methods in teaching his boys. Hornby, evidently, preferred the methods of
recitation and rote practice from a grammar book. Alternatively,
Browning's pedagogical methods played to the interest of his students.
Like Cory before him, he introduced unofficial subjects into the
curriculum, such as art, science, economics, political science and modern
history. As far as Hornby was concerned, Browning's classroom content,
his pedagogical methods, his music and his outside educational pursuits
were all diversions from the 'serious work' he should have been doing. As
a teacher, Browning appeared to be expanding and enjoying his craft,
keeping it alive with experimental lessons and engaging activities for him
and his students. For the more conventionally minded, this might sound
like too much pleasure to be 'real' learning.

Browning arrived at a different conclusion about classroom content and
practice: it is not as important *what* we teach (or even *when* we teach as
demonstrated by his soirées), but *how* we teach it. Regardless of the
subject matter, it is the pedagogy which remains the crux of the successful
educational process. Efficient teaching can bridge the gap between
established curricula and student interest as well as between new
economic forces and waning educational cultures. Educators need to
review how they devise lessons and classroom practices, but this also
assumes that the instructors in front of the class are sufficiently prepared
and knowledgeable about burgeoning disciplines, or humble enough to
learn about them alongside their students. O. B. knew that to achieve
classroom success during a changing era, teachers needed to have a
different relationship with their students. He knew how to instill a sense
of camaraderie in his students, and treated his pupils as companions in
learning. This type of student–teacher relationship was an unusual
approach in Victorian public schools, where the precedent had been to
keep a reserved distance between tutors and students unless, of course,
punishment was involved. Browning infuriated the other traditional
masters, who objected to his free intermingling with students. They
complained that he advised the boys under their trust on various life

issues, including its vices, and they took obvious exception to the boundaries he overstepped.

The close relationship Browning had with George Nathaniel Curzon, later Viceroy of India, would be a major factor leading to Browning's eventual dismissal from his Eton post. David Gilmour, in his biography of Curzon, reports, '[Browning] was also one of those rare teachers capable of identifying and stimulating a boy's latent interests. In return, his favourite pupils were devoted to him. Curzon remained a friend for fifty years and introduced him to his first wife with the words, "Whatever I am, dear, I owe it all to Mr Browning."'[38] In contrast to his admiration of Browning, Curzon detested his own tutor Wolley-Dod, finding him staid and unintellectual. In reaction to Curzon and Browning's friendship, Wolley-Dod lodged a complaint with the Headmaster against Browning and his activities with Curzon, and after numerous warnings the two were forbidden from seeing each other. Curzon's parents, however, fully appreciated the attention O. B. gave their son and, during a following school break, would send him with Browning on a European tour. Unfortunately for Browning his relationships with students and his style of teaching were to be the demise of his career at Eton. Hornby abhorred Browning's (and, previously, Cory's) alternative approaches to dealing with students. The tangle of progressive pedagogy and desire was too much for Eton's conservative contingent to handle. But how else could Hornby justify to Eton's students, parents and institutional authorities, that because Browning employed enjoyable, successful teaching methods he was at fault? In the end, Hornby accused Browning of not following a minor administrative regulation, and sacked him. Yet, during dismissal proceedings, the Headmaster also alluded to Browning's moral misconduct with students. Infuriated, Browning inflated the issue, found a supporting parent with peerage, and finally involved the British Parliament, in the end, to no avail. After 15 years of dedicated teaching, Browning was removed without honour (or pension) from his Eton post.

William Cory wrote to H. E. Luxmoore, another Eton tutor, regarding Browning's dismissal:

> I believe the departure of Oscar Browning will be resented by scores of kindly, intelligent young men to whom he has freely given all that he had to give of those good things of the mind which the old routineers thought should be reserved for the Masters of the Arts...I daresay among these boys will be a few sweet-hearted enthusiasts: they are the people that used to be starved at Eton.

Happily, there are plenty, no, a fair sprinkling – of young teachers who so far resemble B. [Browning] as to make themselves known to the lads: that is the new art or growth in schools. It is, I think, not less than a critical change in education, though, being unconnected with creeds, it has not yet found its biographical historian.[39]

Cory lamented Browning's departure because he saw it as symbolic of the diminishing ranks of gifted teachers and, therefore, productive pedagogy at Eton. He worried about the mere 'fair sprinkling' of a pedagogical tradition that he himself initiated at Eton and, thereafter, Browning perpetuated. First Cory is discharged, then Browning: Hornby was slowly but surely ridding Eton of this 'dangerous' element of (effective) pleasurable pedagogy. Even if he could not expunge it completely, he would give due warning to those who believed in its practice.

Browning is, of course, not the only Victorian educational figure who could be representative of this period, but his historical role offers an alternative perspective of Victorian teaching. O. B. was a unique character, queer, in fact, in all the various and contentious meanings of that word. I chose Oscar Browning because his way of interacting with students altered the typical disciplinary roles that teachers were expected to assume and, because of these unorthodox relationships, his personal desires and professionalism eventually became suspect. This tutor's pedagogical and sexual desires began to interweave and to change the fabric of how instruction could be done and how that affected students' relations with teachers and vice versa. Ian Anstruther writes in his 1983 biography of Browning:

> The complexity of Browning's character seems to be just as difficult to understand today as it was a century ago to those who knew him. He was blessed with talents of a high order – intelligence, charm with stamina, a gift for friendship and a genuine love of youth – which ought to have given him real success in his chosen profession of teaching. At the same time he was cursed with equal and opposite defects – conceit, sloth, narrowness, insensitivity, a genius for upsetting people and an unpleasant homosexual appetite. Over and over again these got him into trouble and stopped him achieving the prizes his talents deserved. The needle on the balance swings back and forward violently between good and bad, and the problem for the biographer which these contradictions pose is formidable.[40]

Browning's character is difficult, yet it is the lens through which he is regarded which engenders how he is viewed and depicted. To revaluate his teaching life, I turn to Queer Theory's ideas regarding difference to illustrate an alternative concept of learning's desires and pleasures. Deborah Britzman explains:

> A queer pedagogy is not concerned with getting identities right or even with having them represented as an end in themselves. [Its point is] to examine and to refuse 'cases of exorbitant normality' whether such cases take the form of heteronormativity, racisms, gender centerings, ability hierarchies, and so on.[41]

Britzman resists teaching practices which fail to look beyond the status quo, which may hinder enrichment. What Browning's teaching life offers is a historical stance for difference – a place from which to approach students' learning with attention to their problems and their pleasures. He approached students' learning from their unique strengths, weaknesses and perspectives and, in doing so, was able to harness their learning capabilities. As a progressive reformer of education, his pedagogical practices challenged normative ways of educating young men in the nineteenth century. His 'queer' methods linked pedagogy and pleasure and, ultimately, were perceived as transgressive as his desires. Retrospectively, this alternative way of conceiving teaching creates a rich resource to reflect upon educational policy and practice.

Yet, generally, Browning has been cast as an educational villain. In a *Room of One's Own*, Virginia Woolf attacks Browning on his educational stances regarding women's learning:

> I will quote Mr Oscar Browning, because Mr Oscar Browning was a great figure in Cambridge at one time, and used to examine the students at Girton and Newnham. Mr Oscar Browning was wont to declare 'that the impression left on his mind, after looking over any set of examination papers, was that, irrespective of the marks he might give, the best woman was intellectually the inferior of the worst man'. After saying that Mr Browning went back to his rooms – and it is this sequel that endears him and makes him a human figure of some bulk and majesty – he went back to his rooms and found a stable-boy lying on the sofa – 'a mere skeleton, his cheeks were cavernous and sallow, his teeth were black, and he did not appear to have the full use of his limbs..."That's Arthur!" [said Mr Browning], "he's a dear boy

really and most high-minded."' The two pictures always seem to me to complete each other.[42]

Furthermore in Woolf's writing, as well as in that of a later Woolfian feminist critic,[43] O. B. is portrayed as a symbol of patriarchal forces. Unaware of how his extensive pedagogical work informs his story, his critics misinterpret his position on women's education. Woolf over-inflates his influence and underestimates his contributions to nineteenth-century educational reform. Woolf's 'two pictures' of Browning – his crass, inexcusable remark, coupled with the emaciated boy-child lounging in his parlour – illustrate a figure who represents a misogynist, patriarchal subjectivity, yet one which is diacritically marked by his homosexual desire. Woolf adopts her narrative about Browning from his nephew's biography where Wortham distinguished O. B. as a rescuer of Arthur rather than his lecherous suitor. Browning is quoted as explaining:

> 'Oh ... that's Arthur ... He's been a stable boy at Chantilly and was shamefully misused. They starved him to get his weight down and then beat him because he lost his strength. Finally, they threw him out. I found him destitute in Paris, and the only thing I could do was to bring him back with me. He's a dear boy really and most high-minded.'[44]

With the 'Arthur story', it is easy to sexualize O. B's intentions because of the disparate power relationships between Browning and Arthur. Woolf underscores his ostensible sexual activities to bolster her argument and to persuade her readership of Browning's sordid character. This reinforces her – in many ways unrelated – arguments about Browning's misogyny. As far as women's issues, Browning, in fact, engaged his students, both at Eton and Cambridge in open-ended discussions about women's suffrage, himself agreeing with suffrage. He, however, did not bully his students into adopting his political opinions, but allowed them to process and draw their own conclusions. Furthermore, Browning's teaching ideas and editorial writing showed that his complaint was not with women in education, but the type of education normally being offered to them.[45] The quality of teaching and knowledge that students received was always Browning's prime concern.

Anstruther, in his biographical portrait of Browning, disagrees with feminist writers, seeing him as a much less omniscient figure, yet he agrees with them on one integral factor: 'When he retired at the age of seventy, he was still only an ordinary Fellow, and had no public reputation except as a Cambridge personality. Something had always blocked his progress, the same something that had made Hornby [his Eton Head-master] determine, come what might, to sack him.'[46] That 'something' that Anstruther refers to is Browning's same-sex desire. In all his portraits, same-sex desire remains an important yet disparaged issue in his life. Their reinterpretations overlook Browning's career and life at Eton and King's College, glossing over his life as an educator. Browning devoted his lifetime to teaching young men and, although all of his biographies include issues about his teaching career, they often ignore the impact that his pedagogy – his particularly quirky stances about teaching – had upon British public schooling and, later, upon reform at King's College. Other educators were as involved in a reforming pedagogical process, but it is O. B.'s particularly queer (read alternative) approach that is idiosyn-cratically representative of transforming educational thinking. Those who have recorded his life have disregarded his teaching practices and philosophies, his scholarly work concerning pedagogy, his dedication to teaching England's gilded youth, and his later teacher-training endeavours with working-class students.

In my revision of his story, I recognise how Browning's desire bonded with his pedagogical thinking. Emphasising his life teaching boys and, later, diverse classes of university men, only underscores a significant part of his often dismissed life. His desire, both his sexuality and his teacherly goals, overlapped. In his 1868 article 'On Science Teaching in Schools' for the Victorian journal *The Chemical News*, Browning discussed the usefulness of science teaching in schools and, further, commented on how different disciplines can suit 'an order peculiar to [each] individual'. In a metaphor of appetite, Browning wrote:

> Experience of boys' minds tends to show me that they are not generally indolent or inactive; that if they are surrounded by healthy conditions, they are really desirous of growth and nourishment. The chief difficulty of the teacher is to discover the precise food which is required at a given time. If this is offered, it is received and assimilated with the greatest ease and rapidity. The most perfect possible education would be given by supplying at the right moment the intellectual food for which the healthy mind was craving.[47]

Browning reiterated how important it is for teachers to attend to students' interests and strengths as a way to supplement their educational regime. If students' aptitudes can be discerned and nurtured, then they can be induced to partake in the remainder of their less favourite scholastic victuals. His sensual rhetoric of desire/appetite co-mingled with learning/teaching reveals his own educational cravings.

Like others who have used him as a symbol, I want to address his teaching career to show the importance of desirous instruction – a pedagogy that acknowledges student need and introduces pleasure into teacherly performances. The driving force of Browning's teaching was his concern with and dedication to his students' interests and pleasures in the service of their scholastic success. Many of his critics, who ignore the effects of desirous teaching, have used this against him, like Anstruther above, who reproaches him for being a lover of boys. They simplistically conflate the teacher's caring actions with the teacher's personal desires without considering the beneficial effects of desire on teacher–student relationships.

With his student-centred approach to learning, Oscar Browning represents a form of teaching full of rich potential because of the non-normative perspectives he brought to the classroom. With his charges' best interests in mind, his desire informed and inspired his teaching which, for his declaimers, undermined his teaching career. David Newsome questions the reasons why men such as Browning would choose to teach young men. His statements define the classroom partnership between students and instructor as 'the mutually vulnerable relationship between the teacher and the taught, the consciousness of some particular or personal rapport becomes quite literally a sort of heart-hunger – an almost irresistible stretching-out towards an intimacy of unions: heart strives to speak with heart'.[48] Newsome acknowledges that to teach students you must care about them and, reciprocally, students must care about you. I appreciate how he sees both the positive side of this desire to teach, while recognising the pitfalls, ones in which both students and teachers become vulnerable. Moreover, his inquiry extends beyond the teaching of boys and strikes a chord resonant with all acts of pedagogy and teacher–student relationships. In investigating a teaching life, such as Browning's, teachers may reflect upon and better understand the advantages and inspirations of this form of desirous pedagogy, while speculating about its possible dangers and limitations.

Even after being removed from his post in 1875, Browning remained true to his ideals of pedagogy, and was to return to his fellowship at King's College, Cambridge, where he incorporated these ideals into his work with university men. One of Browning's most formidable contributions to British education was his work with the Cambridge Day Training College for Men, which grew out of the University Extension Programme and was designed to prepare working-class men for primary and secondary teaching positions. (A similar programme was designed for women also.) Browning was a key figure in the founding and successful initiation of this progressive endeavour in 1891 that continued until 1938 when it evolved into Cambridge's education department. The students involved in this programme matriculated into a university college and followed the regular degree coursework, but with additional coursework concerning the theories and methods of teaching. Some university faculty members found this line of study pointless, but Browning relentlessly justified its role in the university. In a preface for Johann Freidrich Herbart's *The Science of Education*, Browning wrote:

> It is urged by some that a university graduate who has been at a public school needs no special training [to teach], because having had experience of many teachers he can tell for himself what should be imitated and what avoided. It would be as reasonable to assert that an invalid who had passed through the hands of many physicians would make an excellent doctor.[49]

And in a lecture he delivered to a meeting of the Day Training College, he stated:

> In discussing the advantages which teachers derive from training, should we not rather throw the burden of proof on the opponents of training, and call upon them to show why, of all occupations and professions, teaching should be the only one which can be successfully exercised without previous training? The teacher's is one of the most difficult and subtle of occupations, and certainly one of the most important, but it has been one of the most despised and neglected.[50]

In both these passages Browning reacted to the academy's adverse opinions about the significance of progressive pedagogy and teacher training. He realised that without adequate tutoring and guidance, students could not fulfil the 'standards' expected of them. Browning's sarcastic tone showed his passion about the act of teaching and his disdain for those who would diminish its importance. Yet positive commentary about quality teaching always accompanied these sardonic comments:

> A boy is not a fair critic of a master's methods. He is generally struck to an exaggerated degree by some peculiarity, which may be a merit or a defect. Indeed, the best teaching and the highest form

of education are imparted in such a way that the pupil is unconscious of the process. The greatest merit of the teacher is to secure his own effacement. His greatest honour is when the pupil thinks that he has learnt everything by his own unaided efforts.[51]

Yet, Browning was not a sentimentalist regarding the responsibilities of the classroom, and he acknowledged the discipline necessary of the learner and instructor. He wrote:

The mainspring of education is stimulus, the exciting of interest, but the necessary condition precedent of stimulus is discipline. The chief object of the training of a teacher is to secure discipline, discipline resting not on fear or the threat of punishment, but on kindly influence, which makes disorder impossible, because disorder would be the interruption of a genuine pleasure... By the force of training, the influence of the heart has taken the place of pompous pretense and of hard austerity or of hectoring and bullying. The pupil does not fear, he likes and he sometimes loves.[52]

Browning's lifelong dedication to progressive pedagogy and his democratic perspective of education was apparent in how he administered the Day Training College. He knew that many of these predominantly working-class students would be unaccustomed to the expectations and rigours of a university education. Many of them would be the first of their families to attend university and, therefore, would not have the parental support and guidance that his more privileged students assumed. Some of these students were partially supported by Toynbee Hall, a social service founded by Canon S. A. Barnett to uplift the poverty-stricken of East London. Barnett conceived of a plan to invite Oxbridge College men to live in the poor neighbourhoods of London, while also sending working-class students to the ancient universities.[53] These new university students, who in 1891 numbered three under the Principalship of Browning,[54] were the first members of the Cambridge Day Training College (CDTC). While upper-class college men were experiencing and hoping to contribute to the Whitechapel, Stepney, Hackney and Tower Hamlet boroughs of London, working-class students with Browning's guidance acculturated them-selves to academic life.

Both during their time at Cambridge and afterwards, Browning kept close contact with many of these Day Training College participants. He realised that the regular university curriculum, accompanied by the extra work of the CDTC certificate, was a burden on his already disadvantaged students. While at Cambridge, they began studying Greek and Latin, languages with which they had no, or little, previous training, but for which they would be examined. Browning, himself, undertook the task of tutoring them for these exams, while also calling upon the assistance of his university colleagues. In his letters, there are numerous correspondences in which his Day Training College students mailed him Latin or Greek translations to correct for their revision. Browning also helped students gain scholarships, writing to Toynbee Hall representatives for additional funds, procuring financial pledges from the colleges themselves, or sometimes digging into his own pocket. Even after students departed the school, O. B. supported their employment searches with recommendations, encouraged their personal endeavours, and offered experienced advice about their careers. Describing these working-class students, he wrote:

> It was a new and fruitful enterprise to send out every year a number of well-trained and distinguished University men to be elementary schoolmasters, and incidentally our college was a most efficient machine for providing a first-rate University education for exceedingly poor men. Many of our students had not cost their parents anything for their education since they were fourteen or fifteen years of age, and *it was an unspeakable pleasure to me*, who had spent my boyhood and early manhood in the society of the gilded youth of England, too often unconscious and unheedful of the advantages they possessed, to be connected with men of a more virile and self-denying type. Nothing struck me more in my intercourse with these young men than their great force of character and their strong individuality. Their success in their profession has up to the present time been remarkable...[55] [my emphasis]

Unlike many writers of his day, who spoke of education's ability to 'tame' the 'roughness' of the working-class, Browning did not use a negative rhetoric. He neither denounced their backgrounds, nor made excuses for flaws that they, like all students, may have had. He recognised the particular positions and problems associated with those positions and accommodated the 'efficient machine' of learning to their productive means. To put it simply, he unconditionally *taught* them. In his reverence for these working-class men, Browning's 'unspeakable pleasure' exposed a place where his desires and pedagogical ideals became constructively interlinked: his personal penchants informed his pedagogical visions and vice versa.

Throughout his life, Oscar Browning espoused the history of education as a crucial knowledge for teachers. He was convinced that the accrued knowledge and knowhow from former educators should be remembered as a rich resource to our teaching practices. He claimed:

> It is often argued that this study [of the history of education] is of comparatively little value, and should not be given an important place in the curriculum. I cannot agree with this opinion. The History of Education may be treated in various ways. It may deal with the theories of educational thinkers, or with the practice of educational reformers, or it may be chiefly of an antiquarian character, giving an account of obscure writers on educational subjects and of the conduct of famous schools in past ages. This antiquarian lore is of little practical utility, and the prevalence of it has done much to discredit the study of the History of Education, but, apart from the fact that the knowledge of what has been imagined or attempted in the reform of education is valuable possession to every teacher, the History of Education is the best introduction to the study of the Theory and Practice. You cannot deal with one without in some degree touching upon the other, and the fact that the information comes in a concrete form closely connected with the vicissitudes of an individual life, gives the study an interest of its own, assists the memory and stimulates the curiosity.[56]

As Browning suggested, the history of education offers a productive place from which to address policy questions because it offers a dialogue between grounded accounts of actual classroom events and theoretical ideals. While seeing the larger frame of education, Browning wanted us to recognise the significance of the classroom's smaller picture, to understand how crucially informative that picture is to our definition of education. He wanted us to listen to the 'dialogue' between theory and praxis. There is useful information that comes from people who dedicate their lives to teaching, who have close contact with students, and who question their practices carefully and thoughtfully.[57] This informed perspective about the classroom views education differently from policy-makers, who may have vague memories of what it means to be a learning individual and who normally do not have first-hand teaching experience with students. The informed teacher's viewpoint bypasses simplistic solutions to educational 'crises'. A plethora of standards and tests can be implemented, but without careful consideration of how students will learn and teachers will teach, educational criteria and examination results mean relatively little. A pie chart of passes and fails reveals little about people's ability to apply their learning to the improvement of their daily lives. Close attention to student development, although more rigorous an activity, can demonstrate much more about educational behaviours and habits. However, to do this we must be close to our students and be attentive to their backgrounds, problems and needs, as well as their desires and pleasures in the classroom.

When David Newsome looks at the life of various Eton tutors, he cautions that when there are close relationships between teachers and students:

> professional detachment is most severely put to the test. What, after all, is true vocation if it is not the yearning to arouse, to enkindle, to elevate, to improve, to open up new horizons, to share excitement with others, above all – to give? These are all functions, which lie athwart the tenuous dividing line between the intellect and the affections. This line is the tightrope that many schoolmasters have to walk. But not all who walk it can perceive the abyss at their feet; and even those who do, and who are brave enough to keep on walking, cannot always reach the end.[58]

Oscar Browning was not detached, but he was professional. If questioned about his students' pleasures and learning, he would have agreed that they were inextricable. He would also have explained, as he did in his teacher training, how learning could be achieved as a vocation of love and pleasure for both teachers and students. From a historical point of view Browning, and subsequent public school teachers, walked this tightrope with their students, revealing and conveying their desires successfully, constructively and ethically.

To look at the historical lives of teachers is an important project because it allows us to see how schooling changes while, simultaneously, revealing the recurring patterns of educational issues. What may have been similar crises in the Victorian era can inform our own educational crises. Between these two historical eras, educational parallels can be drawn, and certain elements which affected Victorian education, such as job markets, technology and economics, again affect our classrooms today. Within this constant metamorphosis of education, the same questions are often reiterated about the quality, value and accountability surrounding educational goals: Why aren't our students more successful?

What curriculum should be put in place? Who is entitled to higher education? What kind of degree students are we trying to produce? Who should pay for education? More often than not, the same (inadequate) solutions are revisited. Educators, like Browning, question how their educational system can serve the needs of students, especially those who have been formerly excluded. They creatively approach their roles to make the system work for students, and their students consciously work within (or perhaps even against) the system.

Also crucial to students' success are the questions that conscientious and self-aware teachers ask themselves: how much of my time, my efforts and my knowledge do I give to my students? How much do I reveal about myself as a person? If I do not divulge things about myself, how else will students learn about the strengths, weaknesses, certainties and insecurities of an experienced learner? What student–teacher boundaries must I respect and which may be productively crossed? And, how are my students' and *my* scholastic desires both enkindled and quenched by the institutional systems in which we learn and teach? Summed up, these inquiries demand a bigger question; How can I help students yearn to engage fully in their educations? I would like to suggest that, like Browning, teachers who attend to their students' learning pleasures can stimulate a longing to learn even after they become history.

ENDNOTES

1. W. J. Cory, *Ionica* (London: George Allen), p.28.
2. O. Browning, *Memories of Sixty Years at Eton, Cambridge and Elsewhere* (London: John Lane, The Bodley Head; New York: John Lane Company), p. 299.
3. Ibid., p. 305.
4. I. Anstruther, *Oscar Browning, a Biography* (London: John Murray), pp. 16–17.
5. H. E. Wortham, *Victorian Eton and Cambridge – Being the Life and Times of Oscar Browning* (London: Constable and Co. Ltd.), p. 38.
6. J. S. Mill, 'Inaugural Address at St Andrews', in F. A. Cavenaugh (ed.), *James and John Stuart Mill on Education* (Cambridge: Cambridge University Press), p.139.
7. Ibid., p. 140.
8. M. O'Connell, *The Oxford Conspirators; A History of the Oxford Movement 1833–1845* (New York: Macmillan), p. 4.
9. O. Browning, *Introduction to the History of Educational Theories*

(London: K. Paul, Trench and Company), p.10.

10. C. Hollis, *Eton, A History* (London: Hollis and Carter), p. 221.

11. Ibid., p. 221.

12. M. Sanderson, *The Universities and British Industry 1850–1970* (London: Routledge and Kegan Paul), p. 29.

13. F. Crouzet, *The Victorian Economy* trans. by Anthony Forster (New York: Columbia University Press), p. 417.

14. Wortham, *Browning*, pp. 19–20.

15. O. Browning, 'Arnold and Arnoldism', *Education*, 1, p. 309 British Library Manuscripts, p. p. 1187.id.

16. Ibid., p. 309.

17. Ibid., p. 19.

18. O. Browning, Unpublished Letter, 1918, Berg Collection, New York City Public Library, Main Branch.

19. *William Johnson Cory 1823–1892* (Rampant Lions Press, Cambridge), p. 2. Rare Books Collection, New York City Public Library, Main Branch.

20. C. Morris, *King's College, A Short History* (Cambridge: Printed for the College), p. 43.

21. R. Ollard, *An English Education, A Perspective of Eton* (London: Collins), p. 59.

22. W. J. Cory, *Hints for Eton Masters* (London: Henry Frowde Oxford University Press Warehouse Amen Corner E. C.), p. 11, British Library 8304.bbb.4 ff. 1-7.

23. T. Card, *Eton Renewed, A History from 1860 to the Present Day* (London: John Murray Ltd.), p. 65; see Anstruther, Browning, p. 60.

24. A. Hickson, *The Poisoned Bowl. Sex Repression and the Public School System* (London: Constable and Company Limited), p. 59.

25. Morris, *King's*, p. 43.

26. Browning, *Sixty Years*, p. 64.

27. R. Jenkyns, *The Victorians and Ancient Greece* (Cambridge, MA: Harvard University Press), p. 60.

28. Ollard, *English Education*, p. 63.

29. For a fictional account of this Victorian male–male passion in education, read E. M. Forster's *Maurice*.

30. Jenkyns, *The Victorians*, p. 292.

31. Ibid., p. 134.

32. M. van Manen, *Researching Lived Experience: Human Science for an Action Sensitive Pedagogy* (Albany, NY: The State University of New York Press), p. 79.

33. Wortham, *Browning*, pp. 66–7.

34. Ibid., pp. 62–3.
35. Anstruther, *Browning*, p. 61.
36. Card, *Eton*, p. 66–7.
37. Wortham, *Browning*, p. 121.
38. D. Gilmour, *Curzon* (London: John Murray Ltd.), pp. 13–14.
39. F. C. Mackenzie, *William Cory, a Biography* (London: Constable), p. 89.
40. Anstruther, *Browning*, p. 189.
41. D. P. Britzman, *Lost Subjects, Contested Objects* (Albany, NY: State University of New York Press), p. 94.
42. V. Woolf, *A Room of One's Own* (New York: Harcourt Brace Jovanovich Inc.), p. 55.
43. In 'Taking the bull by the udders' and in a book review of Anstruther's biography, Jane Marcus follows Woolf's lead and presents Oscar Browning as the quintessential misogynist, homosexual patriarch.
44. Wortham, *Browning*, p. 247.
45. For the limitations and purpose of this article, it is impossible to elaborate further on this subject. However, the minutes of Browning's student debate group, the Political Society, and his writing and editorial work in the journal he co-edited contrast significantly from feminist accounts of his opinions. For the former, see 'Minutes of Political Society' Browning Archives, King's College Library, Cambridge; for the latter, see *Education, A Journal for the Scholastic World* (1890), British Library, London, p.p.1187.id.
46. Anstruther, *Browning*, p. 9.
47. O. Browning, 'On Science Teaching in Schools', *The Chemical News*, v 17, p. 243 British Library Science Division (P)J00-E(9).
48. D. Newsome, *On the Edge of Paradise: A. C. Benson, the Diarist* (Chicago, IL: University of Chicago Press), pp. 79–80.
49. J. F. Herbart, *The Science of Education*, preface by Oscar Browning (Boston, MA: D. C. Heath and Co., Publishers), p. vi.
50. O. Browning, 'The Importance of the Training of Teachers', Cam.d.906.13 Cambridge University Library, England, p. 1.
51. Herbart, *Science*, p. vi.
52. Browning, 'Importance,' pp. 2–3.
53. S. Meacham, *Toynbee Hall and Social Reform 1880–1914*. (London: Yale University Press), pp. 30–44; and see A. Briggs and A. Macartney, *Toynbee Hall: The First Hundred Years* (London: Routledge and Kegan Paul), pp. 30–5.
54. Wortham, *Browning*, pp. 210–11.
55. Browning, *Sixty Years*, p. 263.

56. Browning, 'Importance,' pp. 9–10.
57. For educational narratives of teaching practices and teacher–student interactions, see the works of S. Perl and N. Wilson, I. Shor, M. Sternglass, L. N. Tolstoy, and L. Weis and M. Fine.
58. Newsome, *Edge*, p. 80.

REFERENCES

Anstruther, I. *Oscar Browning, a Biography* (London: John Murray, 1983).

Briggs, A. and Macartney, A. *Toynbee Hall: The First Hundred Years* (London: Routledge and Kegan Paul, 1984).

Britzman, D. P. *Lost Subjects, Contested Objects* (Albany, NY: State University of New York Press, 1998).

Browning, O. 'On Science Teaching in Schools', *The Chemical News*, 17 (1868), pp. 243–4. British Library Science Division (P)J00-E(9).

— *Introduction to the History of Educational Theories* (London: K. Paul, Trench and Company, 1881).

— 'Arnold and Arnoldism', *Education*, 1 (1890), pp. 309–10. British Library Manuscripts, p. p. 1187.id.

— 'The Importance of the Training of Teachers,' (1906), pp. 1–15. Cam.d.906.13 Cambridge University Library, England.

— *Memories of Sixty Years at Eton, Cambridge and Elsewhere* (London: John Lane, The Bodley Head, 1910; New York: John Lane Company, 1910).

— Unpublished Letter, 1918, Berg Collection, New York City Public Library, Main Branch.

Card, T. *Eton Renewed, A History from 1860 to the Present Day* (London: John Murray Ltd., 1994).

Cory, W. J. *Ionica* (London: George Allen, 1891).

— *Hints for Eton Masters* (London: Henry Frowde Oxford University Press Warehouse Amen Corner E. C., 1898); British Library 8304.bbb.4 ff. 1–7.

Crouzet, F. *The Victorian Economy*, trans. by Anthony Forster (New York: Columbia University Press, 1982).

Forster, E. M. *Maurice* (New York: W. W. Norton and Company, 1971).

Gilmour, D. *Curzon* (London: John Murray Ltd., 1995).

Herbart, J. F. *The Science of Education*, preface by Oscar Browning (Boston, MA: D. C. Heath and Co., Publishers, 1900).

Hickson, A. *The Poisoned Bowl. Sex Repression and the Public School*

System (London: Constable and Company Limited, 1995).

Hollis, C. *Eton, A History* (London: Hollis and Carter, 1960).

Jenkyns, R. *The Victorians and Ancient Greece* (Cambridge, MA: Harvard University Press, 1980).

Mackenzie, F. C. *William Cory, a Biography* (London: Constable, 1950).

Manen, M. van, *Researching Lived Experience: Human Science for an Action Sensitive Pedagogy* (Albany, NY: The State University of New York Press, 1990).

Marcus, J. Book review of *Oscar Browning: A Biography* by Ian Anstruther. *Victorian Studies* 28, 3 Spring (1985), pp. 556–8.

— 'Taking the bull by the udders: sexual difference in Virginia Woolf – a conspiracy theory', in J. Marcus, V*irginia Woolf and the Languages of Patriarchy* (Bloomington and Indianapolis, IN: Indiana University Press, 1987), pp. 136–62.

Meacham, S. *Toynbee Hall and Social Reform 1880–1914* (London: Yale University Press,1987).

Mill, J. S. 'Inaugural Address at St Andrews.' In F. A. Cavenaugh (ed.) *James and John Stuart Mill on Education* (Cambridge: Cambridge University Press, 1931).

Morris, C. *King's College, A Short History* (Cambridge: Printed for the College, 1989).

Newsome, D. *On the Edge of Paradise: A. C. Benson, the Diarist* (Chicago: University of Chicago Press, 1980).

O'Connell, M. *The Oxford Conspirators: A History of the Oxford Movement 1833–1845* (New York: Macmillan, 1969).

Ollard, R. *An English Education, A Perspective of Eton* (London: Collins, 1982).

Perl, S. and Wilson, N. *Through Teachers' Eyes: Portraits of Writing Teachers* (Portsmouth, NH: Heinemann, 1986).

Sanderson, M. *The Universities and British Industry 1850–1970* (London: Routledge and Kegan Paul, 1972).

Shor, I. *When Students Have Power: Negotiating Authority in a Critical Pedagogy* (London: The University of Chicago Press, 1996).

Sternglass, M. *Time to Know Them: A Longitudinal Study of Writing and Learning at the College Level* (Mahwah, NJ: Lawrence Erlbaum Associates, 1997).

Tolstoy, L. N. *Pedagogical Articles/Linen-Measurer, The Complete Works of Count Tolstoy*, Vol. IV (New York: Colonial Press Co., 1904).

Weis, L. and Fine, M. *Beyond Silenced Voices: Class, Race, and Gender in United States Schools* (Albany, NY: State University of New York Press, 1993).

William Johnson Cory 1823–1892 (Cambridge: Rampant Lions Press, 1959)

Woolf, V. *A Room of One's Own* (New York: Harcourt Brace Jovanovich Inc., 1929).

Wortham, H. E. *Victorian Eton and Cambridge – Being the Life and Times of Oscar Browning* (London: Constable and Co. Ltd., 1927).

4

Through Cigarette Cards to Manliness: Building German Character with an Informal Curriculum[1]

GEOFFREY J. GILES

Like other children in England, I used to cut out and collect the cards printed on the side of packets of Typhoo Tea, and then the sets of coloured inserts with Brooke Bond Tea on British wildlife, to which belonged attractive albums. At the end of the twentieth century, collecting cards again became the rage, all too literally in fact. In America the Pokémon craze led some teenagers to break into their classmates' homes and commit assault and robbery, in order to complete their set with rare and valuable cards. Such fanaticism is new, but young people have avidly collected colourful cards for well over a century. They have generally been viewed as educational, but in Germany from the 1920s to the 1940s and beyond they were often designed as character-building and ideological tools as well. During the Second World War they were blatantly tied to anti-British propaganda efforts. For example, a photographic portrait of Queen Victoria in the series 'Robber State England' bears the caption: 'The ruler herself embodied many traits of the British national character: self-righteousness and a sham pious hypocrisy, behind which the ruthless lust for power conceals itself.' In the same series, a reproduction of a French cartoon depicting King Edward VII as a rotund wine barrel, deliberately misinterprets this as a powder keg, with the comment that the artist's vision came true: 'Edward VII became the man responsible for the isolation of Germany and thereby paved the way for the World War.'[2]

The origins of the genre are more innocent. The only German scholar to devote his attention to what he describes as 'series pictures' links them to the rising popularity of the picture postcard in the last quarter of the nineteenth century, and sees them as smaller versions of these, distributed by tradesmen.[3] Printed from the start in attractive colours, they could not have taken off in popularity but for the advances in colour lithography.

73

Information on the relative ease and cheapness of printing from stone, rather than engraving a copper or steel plate, began to spread in the second decade of the nineteenth century. Although the process was patented in England in 1780, for example, it was not until 1840 that a lithotint process patent was taken out for actual colour printing. A high-speed printing machine came into use in 1851, enabling the mass production of coloured illustrations as posters or postcards, and the latter exploded in popularity in the 1870s in many countries.

Erhard and Evamaria Ciolina trace the first ever example of what they term 'advertisement collecting cards' to the Parisian department store, *Au Bon Marché*. The founder of this chain, Aristide Boucicaut, decided to present a small gift card with each purchase, with the addresses of his stores on the back, and a charming or amusing colour picture on the front. Customers gave such a positive response that Boucicaut had whole sets of cards designed, which the former soon began pasting into scrap books.[4] In Germany the Liebig Meat Extract Company seized this marketing idea, beginning in 1872, and publishing a total of over 1,100 short sets of highly attractive chromolithographs (generally comprising six cards per set). The bulk of such card series, however, derive from cigarette companies, and the idea was hatched in the United States in 1880. Later the so-called British–American Tobacco War between rival companies spurred British cigarette manufacturers to compete with their own collectibles at the turn of the century. Regimental and national flags, along with portraits of royalty and generals, struck a patriotic note in Britain during the First World War. Such cigarette cards were printed on silk, and collectors were encouraged to remove them from the card backing and have them sewn into cushion covers. Germany's tobacco industry was slow to come to this form of sales promotion, the majority of pre-war cards being restricted to the food industry. The medium proliferated in that country only toward the end of the 1920s, albeit with a vengeance.[5]

Even before Adolf Hitler came to power, and despite his detestation of smoking,[6] the money-spinning tobacco company owned by the Nazi Party, producing 'Storm' cigarettes for its Stormtroopers in the SA and their supporters, was issuing its own cards and albums. With the theme of 'German Uniforms', they had an ideological bent and promoted militarism from the beginning. The 1930s were the heyday of cigarette-card collecting, and tobacco companies used them aggressively as a marketing tool. However, in Germany this coincided with Hitler's tenure as the country's chancellor, and numerous cigarette manufacturers saw this as a means of demonstrating their support for the values of the Nazi regime. Because the cards were principally directed toward the young, they thus grew to be part of the informal curriculum that was already being privileged by the Nazis over the regular school system. The evidence for direct interference from the state in the design or text is scant, although numerous sets featured pictures from the studio of Hitler's own court photographer, Heinrich Hoffmann, which were sometimes amended or censored and withdrawn from later editions of a set.[7] These items of ephemera are worthy of the attention of the historian of education because of their ubiquity in this period. Cards were swapped on every school playground, and with well over 1 million copies of some albums being distributed, they found their way into a remarkable number of homes.

The contents of these albums can be scrutinised from a number of perspectives, such as outright propaganda as in the wartime example above. In large part they merely filled the role of mini-encyclopedias on birds or animals, like many British card sets. An enormous number dealt with sports heroes from the very start, and another large sub-category focused on the cinema and popular film stars. More revealing for the historian are those series that deal with the state: its history, its politics and the role of the individual in it. Felicity O'Dell, in her analysis of Soviet children's literature, quotes Max Weber's remark, concerning the role of ideology in society: 'The magical and religious forces and the ethical ideas of duty based upon them have, in the past, always been among the most important formative influences on conduct.'[8] This is apparent in National Socialist children's literature as well, and ideological issues became more central in the themes of cigarette cards after Hitler's accession to the chancellorship in January 1933, especially in the biggest tobacco firms, such as Reemtsma in Hamburg, Brinkmann in Bremen, or Greiling in Dresden.[9] The subtle role of cigarette cards in character formation, in producing the model German or the model Nazi, has been previously ignored by historians. The thematic content seems to indicate that the cards were directed more pointedly towards boys than girls, and so it is appropriate to examine in this essay some of the suggestive ways in which these images were trying to lead the male youths of Germany in the 1930s. The question of feminine values will be dealt with in a separate essay.

GENDER BOUNDARIES

From the start gendered messages appeared in some popular sets. The emancipation of women following the First World War was deeply upsetting to many on the political right wing, and the Nazi Party promised to return to traditional gender roles. A card in a set on the recent history of

Germany showed a mass wedding of Stormtroopers and their brides, walking two by two in procession in Berlin in November 1933. The notes, accompanying the card, praised the May 1933 law that had thrown out the concept of equality of the sexes in the workplace. State marriage loans, it claimed, would retain women in the home where they could concentrate on the housework, and create job vacancies for men. It must be remembered that this was written in a period of severe unemployment, following the worldwide depression, when enthusiasm for such prospects of work tended to override such sympathy for equal employment opportunities as the Weimar Republic had only just begun to spark among German men.[10] Germany was not unusual among Western countries at this time in consigning housework to the women of the family. A rare glimpse of men carrying out domestic tasks is given in a photograph of a group of five Stormtroopers peeling potatoes, but that is in the special context of the homosocial and para-military world of the SA. When the men were under canvas, similar pictures of camp kitchens were not uncommon, but this particular scene is placed in what is evidently the 'home' headquarters of the unit.[11] The important point here was that membership in the Nazi SA was not all fun and adventure (which at this time translated largely into marching on parade and beating up Communists), but work too was involved. It had also to be seen that it was useful work, in this case resulting in the feeding of a whole platoon of troops, judging by the size of the laundry tub into which the peeled potatoes were being thrown.

THE NOBILITY OF WORK

A strong message promulgated through National Socialist publications, as Hitler's government strove toward full employment, was that work was good, and indeed ennobling. The regime seems to have taken extra care to put this message across about hard, unskilled, physical labour, into which thousands of men were drafted at first voluntarily, then compulsorily, in order to get them off the unemployment rolls. The Labour Service organised these work schemes, typically involving land reclamation in marshy areas, or road-building in the new *Autobahn* network. Cigarette card sets contained numerous images connected with these (in fact frequently unpopular) programmes and stressed the masculinity of the participants. The photographs sought to combine the manliness of the military (there was a special uniform for the Labour Service draftees) with the tough-guy persona of the manual worker. A set with the strongly propagandistic title, 'The Country of Work and Peace', showed a group of new Labour Service recruits, still in their civilian jackets and overcoats and flat caps, marching off from the city centre (in perfect step!) to break ground, their shovels shouldered like rifles. Not yet the bronzed Adonis types that symbolised much of the Labour Service's publicity, they will nonetheless be transformed through hard labour into such demi-gods. The very last picture in this set, 'The way uphill', depicts them in uniform, marching up a hillside in the country with their spades shouldered. They are silhouetted against the skyline on a summer's day, and the caption clearly suggests that a long struggle still lies ahead. The Nazi leadership relied on the idea of a constant struggle, a permanent revolution, in order to legitimise itself. This particular set was conceived as a celebration of the first anniversary of Hitler's regime. The quick reduction in unemployment figures through work creation schemes was celebrated as a kind of miracle. And, while military metaphors dominate, there do occur some almost religious motifs in the iconography. An illustration at the foot of one page in the album is reminiscent of an altar table, on the front of which one sees depicted yet another phalanx of muscular German workers marching uphill from the darkness – this time with a hammer and sickle (as well as a spade) in a clear reference to the socialist movement, which the Nazis are claiming to have trumped – into the bright, new dawn, over which hangs the old tricolour flag of Germany flanked by two swastika banners.[12]

The basic message that work was good for Germany often appeared in images of masses of men. The thousands of Labour Service conscripts on parade for the Nuremberg Rallies were a favourite theme. One typical picture gives an aerial shot of the units, marching past in rows of about 40 men, not only with their trademark shovels, but with heavy backpacks as well.[13] Yet at the same time there was an emphasis on the benefits for the individual, not least in self-esteem. Nordic-looking pin-ups were highlighted in the same way, as they did service for supposedly typical members of other Nazi Party organisations. A group of half-a-dozen shirtless workers carrying tracks for the building of a field railway are fairly average-looking men on the whole, but in the foreground of the group the photographer has prominently placed a sleek blond, wearing riding breeches and jackboots (unlike the others), evidently a Labour Service NCO. Clearly the picture is deliberately posed in this way [*See illustration no. 1*]. 'Work again at last!' proclaims the caption of a picture of a good-looking young man, in shirtsleeves but wearing a far from shabby waistcoat and flat cap, which were typical workman's clothing at the time. He appears to be about to shovel sand in a sand-pit, so the work is none too exciting, but at least it is a paid job, and his clothes look fairly new.[14] Many were the attempts to glamourise very mundane occupations like this. Being a house painter was not a very interesting job, yet even something like this could be invested with a certain cachet. A card in the set, 'German Labour', the aim of which was to celebrate a whole range of occupations, shows a man painting the wrought iron decorative trimming at the top of a church tower. Part of the caption explained: 'As can be seen from our picture, the work of the painter can also be really dangerous,' which was evidently meant as an encouragement, not a warning. A similar device of marketing danger in positive terms was attempted in the depiction of a coal miner: 'His work is hard down there, a thousand dangers threaten his life, and yet he returns again and again, like his father before him, and his son after him. For the occupation of miner is passed down from generation to generation.' Here we also have ideas of continuity and tradition, reinforced by family pride, working against the mobility of labour that new industries had brought about at the end of the nineteenth century, poaching young men from the occupations of their forefathers.[15] It would happen again in the armaments industries in the 1930s but official policy ran in the opposite direction.

NEVER GIVE IN!

One of the virtues that National Socialist leaders tried to promote in describing occupations of this sort may be described as persistence in the face of adversity. The model for this was the tireless political struggle of Adolf Hitler himself, and the ideological underpinning was the Social Darwinism prevalent in Nazi thought, which insisted that all life was struggle (hence the title of Hitler's book, *Mein Kampf*). One example of this was a photograph of a lonely looking Adolf Hitler, holding forth in the snow on a January day in 1923 on the Marsfeld – Munich's more modest version of Paris's *Champs de Mars*, the allegorical significance of which should not be underestimated. Ranged behind him in no particular formation are a mere nine figures of rather chilled SA officers, a far cry from the meticulously choreographed rallies a decade later. Yet that is the whole point of the picture, to emphasize Hitler's political courage and doggedness in the small beginnings of the Nazi Party, when national success seemed only a pipe dream to most.[16] The same idea is conveyed through a line drawing, illustrating the same album, which happens to focus on Austria, where the Nazis had to wait a further five years after Germany for Hitler's takeover. Here the sun rises as a giant swastika, as a sturdy man in

Lederhosen watches from an adjacent mountain-top. The message: if only the individual will stand proud and tall, the Nazi utopia will dawn in the end. Much was made of the police prosecution of early Nazis. The Austrian album shows Nazis crowding at a prison window, defiantly waving a card with a giant swastika emblem through the bars.[17] This refusal to surrender was a common theme in Germany proper as well. Not only did this highlight the persecution that Nazis liked to claim they had suffered in the 1920s (though in fact they were treated much more leniently than their Communist rivals at the opposite end of the political spectrum), but it permitted the portrayal of their ingenuity in circumventing the law. When at various times the Nazi brown shirt was banned by state governments in an effort to quell potential riots, Storm Troopers would parade either bare-chested, or wearing ordinary white shirts [*See illustration no. 2*].[18]

This stubbornness could also be rooted in distant history. A series examining the history of Germany explained, under a scene depicting the surrender of a fortified town in the Thirty Years' War, that the citizens were honour-bound only to give up when 'all means of resistance had been exhausted, or if the town walls could no longer hold off an attack'.[19] Here was an unspoken allusion to the German General Staff in the First World War, which claimed that it had been unbeaten in the field, and had not wanted to surrender, but had simply been stabbed in the back by the home front. At that time, too, the generals would never have given up, if a slender hope of eventual victory had remained. The message is made more explicit in the very first picture in the set on 'The Post-War Era', which shows a gun crew firing off rounds at the invisible enemy. The caption reads: 'The tough resistance of the German front,' and the commentary goes on to deplore the situation in which the German armies found themselves: abandoned by their allies, the Bulgarians, in September 1918, and by the Austrians in October, they were then faced at home with 'revolutionary cells everywhere' (the stab in the back), so that they were 'no longer fighting out there for victory, but just for an honourable peace' (which the political right wing had always claimed the Versailles Treaty did not give them). In one card like this, a good deal of propagandistic myth could be encapsulated for what was possibly a young person's first encounter with contemporary history.[20] A little further on, another war story was milked to full advantage. The image shows the scuttling of a German battleship at Scapa Flow, while the angry British fire shots at a lifeboat full of unarmed German sailors with their hands up, drifting away from their sinking ship. The incident is captioned, 'The Heroism of Scapa Flow'.[21]

THE CONTINUITY OF HISTORY

History is often viewed by regimes as the great legitimiser, and in recent decades both the German Democratic Republic and the Federal Republic vied for the position of heir to the pre-Nazi, democratic Weimar Republic and to the glorious empire built up by Bismarck. As H.W. Koch has noted: 'National Socialist education carried to the extreme a tendency inherent in German history since the nineteenth century – the concentration upon the "world historical individual". History, it was alleged, could almost be completely taught in terms of political and military biographies.'[22] A cigarette-card album released in 1934 with the title, 'Great Figures of World History', is a good example of the genre, and consisted mainly of Germans, and placed Bismarck himself on the cover. Military might unashamedly framed this series, with Charlemagne gracing the first card, and the generals of the First World War filling the last page. Charlemagne was described as 'the most powerful conqueror of the Germanic West. He subjugated the Langobard empire in Italy, the Bavarians, and above all in long and bloody battles the heathen Saxons led by Widukind.' Otto the Great, the hero of the second card, received similar plaudits. He was 'the most famous conqueror of the Saxon imperial house. With an iron fist he crushed the uprisings of his son Ludolf, his brother Heinrich, and the unruly ducal chieftains.' Otto is hailed as the founder of the 'First Reich' through his creation in the tenth century of the Holy Roman Empire on the basis of his German empire.[23] These historical series did not merely show stereotypical warlords as the makers of history, however. In a scene that goes against the typical Nazi view of students as the antithesis of real men of action, we see the Breslau Professor Steffens (not even a German himself!) haranguing his students in 1813 to leave their classrooms and take up the fight for their fatherland against Napoleon.[24] Another man who was not the stereotypical warrior was Frederick the Great, startled while playing the flute by his angry father, Frederick William I. 'The soldier king disliked it intensely', we are told, 'when Frederick occupied himself with anything but military matters.' Nonetheless Frederick became a great military leader in the end, and in addition an important role model for not surrendering in the face of the many setbacks he suffered. And there was always the foil of his brother, Prince Henry, to hold up as a soldier's soldier. One picture shows him, having just jumped into a ditch ahead of his reluctant men at Prague in 1757, in order to lead them through a swamp to the attack.[25]

Figure 1. Always a blond in the foreground: Labour Service men laying railway tracks.
Source: Cigarette card album *Staat der Arbeit*, p. 38; Geoffrey Giles, private collection.

Figure 2. Defying the ban on Brown Shirts: Stormtroopers parade on Vienna's *Ringstrasse*,
Spring 1933.
Source: Cigarette card album *Ostmark*, p. 48; Geoffrey Giles, private collection.

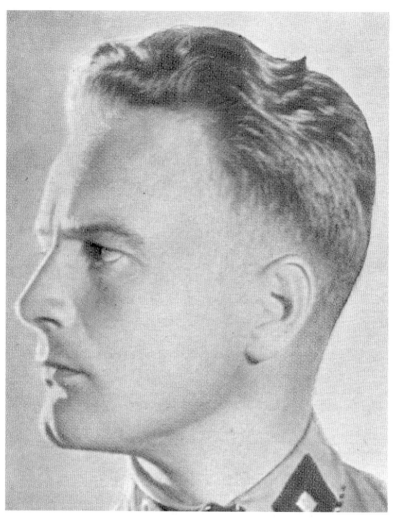

Figure 3. The model Stormtrooper: blond hair, blue eyes, chiselled features, determined gaze.
Source: Cigarette card album *Kampf um's Dritte Reich*, p. 17; Geoffrey Giles, private collection.

Figure 4. Basic training is going to be such fun: German navy recruits respond to the
'comradely heartiness' of their drill sergeant.
Source: Cigarette card album *Reichsmarine*, p. 24; Geoffrey Giles, private collection.

Figure 5. Racing to fight the enemy: a cavalry squadron's bicycle troop.
Source: Cigarette card album *Manöver*, p. 14; Geoffrey Giles, private collection.

Figure 6. A handshake from the Führer for Stormtroopers wounded fighting the Communists. *Source:* Cigarette card album *Ostmark*, opposite p. 56; Geoffrey Giles, private collection.

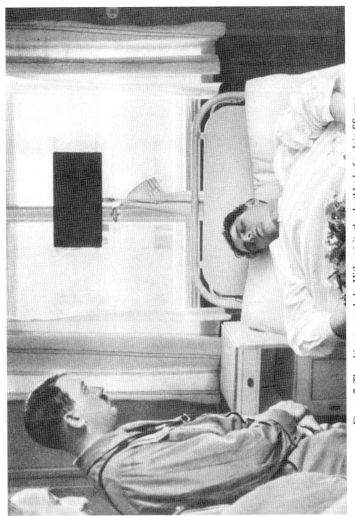

Figure 7. The ultimate accolade: Hitler visits the deathbed of a slain SS man.
Source: Cigarette card album *Deutschland erwacht*, p. 49; Geoffrey Giles, private collection.

Figure 8. 'The picture reveals the character': an allegedly typical Jewish leader of the
revolutionary government of Munich in 1919.
Source: Cigarette card album *Ostmark*, p. 19; Geoffrey Giles, private collection.

Figure 9. Raden Ajeng Kartini (centre standing) with her sisters Roekmini (right) and Soematri, 1901. Kartini described this studio photograph in self-deprecating terms to her Dutch friend, Rosa Adendanon-Mandri. The photograph represents her in the conventional style of the Javanese aristocracy of the day from whom she wished to distance herself.
Source: Koninklijk Instituut voor Taal, -Land en Volkenkunde (KITLV), Leiden, the Netherlands; with whose permission it is reproduced.

Figure 10. Raden Ajeng Kartini (right) and her sister Roekmini in their schoolroom in the grounds of the official residence of the Regent of Jepara, June 1903. Pupils are the children of native civil servants. Shortly afterwards Kartini received a proposal of marriage.
Source: Koninklijk Instituut voor Taal, -Land en Volkenkunde (KITLV), Leiden, the Netherlands; with whose permission it is reproduced.

Figure 11. Miss Rose Gosling (headmistress 1906–34)
and the girls of Bermuda High School.
Source: Winifred Rogers Collection, Bermuda Archives PA 532. Reproduced with the
permission of the Bermuda Archives.

Figure 12. The Korana's rock site. This site is still visible around Wentzeldam,
and the Korana's rock art paintings can be seen all over the vicinity of Hartz River
in Schweizer-Reneke.
Source: Ziphora Moichela, private collection.

THE GLORY OF THE MILITARY

It was important that military and para-military life appear to be attractive and enjoyable, and a number of ploys were used to enhance this image. Thousands of Germans were indeed thrilled when war broke out in 1914, and the famous picture of the smiling Adolf Hitler, listening to the declaration on 2 August in Munich, could not be missing from most books about the Nazi movement.[26] Hitler had rushed to volunteer with the best of them, and the elitism of fighting men was a constant theme that was applied also to the Stormtroopers. Handsome men in SA uniform were portrayed in close-ups, both with determined expressions and rather softer features, generally with the requisite blond hair and blue eyes. They gaze dreamily into the distance [*See illustration no. 3*]. Other pictures featured older men with full, grey beards, in uniform, to show that old warriors, too, were respected and welcomed in the ranks of the SA.[27] Sailors made attractive models, too, and a group of smiling recruits in a series on the navy seemed to suggest that basic training was going to be great fun [*See illustration no. 4*].[28] A photograph of nude sailors, washing themselves down, was certainly not intended to be of homoerotic interest, but rather to show that even heavy labour in a dirty environment, like the work of these stokers, was compensated by unlimited supplies of hot water to wash off the coal dust. It must be remembered that hot water was still something of an expensive luxury at this time. Having cleaned themselves up, the sailors were shown having plenty of time for relaxation in the evenings, with a shipmate around to play the accordion. And as for shore leave: 'In the Café Hollywood or whatever the harbour bars are called, there is dancing, and an atmosphere of lively, good cheer. Not to mention plenty to drink, and the talk and song can become a real racket. When sailors set about something, they do it properly.' Popularity with the local women wherever you went, great sociability amongst your own men, and a life of adventure: what teenager could argue with that?![29]

Cigarette series on the German army sought to make it, too, look attractive to young men. The SA's *Sturm* cigarettes produced sets of cards that focused especially on the several hundred smart and colourful German uniforms down the ages. A lowly trumpeter could appear dazzling in a golden uniform with a scarlet plume, while even the relatively drab, black uniform of a trainee paymaster could seem quite dashing in the hands of the artist.[30] Efforts were also made to de-emphasise the dangers of military service. Cavalry were still sent into action as late as the Second World War, and were clearly highly vulnerable to modern weaponry, but again the stress lay on the sheer fun and skill that filled the lives of cavalrymen. They were depicted in photographs, riding with no hands, doing a handstand on the horse's back, and firing a rifle while standing on top of the saddle of a stationary horse.[31] Actual battle scenes were usually one step removed from real life in such series, by dint of showing them in water-colour sketches, rather than actual photographs. An example of this is a cavalry charge, with shells exploding all around the horses – an exciting action shot, but the viewer somehow feels safe. All the more so, since the set is titled, 'The German Army on Manoeuvres,' so one is reassured that this is not the real thing, and no-one will come to any harm.[32] For those who feared the irrelevance of cavalry in modern warfare, there were appeals to tradition and history. One card showing an encounter in the Thirty Years' War explained: 'Just as in present-day warfare aircraft reconnoitre the enemy, so did the fast cavalry in earlier times. But since the enemy also possessed the weapon of cavalry, lively skirmishes between both patrols were all in a day's work.'[33] Fighter planes certainly did make the troops on the ground feel nervous, but the action paintings were designed to lessen the feeling of vulnerability of the individual. A scene, showing not cavalry but the very latest track-mounted armoured car with gun carriage, catches the unit shooting at the enemy planes diving overhead, with the comment: 'Even while on the move, the troop has machine guns at the ready, which can open fire immediately and make the attack a dangerous undertaking even for the enemy in the air.'

Almost always the situation is made to look rather safer than in real life. A picture of infantrymen charging concentrates on their team spirit – the enemy forces are out of the field of view, and are therefore somehow less threatening. When they reach the barbed wire at the enemy's front line, the soldiers throw grenades to ensure the safety of their next move forward. Here too, the picture emphasises the excitement of battle, while the caption reassures the young reader that close combat means that the artillery of both sides is more or less neutralized here. A close-up of a lone soldier charging through a grassy field is rather too tidy: there is none of the mud of the actual front lines of the First World War, and he might just as easily be running towards his lunch. Nonetheless the caption is a serious one, stressing the need for strength of character in each man: All the supporting heavy armaments 'are in vain, if the brave man is missing who despite all the technology takes the last step of personal action, and gives his all: the hand-to-hand fighter on the attack [*der stürmende Nahkämpfer*]'.[34] The Nazis were great modernisers and enthusiastic users of the latest equipment, such as motorbikes (though in the mud of the Russian campaign these turned out to be less useful than horses after all). With one card showing a motorbike and sidecar team, one can almost hear the screech of tyres, but it is again character as much as action that the caption emphasises: 'Control over his machine, guts and determination mark the face of the motor-cyclist. For him there is scarcely any obstacle that cannot be overcome by will-power and skill. His motto is: "If the heart is out front, then the deed will follow!"' Yet it was again important not to leave out the more humble soldiers with less dramatic equipment. The *Wehrmacht* could not afford as many motorbikes as it would have liked, and some units were provided instead with the more prosaic push-bike. They had to be made to look a crucial part of the big picture, too. Here they were described as 'a valuable supplement to the fighting power' of the cavalry. And though it may not have been saying much, the caption added: 'On suitable terrain the speed of their mobility is considerable.' As if to prove this, the illustration showed clouds of dust being thrown up behind the passing troop of cyclists [*See illustration no. 5*].[35]

THE NOBILITY OF DEATH

The unpleasant, indeed horrific, aspects of war were, on the other hand, treated very gingerly. Sometimes authors created a certain distance by pushing the topic back into history. Atrocity stories had been utilised on both sides during the First World War, but the need to keep 'savage foreign soldiers' at bay, a theme used effectively about the Russians in the Second World War, was relocated in the Thirty Years' War for the moment. The commentary also kept the phenomenon at a distance: 'War fetches up both virtues and vices from the depths of mankind. In every war there are numerous scoundrels, who present the most terrible affliction for the country as marauders, laggers, slackers and profiteers. With the foreign armies in the Thirty Years' War already more or less allowed to run wild, they plundered and pillaged the land, and tortured the peasants to death.' The implication was that the Germans were now much too disciplined and civilised to countenance such behaviour.[36] Pictorial histories of the First World War in general tended to be highly sanitised, and so it is surprising to find a couple of photographs of dead soldiers in an admittedly rather rare album. Yet they are not Germans! Rather the cards show dead Italian and Senegalese soldiers respectively.[37] It was far more common, and safer, to skirt around the subject of death in battle by placing it in the very distant past, among the ancient Germans and in the realms of myth. In that case, a series like 'Glorious Chapters of German History' could plunge straight into the topic of war and battle. The caption to the very first picture of Germanic warriors (in very Wagnerian costumes!)

unmistakably pointed a suggestive finger at the present day, however, in its ringing description of days of old: 'The struggle for freedom from the foreign yoke and for the unification of the whole people stands already at the beginning of German history. Justice and freedom, space and a united state were the motives of Germanic battles.' To anyone with a passing acquaintance with the right-wing literature of the day, this was a reference to the shackles of the Versailles Treaty, and the ethnic Germans living outside the post-1919 borders of the country, not to mention Hitler's demands for *Lebensraum*. The set also celebrated German military victories in the distant past, and an illustration of a particularly bloody massacre in full swing described this *furor teutonicus* that led to the slaughter of the entire enemy Roman force in the Teutoburg Forest in AD 9 as a 'strategic masterpiece'. The ultimate sacrifice could also be removed entirely to the realms of myth, as when a picture of 'dying heroes' contained the comforting words that the ancient Germans believed that they would live on after their death in Valhalla, the home of the heroes in the beyond.

Unhesitating self-sacrifice of one's life, if the Fatherland demanded it, was part of the Nazi rejection of the emancipation of the Weimar years, which they termed 'selfish individualism'. The model was rooted here in medieval times in the person of Winkelried, a hero fighting with the peasants against the evil Austrian knights at the Battle of Sempach in 1386. Faced with an impenetrable wall of spears, he grasped hold of and bunched a number of them together, driving them into his breast, thus creating an opening through which his companions surged to victory. More recent examples conveyed the message that daring action would bring you glory without death. A prime example held up here was Graf Zeppelin's almost foolhardy boldness during the Franco–Prussian War in 1870, when he took off with a mere nine cavalrymen to reconnoître deep inside enemy territory in Alsace, and accomplished his mission unscathed.[38]

If this was the kind of behaviour that was required in the future, then the Nazi Party sought to further legitimise itself by stressing the bravery and self-sacrifice already shown by its own members during the days of its struggle for power. The pitched battles with Communists at political meetings were already the stuff of legend by the time Hitler became chancellor. Both sides tried to disrupt each other's rallies with violent fighting. A full-page colour illustration in one of the card albums shows a Stormtrooper about to swing a chair at an opponent, and bears the caption: 'One can only meet the terror from the left with still harsher terror.' With such sentiments as these, young minds could be acclimatised to the arbitrary violence of SS guards in the concentration camps, or SA thugs in the streets of German towns. Being wounded oneself in the service of the Party counted as a badge of honour. Pictures of wounded Nazis in bandages abounded. An obviously posed photograph of Stormtroopers having their wounds dressed, in 'The Post-War Period,' does not resonate as strongly as the frequent photos of Hitler visiting the sick. On one card, with the caption 'One of the Most Loyal', Hitler has stopped his car to lean out and shake the hand of a supporter with his head bandaged. In another, labelled 'Loyalty for Loyalty' he shakes hands with and delivers his piercing gaze at some young Germans with head bandages and crutches [*See illustration no. 6*]. Finally, following the rape of Czechoslovakia, he warmly greets wounded Czech Germans on stretchers.[39]

It was also in connection with its own members that the Nazi movement not only permitted, but positively encouraged the contemplation of death. 'To die for Germany' was what every young German was meant to be prepared for. Patriots of the Weimar period like Albert Leo Schlageter, who was executed by the French, were memorialized – cigarette cards showed both his tomb, and that of Stormtrooper and pimp Horst Wessel, the most famous Nazi martyr of all, shot by Communists after his landlady had complained to them that he was not paying his rent.[40] And just as Hitler was shown giving special recognition to the wounded, so too he appeared in a well-known photograph at the death bed of a young SS man, allegedly killed by Communists [*See illustration no. 7*]. A whole-page colour painting of a Nazi, standing with head bowed over his fallen comrade, graced one of the albums, with the caption: 'No other thanks can be given than to pledge that we will fight on for Germany, for whom you have died.' As mentioned, even teenagers were expected to be ready to make the supreme sacrifice, and Herbert Norkus, who became Hitler Youth Quex, the hero of a novel that was quickly turned into a film on the eve of the Third Reich, set the example. He was shown on one card in a scene from the film, as his young friends gather round his hospital bed just before his death.[41]

GERMANY'S ENEMIES

One striking aspect of the cigarette cards published during the Third Reich is that they do not contain as many negative stereotypes as one might expect. There were certainly not as many as appeared generally in the Nazi press, and even in some children's literature. The wartime appearance of the openly propagandistic set, 'Robber State England', which attacked the British from every possible angle, was the exception that proved the rule.[42] On the whole, the role models put forward in these series were positive ones. A careful examination reveals but a few examples of negative images of nations and races. A picture of *francs-tireurs* in Bolbec during the Franco–Prussian War, French civilian snipers shooting at the invading Germans from the safety of their homes, was meant to reinforce the image that the German troops always followed the rules of warfare, while other nations cheated. This idea had been repeated in the First World War about the Belgians, and was to have deadly consequences during the Nazi invasion of the Soviet Union in 1941, when Hitler ruled that all Jews were to be treated as partisans, and therefore to fall outside the protection of international law.[43] Anti-Semitic images were rare, but they did occur, again in a late set, printed during the Second World War. The passage in question looked at the German revolution of 1918–19. By 1940 it was assumed that the rest of the Nazi media had done its job in persuading most people that the Jew was the enemy, and so little time was wasted on explanation. The text of the accompanying album merely noted that the revolution's leaders 'were – one could almost say, naturally – Jews, with whom also some terroristic criminals allied themselves. To characterise them, all one needs to do is to look at the pictures of them.' This last statement in itself was a neat summary of the aim of many of these cigarette card sets, as of much Nazi propaganda. Not only were pictures meant to tell the whole story, but in this case physiognomy would act as the key to character, which reflected an assumption behind much of Nazi racial science. Kurt Eisner, the Bavarian prime minister after the First World War, who was murdered by a right-wing student on his way to open parliament, is described as 'the Jewish dictator... this is what our rulers looked like back then'. Under cards showing other politicians, the captions note that: 'Almost all the powers-that-be were Jews', and that another revolutionary was 'one of the leading Jews... at the time of the murder of hostages'. In fact it was the right wing who murdered many times more opponents than the left [*See illustration no. 8*].[44] Another card builds on pre-Nazi racism, showing a (smartly dressed) jazz group, identified in inked-in letters on its bass drum as 'The Nigger Band'. The caption notes critically: 'American imports: jazz and dollar.' The right wing had been appalled in the 1920s by the Americanisation of the entertainment world, especially the popularity of African-American musicians. The Nazis later built on this to condemn jazz as effeminate, primitive and un-German. Teenagers caught dancing to jazz music in the Second World War were sometimes imprisoned and even charged with treason.[45]

CONCLUSION

The late appearance of these negative images reflects the greater urgency of the Nazi leadership in its diabolisation of the enemy during the war. They do not appear to be designed to elicit fear from readers, but rather contempt. The regime was still extremely confident about winning the war in 1940–41, and so the emphasis remained on positive character-building images. The message could remain one of the strength of the German character and nation overcoming all difficulties and opponents. Sometimes this was expressed not so much in the cigarette cards themselves, as in the line-drawings in the albums that were often used to fill blank space at the end of a chapter of text. One of these shows the swastika as a wheel, being pushed by a muscular Nazi, with the Party flag flying proudly behind. In front of the swastika–wheel, a Communist struggles to resist, but has already been forced to the ground, where both he and the hammer-and-sickle flag are about to be crushed.[46] A sketch with a similar message appeared six years later in the *Ostmark* album, and shows a Czech soldier, a Catholic priest and a Jew, a whole set of 'enemies of the state', heavily caricatured and cringing before a Nazi, who wears a swastika armband, and stands tall and defiant before them, his jaw set and his fists clenched. There is no question of who will get the better of the situation here.[47]

What the historian would really like to know is how effective such propaganda images were with young people. Unfortunately no definitive answer can be given to that question – the records of the most important tobacco companies were destroyed in air raids; the personnel files in the Reich Cultural Chamber of such authors of cigarette card albums as can be identified are silent on this aspect of their work; the extensive records of the Propaganda Ministry reveal no discussions of the question; public opinion surveys never mentioned the genre. We have only scattered evidence of the value attached to such albums, plus the fact that families kept them to the present day. Striking visual images do have a lasting impact. Among the relatively few books in my grandparents' home was a treasured copy, eventually passed down to me, of the first-ever Giles cartoon annual, published during the war with its devastating wit turned against Hitler and the Nazi leaders. The cartoons still packed a punch decades later. Nazi Germany relied heavily on the pictorial. During the war, the production of cigarette cards fell victim to the shortage of paper, and to expanding propaganda needs in the occupied territories. The last series appeared in 1941. The popular and very widely circulated, illustrated magazine, *Signal*, which even came out in

English, French, Spanish and Italian versions, was another example of pictorial propaganda, and one that continued until late in the war. As one analyst has written: '*Signal* is atomistic, impressionist in its layout; it entertains the reader with snapshots, if carefully chosen ones, with visual puns, and with light-hearted narratives; occasionally one find echoes of a "northern Romantic" view of modernism, with the individual staring out into an unknown future.'[48] These same points could be made about one or other cigarette card set. The cards were part of a whole arsenal of popular but often ideological, educational materials that were marshalled in support of the objectives of the regime. This is where they principally differ from British series of cigarette cards. In the United Kingdom, there were indeed sets, celebrating the monarchy and the traditional institutions of the land (the army, the universities, and so on), but the small size of the sets (usually 50 cards) and of the cards themselves, together with their tiny albums, did not permit the inclusion of the kind of expansive, explanatory text that filled the German cards, along with whole essays that graced the typical, large-format, German album.

When propaganda is forced down someone's throat, it often misses its mark. The perennial rebelliousness of youth creates a further problem for the propagandist, and young people in Nazi Germany were no exception. As Detlev Peukert has noted: 'The more the Hitler Youth arrogated state powers to itself, and the more completely young people were assimilated into the organisation, the more clearly visible became an emergent pattern of youth non-conformity.'[49] Yet the cleverness of the producers of cigarette cards lay in their creation of something collectible, something that youths *wanted* to have. Boys sought eagerly to complete their sets. German postcards and postage stamps during this period also had some ideological content, but neither of these collectible categories allowed for the amount of text that the cigarette card albums came increasingly to provide. In a country where many in the Nazi leadership had more or less written off the formal education system as a formative influence on character in the desired National Socialist sense, relying largely for this on the Hitler Youth, such informal learning tools were especially welcome. It would be shortsighted not to acknowledge that the *principal* purpose of such cards was to increase sales of cigarettes. The tobacco companies saw them above all as a brilliantly successful marketing device, with which to overtake their rivals. Thus the cards and their albums became increasingly lavish. Greiling's Zeppelin set came with a foil-covered card that looked like a real medallion.[50] Reemtsma pioneered the idea of merely placing coupons, not actual cards, in cigarette packs, which could then be exchanged, when sufficient points had been earned, for something grander, especially for series with a Nazi theme. The illustrations for its album on Adolf Hitler, still meant to be stuck into the album individually by the owner, were high-quality photographic reproductions up to 17 cm × 12 cm.[51] And it certainly outdid all the competition with its magnificent, fold-out photograph in another album of a crowd of tens of thousands of uniformed Nazis at a Nuremberg Rally, which measured a staggering 103 cm × 31 cm.[52]

The youth of Nazi Germany were no walkover for Nazi propagandists, but there is no doubt that there were susceptible areas. Peukert sums up the situation neatly:

> The ideological content of National Socialism remained much too vague to function as a self-sufficient educational objective. In practice, young people selected from competing information sources and values that were on offer: fragments of ideas of racial and national arrogance, mingled with traditional pedagogic humanism; the model of the front-line soldier, along with the supposition that there was an especially profound and valuable 'German' culture; backward-looking agrarian Romanticism, along with enthusiasm for modern technology.[53]

All these themes resonated in various cigarette card sets. And they were not simply 'on offer': they were alluringly presented to frequently avid collectors. If they were relatively restrained in their negative propaganda, then young people could see plenty of that elsewhere: in the pictorial images in the press, and on posters.[54] Yet the character-building function of such cards should not be underestimated. Of course, other countries made similar efforts in a similar direction, most frequently through children's literature and magazines. Yet the goal was not the same. As George Mosse puts it:

> There is, surely, a world of difference between the clean-cut Englishman, the all-American boy, and the ideal member of the SS. Yet all shared essentially the same masculine stereotype with its virtues, strength, and aesthetic appeal, whether it was restrained, nonviolent, and even compassionate, or uncompromising, ready to do battle by all means at hand. Fascism, and especially National Socialism, demonstrated the awesome possibilities inherent in modern masculinity when it was stripped down to its warlike functions.[55]

It took more than cigarette cards to produce the model Nazi. Yet their role does not deserve to be ignored. Because their content was different, more ideological, than that of the genre elsewhere in Europe, they did play a significant part in the ideological education of Germany's youth. The young men who went to war for Hitler had spent all their formative years in the very heyday of cigarette-card collecting. Many of the 1.5 million youths who owned the album for the ideologically saturated set, 'Germany awakes', must have felt convinced that they were fighting for a just and noble cause.

ENDNOTES

1. The kind invitation to deliver a keynote address at the annual meeting of the History of Education Society spurred the writing of this essay. Its revision was greatly facilitated by my tenure as Shapiro Senior Scholar-in-Residence at the Center for Advanced Holocaust Studies, United States Holocaust Memorial Museum, Washington, DC.
2. *Raubstaat England* (Reemtsma Nr. 16) (Hamburg-Bahrenfeld: Cigaretten-Bilderdienst), pp. 84 and 106.
3. E.Wasem, *Sammeln von Serienbildchen. Entwicklung und Bedeutung eines beliebten Mediums der Reklame und der Alltagskultur* (Landshut: Trausnitz), pp. 8–11; also idem, *Das Serienbild. Medium der Werbung und Alltagskultur* (Dortmund: Harenberg), pp. 9–17.
4. E. and E. Ciolina, *Garantirt Aecht. Das Reklamesammelbild als Spiegel der Zeit* (München: Edition Wissen and Literatur), p. 17.
5. For more on the history of such cards, see also G. J. Giles, 'Popular education and the new media: the cigarette card in Germany', in M. Depaepe and B. Henkens (eds), *The Challenge of the Visual in the History of Education*. Paedagogica Historica Supplementary Series, Volume VI (Gent: *Paedagogica Historica*), pp. 449–69.
6. In a rather paradoxical choice for a cigarette card, an illustration of the interior of Hitler's tent at the 1933 Nuremberg Rally shows a large no-smoking sign, warning 'Rauchen verboten!'. *Männer und Ereignisse unserer Zeit* (Dresden: Bilderstelle Lohse), No.148.
7. For two different versions of the same photograph, with and without the murdered SA chief, Ernst Röhm, see G. J. Giles, 'Die erzieherische Rolle von Sammelbildern in politischen Umbruchszeiten', in Dietrich Papenfuß and Wolfgang Schieder (eds), *Deutsche Umbrüche im 20. Jahrhundert* (Köln/Weimar/Wien: Böhlau), pp. 260–1.

8. F. O'Dell, *Socialisation through Children's Literature: The Soviet Example* (Cambridge: Cambridge University Press), pp. 175–6.

9. C. Kamenetsky, *Children's Literature in Hitler's Germany: The Cultural Policy of National Socialism* (Athens, Ohio/London: Ohio University Press) looks at a number of genres but is altogether silent on the question of cigarette cards.

10. Picture for November 1933, *Die Nachkriegszeit. Historische Bilddokumente 1918–1934* (Dresden: Eckstein-Halpaus).

11. The caption reads: 'Peeling potatoes is SA duty, too.' *Deutschland erwacht. Werden, Kampf und Sieg der NSDAP* (Reemtsma Nr. 8) (Hamburg-Bahrenfeld: Cigaretten-Bilderdienst). Peeling potatoes as part of the 'jolly camp life of the SA' (*Lustiges Lagerleben der SA*, the caption for the photo) in the set on the 1933 Nuremberg Rally, *Parteitag der N.S.D.A.P. Nürnberg 1933* (Dresden: Lande), No. 34.

12. 'Abmarsch zum ersten Spatenstich', p. 13; 'Der Weg bergauf!' p. 97; illustration by Felix Albrecht, p. 42, *Der Staat der Arbeit und des Friedens. Ein Jahr Regierung Adolf Hitler* (Altona-Bahrenfeld: Cigaretten-Bilderdienst).

13. *Wie die Ostmark ihre Befreiung erlebte. Adolf Hitler und sein Weg zu Großdeutschland* (München: Austria), p. 80.

14. 'Feldbahnbau', *Staat der Arbeit*, p. 14.

15. 'Anstreicher', p. 16; 'Bergmann,' p. 19, *Deutsche Arbeit* (Hamburg: GEG). Hitler mentioned the risky nature of the latter occupation in one of his late-night monologues during the war, as noted by his stenographer: 'Two dangerous trades: the miner's and the sailor's'. H. Trevor-Roper, *Hitler's Table Talk 1941–1944: His Private Conversations* (New York: Enigma), p. 209.

16. 'Der Führer spricht auf dem Marsfeld, Januar 1923', *Ostmark*, p. 21.

17. 'Gefangene Nationalsozialisten,' ibid., pp. 31 and 50. The swastika is clearly and rather crudely touched up in the photograph, and may be a complete fabrication.

18. 'Braunhemdverbot', ibid., p. 48, takes the opportunity of displaying a strong image of a strikingly muscular, bare-chested, young Storm-trooper, carrying his brown shirt over his arm, but unfortunately places him in the middle of a ragbag platoon including a couple of rather laughable characters with Hitler moustaches. In another set, an early platoon of motorised SA men on parade with no shirts looks positively flabby. 'Das Braunhemd konnte man ihnen nehmen, die Treue nicht', *Deutschland erwacht*, p. 51.

19. 'Übergabe einer Stadt', No. 95 in *Deutsche Kulturbilder. Deutsches Leben in 5 Jahrhunderten 1400–1900* (Altona: Cigaretten-Bilderdienst).

91

20. 'Tapferes Heer', *Nachkriegszeit*, No. 1.
21. 'Das Heldentum von Scapa Flow,' ibid., No. 18.
22. H. W. Koch, *The Hitler Youth: Origins and Development 1922–1945* (New York: Barnes and Noble), p. 173.
23. The first card gives Dürer's portrait of Charlemagne in his coronation robes, while Otto is shown in the midst of battle, brandishing his spear. The last four cards in the series depict Grand Admiral Tirpitz, who was responsible for the naval race that worsened international tensions at the turn of the century in the first place; General von Einem, minister of war on the eve of the First World War; General von Moltke, nephew of the famed general of Bismarck's wars, and successor to Schlieffen as chief of the general staff of the army in 1906, who nevertheless had a nervous breakdown early on during the First World War; and General Falkenhayn, Prussian Minister of War, and Moltke's replacement after the Battle of the Marne. *Die Großen der Weltgeschichte* (Dresden: Eckstein-Halpaus).
24. *Ruhmesblätter deutscher Geschichte* (Dresden: Eckstein-Halpaus), No. 154.
25. Friedrich and his music teacher are depicted both in *Ruhmesblätter*, No. 80, and *Bilder deutscher Geschichte* (Reemtsma Nr. 12) (Hamburg-Bahrenfeld: Cigaretten-Bilderdienst), No. 60. Prinz Heinrich appears in the latter set, No. 69.
26. '2. August 1914. Adolf Hitler auf dem Odeonsplatz in München', *Kampf um's Dritte Reich. Eine historische Bilderfolge* (Altona-Bahrenfeld: Cigaretten-Bilderdienst), p. 9.
27. 'SA-Mann' (3 portraits), *Kampf*, p. 17; 'Bayerns ältester SA-Mann', *Staat der Arbeit*, p. 30.
28. Two portraits of sailors clearly selected for their good looks in *Unsere Reichsmarine. Bilder aus dem Leben der Matrosen* (Berlin: Caid), p. 9; and smiling recruits on p. 24. In a series on the army, a positively beaming soldier doing push-ups suggests that he is having a good time. *Die deutsche Wehrmacht* (Dresden: Cigaretten-Bilderdienst), No. 37.
29. Nude stokers in *Unsere Reichsmarine*, p. 45; and dancing onboard and ashore, pp. 52 and 53.
30. Trompeter, No. 405, and Zahlmeisteraspirant, No. 432, *Deutsche Uniformen, 1864–1914. Band II: Das Zeitalter der deutschen Einigung* (Dresden: Sturm). This was the fourth album in a series that stretched from the time of Frederick the Great. A fifth album highlighted the uniforms of the Nazi movement itself.
31. *Wehrmacht*, Nos. 40, 47 and 69.

32. *Das deutsche Heer im Mänover. Eine Bildfolge vom Wirken unseres Heeres* (Dresden: Cigaretten-Bilderdienst), No. 39.
33. 'Reiterkampf,' *Deutsche Kulturbilder*, No. 91.
34. *Manöver*, Nos. 120, 89, 192, and 90.
35. Ibid., Nos. 17 and 23.
36. The illustration shows a seventeenth-century farmer being tortured while his wife wrings her hands, and their farm is burnt to the ground in the background – precisely the kind of atrocity perpetrated by the German military on the Eastern front just five years later. 'Kriegsgreuel', *Deutsche Kulturbilder*, No. 94.
37. Black soldiers were especially feared by the German troops, so this picture aimed to reassure, even though it did only show three dead Senegalese, as opposed to a whole platoon of Italians in the other photograph. *Weltkriegsbilder 1914–1918* (Obercunnersdorf: Reunion), p. XVIII. In a series on the weaponry of other countries, black soldiers of the French army were treated as though they were themselves some sort of secret weapon. A caption read: 'French colonial cavalry troop. This troop especially is maintained, for it commands great endurance and fighting strength.' *Wie die Anderen gerüstet sind! ...trotz vertraglicher Abrüstungspflicht* (Bremen: Yosma, 1934), No. 34.
38. *Ruhmesblätter deutscher Geschichte* (Dresden: Eckstein-Halpaus), Nos. 1, 4, 5, 30 and 194.
39. SA first aid station in *Nachkriegszeit*, No. 187; 'Einer der Treuesten', *Kampf um's Dritte Reich*, p. 46; 'Treue um Treue!', a full-page photograph, *Ostmark*, p. 56; Wounded students in Prague, ibid., p. 90.
40. *Nachkriegszeit*, Nos. 65 and 146. For details of the myth-making, surrounding Schlageter, see J. W. Baird, *To Die for Germany: Heroes in the Nazi Pantheon* (Bloomington: Indiana University Press), pp. 15–40.
41. '"Gefallen für Deutschlands Auferstehung." Von den Kommunisten ermordet. Der Führer am Sterbebett eines SS-Kameraden, 1931', *Deutschland erwacht*, p. 49; 'Es gibt keinen anderen Dank als zu geloben, daß wir für Deutschland weiter kämpfen wollen, für das ihr gestorben seid,' ibid., opposite p. 48; 'Szene aus dem Film "Hitlerjunge Quex"', *Staat der Arbeit*, p. 66. The novel about Norkus sold over 190,000 copies within two years, cf. Baird's chapter on him in *To Die*, pp. 109–29.
42. *Raubstaat England*. See note 2 above.
43. *Ruhmesblätter*, No. 227.
44. *Ostmark*, p. 20, and photographs of Kurt Eisner, Levinié-Nissen, and Max Levien, p. 19.

45. *Nachkriegszeit*, No. 86.
46. This is another drawing by Felix Albrecht, *Staat der Arbeit*, p. 12.
47. *Ostmark*, p. 94.
48. F. Bokel, '"Great Days" in Germany: Third Reich Celebrities as Mediators between Government and People' PhD thesis, University of Texas, Austin, p. 370.
49. D. Peukert, *Inside Nazi Germany: Conformity, Opposition, and Racism in Everyday Life* (New Haven: Yale University Press), p. 153.
50. *Zeppelinweltfahrten* (Dresden: Greiling) No. 177.
51. The size of the album page was 23 cm × 31 cm, and full-page illustrations were an added bonus beyond the cards themselves. *Adolf Hitler. Bilder aus dem Leben des Führers* (Hamburg/Bahrenfeld: Cigaretten-Bilderdienst).
52. 'Standartenweihe im Luitpoldhain 1933', *Deutschland erwacht*, opposite p. 154.
53. Peukert, p. 145.
54. Poster art was especially dangerous, because it thrust itself at everyone, even if they did not subscribe to newspapers, read books, or collect cigarette cards. For some crude poster images of Jews and Bolsheviks as the enemy, see R. Rohrbach, *'bis zum letzten Atemzuge...': Propaganda in der NS-Zeit. Texte und Materialien zur Ausstellung des Museumsverbundes Südniedersachsen* (Göttingen: Museumsverbund Südniedersachsen).
55. G. Mosse, *The Image of Man: The Creation of Modern Masculinity* (New York: Oxford University Press), p. 180.

REFERENCES

Adolph Hitler, Bilder aus dem Leben des Führers (Hamburg/Bahrenfeld: Cigaretten-Bilderdienst, 1936).

Baird, J. W. *To Die for Germany: Heroes in the Nazi Pantheon* (Bloomington: Indiana University Press, 1990).

Bilder deutscher Geschichte Reemtsma Nr. 12 (Hamburg-Bahrenfeld: Cigaretten-Bilderdienst,1936).

Bokel, F. '"Great Days" in Germany: Third Reich Celebrities as Mediators between Government and People', Unpublished PhD. thesis, University of Texas, Austin, 1995.

Ciolina, E. and E. *Garantirt Aecht. Das Reklamesammelbild als Spiegel der Zeit* (München: Edition Wissen and Literatur, 1987).

Das deutsche Heer im Manöver: Eine Bildfolge vom Wirken unseres

Heeres (Dresden-A: Cigaretten-Bilderdienst, 1936).

Der Staat der Arbeit und des Friedens: Ein Jahr Regierung Adolf Hitler (Altona-Bahrenfeld: Cigaretten-Bilderdienst, 1934).

Deutsche Arbeit (Hamburg: GEG, 1934).

Deutsche Kulturbilder: Deutsches Leben in 5 Jahrhunderten 1400–1900 (Altona: Cigaretten-Bilderdienst,1936).

Deutsche Uniformen Band 2. Das Zeitalter der deutschen Einigung. Album IV: Die Zeit von 1870 bis 1888 (Dresden: Sturm-Zigaretten, 1933).

Deutschland erwacht. Werden, Kampf und Sieg der NSDAP Reemtsma Nr. 8 (Hamburg-Bahrenfeld: Cigaretten-Bilderdienst, 1933).

Die deutsche Wehrmacht (Dresden: Cigaretten-Bilderdienst, 1936).

Die Großen der Weltgeschichte (Dresden: Eckstein-Halpaus, 1934).

Die Nachkriegszeit: Historische Bilddokumente 1918–1934 (Dresden: Eckstein-Halpaus, 1935).

Die Reichswehr (Dresden: Haus Neuerburg/Waldorff-Astoria/Eckstein-Halpaus, 1933).

Giles, G. J. 'Die erzieherische Rolle von Sammelbildern in politischen Umbruchszeiten', in D. Papenfuß and W.Schieder (eds), *Deutsche Umbrüche im 20. Jahrhundert* (Köln/Weimar/Wien: Böhlau, 2000), pp. 241–65.

— 'Popular education and the new media: the cigarette card in Germany', in M. Depaepe and B. Henkens (eds), *The Challenge of the Visual in the History of Education*. Paedagogica Historica Supplementary Series, Volume VI (Gent: Paedagogica Historica, 2000), pp. 449–69.

Kamenetsky, C. *Children's Literature in Hitler's Germany: The Cultural Policy of National Socialism* (Athens, Ohio/London: Ohio University Press, 1984).

Kampf um's Dritte Reich: Eine historische Bilderfolge (Altona-Bahrenfeld: Cigaretten-Bilderdienst, 1933).

Koch, H. W. *The Hitler Youth: Origins and Development 1922–1945* (New York: Barnes and Noble, 1996).

Männer und Ereignisse unserer Zeit (Dresden: Bilderstelle Lohse, 1934).

Mosse, G. L. *The Image of Man: The Creation of Modern Masculinity* (New York: Oxford University Press, 1996).

O'Dell, F. *Socialisation through Children's Literature: The Soviet Example* (Cambridge: Cambridge University Press, 1978).

Parteitag der N.S.D.A.P. Nürnberg 1933 (Dresden: Lande, 1933).

Peukert, D. *Inside Nazi Germany: Conformity, Opposition, and Racism in Everyday Life* (New Haven: Yale University Press, 1987).

Raubstaat England Reemtsma No. 16 (Hamburg-Bahrenfeld: Cigaretten-Bilderdienst, 1941).

Rohrbach, R. '...*bis zum letzten Atemzuge*...': *Propaganda in der NS-Zeit. Texte und Materialien zur Ausstellung des Museumsverbundes Südniedersachsen* (Göttingen: Museumsverbund Südniedersachsen, 1995).

Ruhmesblätter Deutscher Geschichte (Dresden: Eckstein-Halpaus, 1934).

Trevor-Roper, H. *Hitler's Table Talk 1941–1944: His Private Conversations* (New York: Enigma, 2000).

Unsere Reichsmarine: Bilder aus dem Leben der Matrosen (Berlin: Caid, 1934).

Wasem, E. *Sammeln von Serienbildchen. Entwicklung und Bedeutung eines beliebten Mediums der Reklame und der Alltagskultur* (Landshut: Trausnitz, 1981).

— *Das Serienbild. Medium der Werbung und Alltagskultur* (Dortmund: Harenberg, 1987).

Weltkriegsbilder 1914–1918 (Obercunnersdorf: Reunion, 1933).

Wie die Anderen gerüstet sind!...trotz vertraglicher Abrüstungspflicht (Bremen: Yosma, 1934).

Wie die Ostmark ihre Befreiung erlebte: Adolf Hitler und sein Weg zu Großdeutschland (München: Austria, 1940).

Zeppelin-Weltfahrten (Dresden: Greiling, 1933).

SECTION 2

GENDER, POLITICS AND THE EXPERIENCE OF EDUCATION

5

'Like the Spirit of the Army': Fascistic Discourse and the National Association of Schoolmasters, 1919–39[1]

DAVID LIMOND

By contrast to its long-time rival, the National Union of Women Teachers (NUWT),[2] the National Association of Schoolmasters (NAS) has attracted relatively little academic interest,[3] and that which it has attracted has been hostile.[4] The NUWT is now defunct[5] but the NAS endures, in an unwieldy sounding alliance with the Union of Women Teachers (UWT)[6] as the NASUWT.[7] In what follows I shall argue that the all-male NAS of the inter-war years was never more fully or acutely described than by the member who likened it to the army. In doing so he captured the essence of its appeal to its members: masculinist solidarity along quasi-militaristic lines, in effect the appeal of fascism.

In common with the NUWT, the NAS began its life as a pressure group within the oldest and largest of the English/Welsh[8] teaching unions, the National Union of Teachers (NUT).[9] The NAS was first the National Union of Men Teachers (NUMT) and dates its existence from 22 April 1919 when it coalesced from the 'many cells of the men's movement'.[10] Foremost amongst these was the London Schoolmasters' Association (LSA), a breakaway from the London Teachers' Association (LTA),[11] but most senior was a group from Cardiff founded as early as 1911.[12] (The LSA's prominence within the NAS lay in its large membership and the fact that it started what was to become the official journal of the NAS, *The New Schoolmaster* (*TNS*)).[13] By 1920, the newly renamed NAS was well enough organised to be able to produce an annual report/yearbook.[14] Two years later, despite some internal opposition, the NAS split from the NUT.[15]

The NAS is generally known to modern readers only through commentaries on its rival, the pro-equal pay NUWT, where its position has been summarised by authors intent on explaining the aims of the latter.[16] Substantially unaltered in the two decades thereafter, the position outlined in 1920 was as follows. Addressing first 'the Marriageable Woman' the putative NAS made these points.

1. If you want to marry, Equal Pay will spoil your chance.
2. Equal pay means Elimination of Proposals for you.
3. What's the good of a good time now, if you lose a husband by it.
4. As a future wife, don't rob your future husband.
5. As a future wife, ask for equal pay for wives.
6. More money for men – more marriages for women.
7. Child-bearing is more important than teaching.
8. No mothers, no scholars; no jobs for teachers.
9. If you want to be a wall-flower, attack men.
10. Men and their wives can outvote spinsters.
11. Boy-teaching is a man's job. If you want to remain feminine, keep out of boys' schools.
12. If you believe in equality of opportunity, you can't be an equal payite.

These it paralleled with twelve claims addressed to 'the Married Man'.

1. Boy-teaching is a man's job, worth a man's pay.
2. Parents ask for: 'Men Teachers for Boys!'
3. Preservation of Population is the State's first law. Equal Pay means extirpation of Population.
4. Demand equal pay for your wife, and equality of opportunity for your children.
5. A man's responsibilities are legal, a woman's sentimental.
6. Co-education is a dodge to get Equal Pay by Inches. Boys and Girls seven to fourteen years are best taught apart.
7. Don't let a single woman limit your salary to what she can secure. Your duty is your wife and children.
8. Ask for a separate scale of salaries for Boys' schools.
9. Men and their wives can always outvote the equal payites. Tell your MP's and councillors that.
10. Separate consideration is logical. It is the only scheme which secures economic equality for wives.
11. The public is on the Parents' side. The State is bound to be.
12. Till state allowances are granted for everybody (not teachers only), separate consideration for the sexes is the only fair way.[17]

As the *Yearbook* suggests, by 1919 it was established practice for Local Education Authorities in England and Wales, almost without exception and in common with other public sector employers,[18] to pay female elementary teachers on scales which both started lower and ended lower than those of their male colleagues.[19] A less well-qualified and less experienced man might therefore be paid more highly than a more qualified and experienced woman.[20] The NAS was committed to the retention of these differentials and to this it added a policy of 'job reservation' for male teachers – 'Boy teaching is a man's job, worth a man's pay.' But the platform on which the NAS stood was never simply economic. It arose from a set of gendered expectations, parallel constructions of masculinity and femininity. 'Boys and Girls seven to fourteen' would both benefit from being taught separately. Though this was apparently especially important for boys, a fact seemingly endorsed variously by parents ('Parents ask for: "Men Teachers for Boys!"') and the public, which was said to be 'on the Parents' side' (though no evidence was produced to verify these claims). 'The State' in turn was apparently 'bound' to side with this coalition of parents, public and the NAS. But women's interests were also to be considered. Wives (and children) would be adversely affected if equal pay entailed the general level of salaries being driven down but more than this, women teachers themselves were at risk of falling victim to a demographic catastrophe of their own making did they but know it. 'Equal pay means Elimination of Proposals', this would lead to fewer marriages: 'No mothers, no scholars; no jobs for teachers.' In the last analysis 'Equal Pay... [would bring] extirpation of Population'. Thus if women would only marry and have children ('Child-rearing is more important than teaching'); and men were left alone to teach boys over the age of seven (which was dangerous work for women anyway, 'If you want to keep feminine, keep out of boys' schools'), all would be well.

After abortive attempts by activists in the NUT before and during the First World War to have their union adopt a policy of equal pay regardless of gender, a motion to this effect was successfully passed at the union's conference in 1918 and ratified in a referendum of the membership.[21] Those who subsequently made up the first branches of the NAS were of the view that this endorsement had been achieved only because many male NUT members were on active service.[22] Those men attracted to the NAS were hardly likely to remain in a union committed to a policy of supporting equal pay for long. The split of the NUWT from the NUT has been described as 'more difficult to understand'[23] than that of the NAS, but it was occasioned by a sense that the NUT's leadership was far from committed to using the uniform pay negotiating procedures established under the auspices of the Burnham Committee in 1919 to pursue the equal pay issue.[24] Thus by the early 1920s, there existed amongst teachers not so much a vicious circle as a triangle of enmity. Members of the NAS, were not confident that the NUT would *not* push vigorously for equal pay while members of the NUWT were not confident that the NUT *would* do so.[25]

In the inter-war period, NAS membership neither fell below 5,000, nor did it rise above 10,000.[26] This tally placed it on a par with the NUWT which 'in the mid-1920s... had about 8,500 members... [making it] a reasonably sized trade union'.[27] Thus, although the NAS and the NUWT were far smaller than the NUT, which already had a membership in six figures (101,994) by 1918,[28] they were more or less equally matched. Both the NAS and the NUWT were always oppositional and activist unions. It took a distinct decision to join either in preference to the 'default position' for elementary teachers of joining the NUT.

> Any prospect of industrial action was eschewed by the majority [in this period], for whom the union was seen either in terms of practical security and support, or, in a much deeper sense as an emblem of elementary teachers' traditions, history, and shared interests.[29]

This was a position which the NUT had 'earned' by the inter-war period in virtue of its longevity. Indeed, the 'tact and pragmatism' of the NUT, both at branch level[30] and in its national leadership,[31] may have contributed to the forging of a changed popular view of elementary teachers. This view was more accepting of the 'new type of elementary teacher', as a far more respectable figure, that had emerged by the early twentieth century. Marion Mortimer, born in 1905 and an elementary teacher in the inter-war period, recalls: 'We more or less had to be in the NUT. I joined for peace and quietness.'[32] While this certainly did not hold true for all NUT members it may well have been so for many, perhaps even most. But it *could not* have been true for NAS (and NUWT) members.

In the circumstances it can be a little difficult to see what the members of the NAS, especially those who had actually played some part in the First World War, had to worry about. Being an ex-serviceman (re-)entering a career in teaching might well have been an advantage in certain circumstances. When A. S. Neill took up a post at the independent, progressive King Alfred School in London he was introduced in the school's magazine in terms that stressed his military rank (Lieutenant) and his academic credentials (MA, University of Edinburgh) in equal measure.[33] Neill's war record was in fact far from distinguished but there was evidently sufficient glamour attaching to his rank, with its implication (unfounded) of battlefield experience, that it was deemed worth mentioning. And any (male) teacher, officer or not, who had been in the services coming to an ordinary elementary school, might be able to trade on some degree of glamour. This could be added to an odour of the patriotism exhibited by self-sacrifice in war – useful for impressing employers – and perhaps a hint of toughness imbued by military life and combat – useful for subduing pupils. Further, overall, teachers' salaries were not eroded in the period between the end of the First World War to the end of the Second as they, too, benefited from the 'remarkable improvement in wages and living standards brought about by the First World War' which ensured that 'by 1945 average real earnings for those in regular employment stood more than a third higher than in 1913'.[34] (Though of course this latter fact was hardly obvious at the time.) However, the cause of the NAS was never purely economic.

The precise relationship between the putative NUMT/NAS and the apparently short-lived National Association of Ex-Service Teachers seems obscure[35] but it is clear that from the start the new movement amongst male teachers was significantly influenced by returning servicemen. Some degree of more or less organised opposition to equal pay and generalised concern, amongst certain groups of men, as to the implications of the increasing feminisation of elementary teaching certainly existed before the First World War. Attempts by members of precursor bodies to the NUWT to align the NUT behind the cause of equal pay were first made a decade before the war but were always voted down. Men's 'ginger groups' concerned with these issues also pre-dated 1914.[36] However, it is central to the thesis pursued in this chapter that the events of 1914–1918 had a galvanising effect on that opposition, an opposition which was the defining feature of the culture of the NAS.

To appreciate this argument fully it is necessary to root the NAS in the *milieu* of the network of groups formed to protect the rights and serve the interests of returning servicemen. These groups included the National Federation of Discharged and Demobilised Sailors and Soldiers, the National Association of Discharged Sailors and Soldiers, the Comrades of the Great War, the Officers' Association, the British Legion, the Military Medallist Association and the Association of Ex-Prisoners of War.[37] Though diverse or even contradictory in their aims[38] they all 'attempt[ed] to ... [employ] ... wartime male bonding in a new way within civilian [life]'.[39] It was certainly this language of (supposedly) 'non-sectarian, non-political, and all-embracing [but of course not non-gendered] ... mateship'[40] which 'HM' invoked when he described the NAS as 'like the spirit of the army', with 'common calling...a bond of union'.[41] Amongst erstwhile servicemen rejection of fraternal post-war groups was widespread. This was caused in part by disillusionment at their fractiousness – they hardly displayed the solidarity they advocated – and partly by an unwillingness amongst many returning combatants to accept a rhetoric that ironed out the various social inequities which had been the actual stuff of wartime life for most soldiers.[42]

However, anti-feminist male schoolmasters differed from other post-war groups in their true cohesiveness of purpose. Unlike the Military Medallist Association, with its generalised appeal for those returning from the war to be 'interdependent one upon the other [now as] *then*'[43] (original emphasis), the NAS had a definite cause. Further, ex-service groups suffered from the existence of a disjunction between the competing calls of domesticity and militarism. This had the effect of making it largely 'impossible to apply military *esprit de corps* to men whose [post-war] sense of identity remained lodged within their civilian domestic environment'.[44] However, the NAS could offer to employ that distinctive military cohesiveness in defence of domestic values. This being so, it was a beneficiary of the special solidarity the war was suggested by some to have occasioned. That is: the NAS was built on something like Mussolini's *trincerocrazia* – in English, 'trenchocracy'.[45] Admission to this 'aristocracy of the trenches'[46] was open only to those 'demobilised soldiers...conscious of what [they have]...achieved' whom he predicted would soon 'cause shifts in the equilibrium of society'.[47] Here was the emergent outline of a fascist programme of action.

Anyone attempting to summarise the nature of fascism enters a quagmire. For some fascism is a more or less straightforward projection of power in defence of certain class interests – it has a single, simple purpose, to protect wealth and property.[48] For others (amongst whom I count myself) fascism is replete in contradictions and complications. But even those who subscribe to the idea of 'fascist eclecticism' (fascism is no simple continuation of class war by other means but a coming together of diverse imperatives, causes and impulses – 'a sort of modernist *bricolage*')[49] are as much divided as united. Not least they are divided sharply between those for whom national socialism is a species of the fascist genus[50] and those who subscribe to what might be called Nazi exceptionalism (Nazism is not a variety of fascism at root though it has many similarities in its poisonous fruits).[51] I am persuaded that there are fundamental differences between Nazism and fascism, a fact always obvious to Nazis though not always to fascists.[52] Because disputes of this sort as to the nature of fascism have proven to be complex, the following description points to some general characteristics of fascism, rather than attempting to make them cohere into a definition.

Fascism can be construed as irrationalist, authoritarian and corporatist. That is: it does not encourage thought, it prefers loyalty and obedience. In return for these it offers collective rather than individual gratification and advancement, 'a basic shifting of legitimacy...from the citizen to the group'.[53] Through group cohesion, fascists exchange freedom for power. Fascism is also violent.[54] In place of rational argument it puts orders which brook contradiction only on pain of violence. Fascism is thus violent in itself because it cannot tolerate opposition, disagreement or difference. Its violence is the inevitable product of the fusion of its irrationalism (no time for argument), authoritarianism (no allowance for dissent) and its corporatism (no toleration of individuality). Confronted with argument, dissent and individuality fascism cannot but be violent. Fascism is militarism – 'the spirit of the army' – writ large and run wild. Fascism is also apolitical politics: politics with the debate and disagreement left out.

Amongst the first wave of fascist recruits in Italy itself[55] and in other countries[56] it is possible to number many returning servicemen.[57] 'The presence of war in people's lives led to a certain brutalization of postwar politics...Few, at first, dared to say so in public, and yet a new harshness and even brutality entered the postwar political scene.'[58] Early fascists were typically drawn from amongst the ranks of those who had had 'a good war': 'imposing upon the bloody fields of war their own individual, and often complex, pleasurable landscapes'.[59] Fascism offered them a continuation of both the struggle of war and the cohesiveness of military life.[60] It is possible to have either without the other but fascists were seemingly drawn to both in equal measure, blending them together in 'remembrance of the glory and the camaraderie, and the sense of purpose that infused an ordinary life'.[61] Whether or not modern war was attractive to many more men than has hitherto been imagined[62] is a moot point.[63] What matters here is that it was attractive to some and that of those to whom it was attractive a proportion in turn translated their interest into early fascism.

However, the war had been a largely male preserve[64] and, more to the point, (because the two are not one) it had certainly been a *masculinist* phenomenon, as wars have ever tended to be.[65] Describing in detail the relationship[s] between masculinity and warfare (which is not strictly synonymous with militarism nor with violence) would be a difficult and time-consuming task in itself and lies beyond the present scope. I confine myself to some remarks from David Morgan's essay 'Theater of War: Combat, the Military and Masculinities'.

> The gendered associations of war and soldiering have
> [traditionally] been...one of the abiding features of the sexual
> division of labor...women are often formally barred from
> [military]...activities...combat and military experience separate
> men from women while binding men to men...[which contributes
> to] highlighting...[the] contrasts between active masculine
> animality and female passivity.[66]

Facism traded on the desire of some men to return to warlike
conditions[67] – the simplistic thrill of violence coupled with 'the ecstatic
evasion of thought',[68] which can live in the obeying of orders[69] and both of
these in an essentially masculine environment.

If fascism was an expression and continuation of masculinist militarism
then it followed that it had little room for women. Martin Durham has
recently argued that 'fascism is [not] to be seen as by definition a
masculine movement pursuing a misogynist agenda'.[70] The position of
women in English/Welsh inter-war fascism was highly ambiguous and
contradictory.[71] On the one hand, women could certainly be fascist
activists.[72] Indeed, they could even be more active and committed than
men. Trevor Grundy's father was interned for the duration of the Second
World War for his loyalty to Oswald Mosley's British Union of Fascists
(BUF). However, after the death of his wife (herself from a family of
Jewish converts) he confessed to his son that he 'only got involved with
Mosley because of her'.[73] What fascism held out to selected women was
the possibility of being initiated into its essentially masculinist culture of
militaristic authoritarianism, corporatism, irrationality and violence. Thus
they might enjoy power of a sort but only individually and at the expense
of the vast majority of women who always stood to be significantly
disadvantaged by fascist policies when enacted.[74]

The concerns made manifest in the NAS pre-dated the First World War;
but in war's wake, men who were (re-)entering a highly feminised sphere
(elementary teaching) looked for defence of their interests to the least
feminised institution they knew, the military services from which so many
had recently been discharged. In doing so they paralleled aspects of the
thinking, if not the actions, of those men who turned towards fascism in
the same period.

It is possible to show that, although membership of trade unions was
uncommon in the ranks of the BUF,[75] many of those fascists who were also
trade unionists were either journalists or teachers;[76] and, indeed, it is
possible to 'run to ground' individual fascist teachers sufficiently active
immediately before the Second World War as to have been thought to

warrant detention for at least some part of its duration.[77] (Though there was probably greater wartime animosity towards socialist-pacifist conscientious objectors.)[78] The claim here is not so much that there were crossovers between the NAS, the BUF and other fascist (and pro-Nazi) groups, though instances of these certainly existed.[79] Guilt by association is no guilt at all and whatever else it was, the NAS was no fascist or pro-Nazi front organisation. However, the NAS did represent what can be described as 'an English [ideal of] masculinity arguably not *far distant* from a category of manliness mobilised by European fascism' (emphasis added).[80] It is here that we can turn to consideration of the discourse of the NAS, its way of talking to itself, about itself and of constructing itself through language. The study of discourse pioneered in the works of Michel Foucault (which is not the same thing as the precise discourse analysis of the linguists)[81] has become commonplace in the portmanteau discipline of education studies in recent years in the UK and elsewhere. The reasons for this are many and various,[82] and this 'linguistic turn' has not been without controversy,[83] but if all learning is essentially language learning then it would seem to follow that there would be a considerable attraction for those interested in studying education in the qualitative assessment of language persistently used in certain contexts. Studying discourse can be thought of as the investigation of 'set[s] of terms, images, and concepts, which organize thinking and experiences about the past, present, and future of society, doing so in a way which enigmatically surpasses the specific claims they put forth'.[84] It is my contention here that the discourse of the NAS was essentially fascistic in the period 1919–39. That is to say, it drew on imagery, references and forms of argument which fascism also typically invoked. The most resolute linking of fascism, masculinity and militarism through shared language comes in the work of Klaus Theweliet on the German proto-fascistic *freikorps* of the 1920s. Theweleit overtly identifies his theme as thwarted masculinity seeking relief through orgiastic violence and ecstatic [a]politics.[85]

How can the discourse of the NAS be said to be fascistic? Here several elements can be identified. Most obviously, as an organisation based on, and actively advocating, corporatist gender separation, the NAS inclined towards fascism in its very nature. More than this, masculinist values were invoked in the criticism of opponents, typically as 'effete'.[86] Intellectualism was denigrated and derided.[87] Apolitical unity was often appealed to as the organisation's distinctive strength,[88] (and NAS leaders could be forcefully reminded of this heritage by the membership when they seemed to have strayed from the path it prescribed).[89] There was also a marked preference for direct, authoritarian, even militaristic leadership.[90]

Formally the NAS was committed to the cause of world peace (or at least order) through the conventional means of support for the League of Nations. From as early as 1931 it was being 'suggested [by the leadership] that... local associations should co-operate... with branch[es] of the League of Nations Union'.[91] As the international situation worsened there was little support at the association's conference for the suggestion, by one delegate, that Italian aggression in Abyssinia should be excused, or even supported by the world at large.[92] By 1938, late as it was, there was 'unqualified approval' from the floor for proposals to support the League,[93] but in the overriding cause of gender difference/separation amongst teachers and pupils alike, NAS members were prepared to make strange 'bed fellows' indeed. Thus reports of gendered schooling in Nazi Germany and even imperial Japan were tendered by members and printed, apparently with approval.[94] The article 'A Boys' School in Germany'[95] is worth some detailed consideration.[96] Certain lacunae in the description make it difficult to be precise in any identification of the school being visited but it seems most likely to have been an example of the *Nationalpolitische Erziehungunstalten* schools (literally National Political Institutes of Education, or Napolas) established in 1933.[97] It most certainly was not a mixed elementary school.[98] This was an elite, selective institution and it was decidedly single sex. The article's author enthused over this 'large boys' school of a particularly modern type' where 'the headmaster and... staff [were] all in uniform and wearing Nazi armlets' containing 600 boys who had all 'gained admission after a thorough examination and a severe medical test'.[99] The tone was obviously approving throughout, in a way 'surpassing the specific claims' being made – here was a vindication of all that the NAS had campaigned for over some 20 years. Here was a school offering to foster and protect masculinity in the isolation from femininity it needed and craved and to give it its fullest, most compete expression through obedience, conformity and the only barely restrained violence of these 600 'severe[ly] medical[ly] test[ed]' boys and their uniformed para-military masters.

Despite repeated claims to the contrary,[100] the NAS was anti-feminist, in so far as it was masculinist. That is: to its core. It was built on the conviction that separate provision for boys and girls was necessary if boys were not to be feminised and if girls were not to be denied the opportunity to be feminised. It was an organisation proud of its formation by 'strong men',[101] 'good and strong men'.[102] Its appeal to members was comparable (though not identical) to that of the fascist parties of the 1920s and 1930s. It offered to recapitulate the life and values of the military. These values it reflected in its language (in its official statements and in its members' own writings).

> [T]he first [twentieth century] crisis of masculinity came to a temporary end with the outset of World War I when many young males enthusiastically saw war as the ultimate homosocial institution in which adult men, separated from women, could engage in masculine activities.[103]

That crisis was, however, only temporarily abated by the war and indeed it was deepened for many of those who returned to a disturbed and dislocated world. That dislocation would spawn both socio-political and aesthetic changes.[104] The NAS was a refuge from the post-war storm for its members. It was also a means of expressing their especially militant anti-feminism, their suspicion that effeminacy resulted in degeneration, threatened population (corporate well being) and subverted hierarchy. The post-war 'crisis of masculinity' (the fear that masculinity, the supposed perfect expression of which had been seen in wartime, was now even more undermined than it had been before the war) that drew some men to fascism was far from universal.[105] But it was sufficiently widespread to warrant recognition as a contributory factor in fascism's birth and in the emergence and growth of the NAS.

'The involvement [or not] of men in the education of boys has become an important part of recent debates.'[106] In the UK and elsewhere the contemporary [non-]availability of male teachers (usually in primary schools but sometimes also in secondary) and the implications of this for the learning of boys is rarely depicted as an opportunity or simply a fact having no moral significance.[107] When the situation is treated as a 'shortage', as a problem, it is certainly invested with such a degree of (malign) significance. Thus does something of the discourse of the NAS endure.

ENDNOTES

1. 'HM', 'Conference viewed by the new member', *The New Schoolmaster*, May, (1924), p. 29.
2. Founded: 1903 as the Equal Pay League, became the National Federation of Women Teachers in 1906 and re-named again on secession from the National Union of Teachers in 1920.
3. Other than works cited below, see, for example: H. Kean, *Challenging the State?* (Lewes: Falmer Press); A. Oram, '"Men

must be educated and women must do it"; The National Federation (later Union) of Women Teachers and contemporary feminism, 1910–1930', *Gender and Education*, 2, 2, pp. 147–67; S. King, 'Feminists in teaching: the National Union of Women Teachers, 1920–1945', in M. Lawn and G. Grace (eds), *Teachers: The Culture and Politics of Work* (Lewes: Falmer Press); A. Oram, 'Inequalities in the teaching profession: the effect on teachers and pupils, 1910–1939', in F. Hunt (ed.), *Lessons for Life: The Schooling of Girls and Women, 1850–1950* (Oxford: Basil Blackwell), pp. 101–23; A. Oram, '"To Cook Dinners With Love in Them"?: Sexuality, marital status and women teachers in England and Wales, 1920–1939', in K. Weiler and S. Middleton (eds), *Telling Women's Lives: Narrative Inquiries in the History of Women's Education* (Buckingham: Open University Press), pp. 96-112.

4. M. Littlewood, 'Makers of men', *Trouble and Strife*, 5, pp. 23–9.

5. Disbanded: 1961.

6. Founded: 1966.

7. The NAS and the UWT formally merged in 1978 when single sex trade unions were no longer legal. The present day NASUWT is in effect only nominally related to its all-male ancestor. Thus, for example, the tone of a recent book by an NASUWT president is far removed from that of erstwhile NAS publications. See: M. Johnson, *Failing School, Failing City: The Reality of Inner City Education* (Charlbury: Jon Carpenter). Despite conspicuously little comradeship in the past, the NASUWT and the NUT, both of which are represented in the Trade Union Congress, have been able to co-operate more recently. See: N. Barnard, 'Unions Unveil Wishlist', *Times Educational Supplement*, 18 August, (2000), p. 2.

8. Unlike the NUT, the NASUWT operates throughout Britain and is thus to be found in Scotland as well as England and Wales. The origins of the NASUWT's operation in Scotland lie in the Scottish Schoolmasters' Association, a lobby-group within the Educational Institute of Scotland from 1932; a separate body linked to the NAS from 1954. G. Livingstone, 'Teachers' professional organisations', in T. G. K. Bryce and W. M. Humes (eds), *Scottish Education* (Edinburgh: Edinburgh University Press), p. 978. In 1961 a Northern Ireland Association of Schoolmasters came into being extending the NAS throughout the UK. The present remarks are however confined to England and Wales.

9. The National Union of Elementary Teachers (NUET) until 1870, renamed in 1888.

10. B. Morton, *Action 1919–1969: A Record of the Growth of the National Association of Schoolmasters* (Hemel Hempstead: NAS), p. 9.
11. A. Tropp, *The School Teachers: The Growth of the Teaching Profession in England and Wales from 1800 to the Present Day* (London: Heinemann), p. 216.
12. Morton, *Action 1919–1939*, p. 8.
13. *The New Schoolmaster* was so named in opposition to the *Schoolmaster*, founded in 1871 effectively as the journal of the NUET/NUT, though only fully controlled by that union from 1909. R. S. Betts, 'The National Union of Teachers, the Educational Newspaper Company and the *Schoolmaster*, 1871–1909', *Journal of Educational Administration and History*, 2, 1, pp. 33–40.
14. *National Association of Schoolmasters First Annual Report and Yearbook*, (1920), Modern Records Centre, University of Warwick, MSS.38A/4/3/1.
15. Bernard, *Action 1919–1939*, p. 9.
16. The policy platform of the NUWT in its own words can be found in A. M. Pierotti, *The Story of the National Union of Women Teachers* (Southend-on-Sea: NUWT).
17. NAS, *Yearbook*, pp. 27–8.
18. On the 'bigger picture' concerning equal pay in the public sector, see: H. L. Smith, 'British Feminism and the Equal Pay Issue in the 1930s', *Women's History Review*, 5, 1, pp. 97–110.
19. G. Partington, *Women Teachers in the 20th Century in England and Wales* (Windsor: NFER), p. 21.
20. This position was mirrored in the secondary sector, though women teachers were less common in secondary than in elementary schools where they made up some 70 per cent of the teaching force by the start of the First World War. My remarks here are confined to the elementary sector. H. Bradley, *Men's Work, Women's Work: A Sociological History of the Sexual Division of Labour in Employment* (Cambridge: Polity Press), pp. 207–8.
21. A. Oram, *Women Teachers and Feminist Politics, 1900–1930* (Manchester: Manchester University Press), pp. 124–6.
22. Morton, *Action 1919–1939*, p. 8.
23. Partington, *Women Teachers*, p. 19.
24. Oram, *Women Teachers*, p. 3.
25. A version of the NUT's official understanding of its contribution to the equal-pay struggle is given in M. Darke, 'The NUT and the Equal Pay Campaign', *Education Review*, 6, 1, pp. 23–7.

26. The lowest figure recorded is 5,100 in 1923 and the highest 9,405 in 1934. Oram, *Women Teachers*, Appendix, Table 10, p. 235.
27. Oram, *Women Teachers*, p. 3.
28. Ibid. Appendix, Table 1, pp. 226–7.
29. P. Gardner, 'Reconstructing the classroom teacher, 1903–1945', in I. Grosvenor, M. Lawn and K. Rousmaniere (eds), *Silences and Images: The Social History of the Classroom* (New York: Peter Lang), p. 142.
30. C. Griggs, 'The National Union of Teachers in the Eastbourne area 1874–1916: a tale of tact and pragmatism', *History of Education*, 20, 4, pp. 235–340.
31. R. Betts, '"A New Type of Elementary Teacher": George Collins 1839–1891', *History of Education*, 27, 1, pp. 15–27; and R. Betts, *Dr Macnamara 1861–1931* (Liverpool: Liverpool University Press).
32. Quoted in Betts, *Dr Macnamara 1861–1931*, p. 142.
33. J. Croall, *Neill of Summerhill: The Permanent Rebel* (London: Routledge and Kegan Paul, 1983), p. 87.
34. N. Bosanquet, 'From Bermondsey to Canary Wharf: the social context of change in industrial relations, 1800–2000', *British Journal of Industrial Relations*, 31, 2, p. 240.
35. Tropp, *The School Teachers*, p. 216, note 18.
36. Morton dates the Cardiff group to 1911 though both Tropp and Oram (*Women Teachers*, p. 131) prefer 1913.
37. J. Bourke, *Dismembering the Male: Men's Bodies, Britain and the Great War* (London: Reaktion Books), pp. 153–5.
38. 'Men considering joining a comrades' organization had to choose from a large array of groups, all competing vigorously (and sometimes viciously) for limited resources... [for example,] limbless ex-servicemen fought for preferential treatment against associations dominated by the able-bodied', ibid. p. 155.
39. Ibid. p. 153.
40. Ibid. p. 155.
41. 'HM', 'Conference Viewed by the New Member', p. 29.
42. Bourke, *Dismembering the Male*, p. 155. For an extensive discussion of class-based culture[s] in the army on the western front see: J. Bourne, 'The British Working Man in Arms', in H. Cecil and P. H. Liddle (eds), *Facing Armageddon: The First World War Experienced* (London: Leo Cooper), pp. 336–52.
43. Quoted in Bourke, *Dismembering the Male*, p. 154.
44. Ibid. p. 170.
45. B. Mussolini, 'Trincerocrazia', *Il Popolo d'Italia*, 15 December,

(1917), extract in R. Griffin (ed.), *Oxford Readers: Fascism* (Oxford: Oxford University Press), document 5, pp. 28–9.

46.   Ibid. p. 28.

47.   Ibid. p. 29.

48.   For example, D. Renton, *Fascism: Theory and Practice* (London: Pluto); and D. Renton, 'Was Fascism an Ideology? British Fascism Reconsidered', *Race and Class*, 41, 3, (2000), pp. 72–84 in which he responds to authors, including Griffin and Sternhell *et al.*, who do not share his position.

49.   R. Ben-Ghiar, 'Italian Fascism and the Aesthetics of the "Third Way"', *Journal of Contemporary History*, 31, 2, (1996), p. 297.

50.   For example, R. Griffin, *The Nature of Fascism* (London: Routledge) and M. Durham, *Women and Fascism* (London: Routledge).

51.   For example, Z. Sternhell, M. Sznajder and M. Asheri, translated by D. Maisel, *The Birth of Fascist Ideology: From Cultural Rebellion to Political Revolution* (Princeton: Princeton University Press) and D. S. Lewis (ed.), *Illusions of Grandeur: Mosley, Fascism and British Society, 1931–1981* (Manchester: Manchester University Press).

52.   See: D. Orlow, 'A difficult relationship of unequal relatives: the Dutch NSB and Nazi Germany, 1933–1940', *European History Quarterly*, 29, 3, pp. 349–80. Other examples of Nazi disdain for European fascists are given at length in R. E. Herzstein, *When Nazi Dreams Come True* (London: Abacus).

53.   J. Ralston Saul, *The Unconscious Civilization* (Harmondsworth: Penguin), p. 18.

54.   It may be that certain fascist groups have not been as violent in practice as has often been assumed, but this does not militate against my point. Fascism is violent in its nature. See: S. M. Cullen, 'Political violence: the case of the British Union of Fascists', *Journal of Contemporary History*, 28, 2, pp. 245–67. A more customary evaluation of BUF violence is given in Renton, 'Was Fascism an Ideology?' in reply to such claims by Cullen and others.

55.   Griffin, *The Nature*, p. 64.

56.   The Irish Blueshirts, formally the Army Comrades Association, can serve as an example of this that is highly relevant both for proximity to the UK and in the explicit linking of erstwhile soldiers and new-made fascists. (That the Blueshirts were 'truly' fascist has been doubted but here I follow Cronin's judgement that they should be viewed as having been at least 'potential

"para-fascists"'. M. Cronin, 'The Blueshirt Movement, 1932–5: Ireland's Fascists?', *Journal of Contemporary History*, 30, 2, p. 327.)

57. It was not strictly necessary that ex-military (proto- or quasi-) fascists in the inter-war period should have been radicalised by the First World War itself. The fascistic Protestant Action group in Scotland was led by and drew support from men who had seen action fighting the IRA in Ireland rather than anywhere else. See: A. Calder, 'Miss Brodie and the Kaledonian Klan', in A. Calder, *Revolving Culture: Notes from the Scottish Republic* (London: I. B. Taurus), pp. 152–5, and S. Bruce, *No Pope of Rome: Militant Protestantism in Modern Scotland* (Edinburgh: Mainstream), pp. 83-107.

58. E. L. Mosse, *Fallen Soldiers: Reshaping the Memory of the World Wars* (Oxford: Oxford University Press), p. 156.

59. J. Bourke, *An Intimate History of Killing: Face-to-Face Killing in Twentieth-Century Warfare* (London: Granta Books), p. 345.

60. The process by which ex-service men might be drawn towards fascism is, to my mind, nowhere more eloquently mapped out than by the late James Leslie Mitchell (sometimes still better known under his sobriquet, Lewis Grassic Gibbon). His novel *The 13th Disciple*, first published in 1931, charts the flirtation with fascism, in the guise of the fictional 'Secular Control Group', of its hero Malcolm Maudsley. J. L. Mitchell, *The 13th Disciple* (Edinburgh: B and W Publishing), especially p. 211ff.

61. Mosse, *Fallen Soldiers*, p. 114.

62. As suggested in N. Ferguson, *The Pity of War* (Harmondsworth: Penguin), pp. 357–66 and developed in Bourke, *An Intimate History*, see especially pp. 370–1.

63. War also traps in its inexorable, mechanistic logic as well as inviting willing participation. See: J. Glover, *Humanity: A Moral History of the Twentieth Century* (London: Jonathan Cape), p. 155ff.

64. Women were of course involved in the war in many ways. Primarily they were non-combatants caught up in it, but others were active participants often in a variety of [quasi-]military medical formations. See: for example, I. Ross, *Little Grey Partridge: First World War Diary of Isobel Ross Who Served With the Scottish Women's Hospitals Unit in Serbia*, J. Dixon (ed.), (Aberdeen: Aberdeen University Press). Others again were involved vicariously through their enduring links with men at the various fronts. A. Wollacott, 'Sisters and brothers in arms: family, class, and gendering in World War I Britain', in M. Cooke and A. Wollacott (eds), *Gendering War Talk* (Princeton: Princeton University Press), pp. 128–47.

65. D. H. J. Morgan, 'Theater of war: combat, the military, and masculinities', in H. Brod and M. Kaufman (eds), *Theorizing Masculinities* (Thousand Oaks: Sage), p. 165.

66. Ibid. pp. 166–7.

67. An early signalling of Oswald Mosley's putative fascism came when, on first assuming his seat in parliament, 'he joined the New Members Coalition Group which comprised ex-soldiers determined to extend the spirit of war into politics, avoiding class conflict'. C. Cook, 'A Fascist Memory: Oswald Mosley and the Myth of the Airman', *European Review of History*, 4, 2, p. 151.

68. H. G. Wells, *Travels of a Republic Radical in Search of Hot Water* (Harmondsworth: Penguin), p. 378.

69. See, for example: E. Fromm, *The Erich Fromm Reader*, R. Funk (ed.), (New Jersey, Humanities Press), especially pp. 33–8.

70. Durham, *Women*, p. 182.

71. The first overtly fascist group in Britain, the British Fascists, had a woman, Rotha Lintorn-Orman, as its founder.

72. Durham, *Women*, especially pp. 49-73.

73. T. Grundy, *Memoir of a Fascist Childhood: A Boy in Mosley's Britain* (London: Heinemann), p. 200.

74. A theme discussed at length in, V. de Grazia, *How Fascism Ruled Women: Italy, 1922–1945* (Berkley, University of California Press).

75. S. Rawnsley, 'The membership of the British Union of Fascists', in K. Lunn and R. Thurlow (eds), *British Fascism* (London: Croom Helm), p. 151.

76. J. D. Brewer, 'The British Union of Fascists: some tentative conclusions on its membership', in S. Ugelvik Larsen, B. Hagtvet and J. P. Myklebust (eds), *Who Were the Fascists? Social Roots of European Fascism* (Bergen: Universitetsforlagen), p. 547.

77. A. W. B. Simpson, *In the Highest Degree Odious: Detention Without Trial in Wartime Britain* (Oxford: Oxford University Press), p. 400. Simpson gives three cases, one of whom was female, thus ineligible for NAS membership.

78. D. Limond, '"Only Talk in the Staffroom": "subversive" teaching in a Scottish school, 1939–1940', *History of Education*, 29, 3, pp. 239–52 and R. Barker, *Conscience, Government and War* (London: Routledge) p. 38.

79. An occasional writer in the pages of *TNS* was Meyrick Booth, an educational psychologist, and 'an indefatigable pro-Nazi'. R. Griffiths, *Fellow Travellers of the Right: British Enthusiasts for Nazi Germany, 1933–1939* (London: Constable), p. 296. Booth generally wrote for

TNS on educational subjects, especially the efficacy of separate schooling, but on one occasion he did reveal his politics directly with a letter in which he specifically solicited members for the pro-Nazi Link organisation. M. Booth, letter, *TNS*, January, (1939), p. 12.

80. K. Holden, 'Formations of discipline and manliness: culture, politics and 1930s women's writing', *Journal of Gender Studies*, 8, 2, p. 141.

81. S. Trombley, 'Discourse', in A. Bullock and O. Stallybrass (eds), *The Fontana Dictionary of Modern Thought* (London: Collins), p. 230.

82. F. Schrag, 'Why Foucault Now?', *Journal of Curriculum Studies*, 31, 4, pp. 375–83.

83. D. Macey, 'Michel Foucault: J'Accuse', *New Formations*, 25, pp. 5–13.

84. P. Rabinow, 'Introduction', in M. Foucault, *The Foucault Reader: An Introduction to Foucault's Thought*, P. Rabinow (ed.), (Harmondsworth: Penguin), p. 25.

85. K. Theweliet, *Male Fantasies: Women, Floods, Bodies and History*, translated by E. Carter and C. Turner (Cambridge: Polity Press); and K. Theweliet *Male Fantasies, Male Bodies, Psychoanalyzing the White Terror*, translated by E. Carter, C. Turner, S. Conway (Cambridge: Polity Press).

86. 'Getting Gray', letter, *TNS*, May (1921), p.14. The habit of publishing letters and articles under pseudonyms or other devices can be irritating for the modern reader but I have reproduced the names/titles used in each case as they appeared.

87. Anon, 'On Theorising', *TNS*, October (1921), pp. 13–14.

88. R. Winston, 'A Pleasing Valediction', *TNS*, January (1922), p. 27.

89. W. H. Young, 'An Open Letter to the President', *TNS*, December (1932), p. 31.

90. Anon, 'Napoleon and Teaching', *TNS*, July (1921), p. 15.

91. Anon, 'Pioneering for Peace', *TNS*, June (1931), p. 28.

92. Anon, 'Conference Report: First Public Session', *TNS*, May (1936), p. 30.

93. Anon, 'The Thirteenth Annual Conference at Coventry', *TNS*, May (1938), p. 12.

94. H. F. Escott, 'This Education Business in Progressive Japan', *TNS*, July (1934), pp. 17–18. On Japan's variety of fascism, see Griffin, *The Nature*, pp. 153–6 and Y. Khan, 'Schooling Japan's imperial subjects in the early Shôwa period', *History of Education*, 29, 2, pp. 213–23.

95. M. Bailey, 'A Boy's School in Germany', *TNS*, June (1935), pp. 22–3.

96. In making particular use of this piece I do not repudiate my

earlier contention that fascism and Nazism are not one and the same. Germany had inter-war fascism, most obviously represented by such a figure as Ernst Jünger, but the fact that Nazism's ascendance was the cause of German fascism's fall was lost on many fascists, then as now. Griffin, *The Nature*, pp. 92–3.

97. James Bowen, *A History of Western Education*, vol. III, (London: Methuen), p. 481. The even more selective Adolf Hitler Schools were not founded until 1937. Ibid. p. 482.

98. Nazi Germany's elementary schools did also receive approval, G. H. Pumphrey, 'An Elementary School in Germany', *TNS*, December (1938), pp. 11–12.

99. Bailey, 'A Boys' School', p. 22. A note from the editor later (July 1935, p. 4) pointed out that this article had prompted much interest and details were provided of companies offering tours of Germany.

100. For example: 'A SCHOOLMASTER WHO IS ACTUALLY INTERESTED IN HIS WORK', letter, *TNS*, May (1921), p. 15 – 'we are not out merely for filthy lucre or as anti-feminists'. And, Morton, *Action, 1919–1969*, p. 10 – 'It should be stated clearly that ...[the NAS] was not an opposition to feminism generally.'

101. *Action, 1919–1969*, p. 11.

102. Ibid. p. 12.

103. M. A. Messner, *Politics of Masculinities: Men in Movements* (Thousand Oaks: Sage) p. 9.

104. Aesthetic change is described in, M. Eksteins, *Rites of Spring: The Great War and the Birth of the Modern Age* (London: Black Swan); and A. Becker, 'The Avant-Garde, Madness and the Great War', *Journal of Contemporary History*, 35, 1, pp. 71–84.

105. L. A. Hall, 'Impotent ghosts from no man's land, flappers' boyfriends, or crypto-patriarchs? Men, sex and social change in 1920s Britain', *Social History*, 21, 1, pp. 69–70.

106. R. Gilbert and P. Gilbert, *Masculinity Goes to School* (London: Routledge), p. 242. *See also*, K. Roulston and M. Mills, 'Male teachers in feminised teaching areas: marching to the beat of the Men's Movement drums?', *Oxford Review of Education*, 26, 2, pp. 221–37.

107. See: J. Howson, 'Men Fail to Get Places', *Times Educational Supplement*, 22 September (2000), p. 23; W. Mansell, 'More Male Teachers Needed to Help Boys', *Times Educational Supplement*, 1 September (2000), p. 9; A. Wade, 'The Boy Can't Help It', *Spectator*, 2 September 2000, p. 26; A. Ross and D. Thomson,

'The Vanishing Male Maths Teacher', *Times Educational Supplement*, 12 November (1999), p. 24.

I am grateful to Dr Alison Oram for comments on this chapter.

REFERENCES

'A SCHOOLMASTER WHO IS ACTUALLY INTERESTED IN HIS WORK', letter, *TNS*, May (1921), p. 15
Anon., 'Conference Report: First Public Session', *The New Schoolmaster (TNS)*, May (1936), pp. 25–30.
— 'Napoleon and Teaching', *TNS*, July (1921), p. 15.
— 'On Theorising', *TNS*, October (1921), pp. 13–14.
— 'Pioneering for Peace', *TNS*, June (1931), p. 28.
— 'The Thirteenth Annual Conference at Coventry', *TNS*, May (1938), pp. 1–16.
Bailey, M. 'A Boys' School in Germany', *TNS*, June (1935), pp. 22-3.
Barker, R. *Conscience, Government and War* (London: Routledge, 1982).
Barnard, N. 'Unions Unveil Wishlist', *Times Educational Supplement*, 18 August, (2000), p. 2.
Becker, A. 'The Avant-Garde, Madness and the Great War', *Journal of Contemporary History*, 35, 1 (2000), pp. 71–84.
Ben-Ghiar, R. 'Italian Fascism and the Aesthetics of the "Third Way"', *Journal of Contemporary History*, 31, 2 (1996), pp. 293–316.
Betts, R. S. 'The National Union of Teachers, the Educational Newspaper Company and the Schoolmaster, 1871-1909', *Journal of Educational Administration and History*, 2, 1 (1993), pp. 33–40.
— '"A New Type of Elementary Teacher": George Collins 1839–1891', *History of Education*, 27, 1 (1998), pp. 15–27.
— *Dr Macnamara 1861–1931* (Liverpool: Liverpool University Press, 1999).
Booth, M. letter, *TNS*, January, (1939), p. 12.
Bosanquet, N. 'From Bermondsey to Canary Wharf: the social context of change in industrial relations, 1800–2000', *British Journal of Industrial Relations*, 31, 2 (1992), pp. 237–53.
Bourke, J. *Dismembering the Male: Men's Bodies, Britain and the Great War* (London: Reaktion Books, 1996).
— *An Intimate History of Killing: Face-to-Face Killing in Twentieth-Century Warfare* (London: Granta Books, 1999).
Bourne, J. 'The British working man in arms', in H. Cecil and P. H. Liddle

(eds), *Facing Armageddon: The First World War Experienced* (London: Leo Cooper, 1996), pp. 336–52.

Bowen, J. *A History of Western Education*, vol. III, (London: Methuen, 1980), p. 481.

Bradley, H. *Men's Work, Women's Work: A Sociological History of the Sexual Division of Labour in Employment* (Cambridge: Polity Press, 1989).

Brewer, J. D. 'The British Union of Fascists: some tentative conclusions on its membership', in S. Ugelvik Larsen, B. Hagtvet and J. P. Myklebust (eds), *Who Were the Fascists? Social Roots of European Fascism* (Bergen: Universitetsforlagen, 1980), pp. 542–56.

Bruce, S. *No Pope of Rome: Militant Protestantism in Modern Scotland* (Edinburgh: Mainstream, 1985).

Bullock, A. and Trombley, S. (eds), *The New Fontana Dictionary of Modern Thought* (London: Collins, 1977), p. 175.

Calder, A. 'Miss Brodie and the Kaledonian Klan' in A. Calder (ed.) *Revolving Culture: Notes from the Scottish Republic* (London: I. B. Taurus, 1994) pp. 152–5.

Cook, C. 'A Fascist Memory: Oswald Mosley and the Myth of the Airman', *European Review of History*, 4, 2 (1997), pp. 147–61.

Croall, J. *Neill of Summerhill: The Permanent Rebel* (London: Routledge and Kegan Paul, 1983).

Cronin, M. 'The Blueshirt Movement, 1932–5: Ireland's Fascists?', *Journal of Contemporary History*, 30, 2 (1999), pp. 311–32.

Cullen, S. M. 'Political violence: the case of the British Union of Fascists', *Journal of Contemporary History*, 28, 2 (1993), pp. 245–67.

Darke, M. 'The NUT and the Equal Pay Campaign', *Education Review*, 6, 1 (1992), pp. 23–7.

de Grazia, V. *How Fascism Ruled Women: Italy, 1922–1945* (Berkeley: University of California Press, 1992).

Durham, M. *Women and Fascism* (London: Routledge, 1998).

Eksteins, M. *Rites of Spring: The Great War and the Birth of the Modern Age* (London: Black Swan, 1990).

Escott, H. F. 'This Education Business in Progressive Japan', *TNS*, July (1934), pp. 17–8.

Ferguson, N. *The Pity of War* (Harmondsworth: Penguin, 1998).

Fromm, E. *The Erich Fromm Reader*, R. Funk (ed.), (New Jersey: Humanities Press, 1994).

Gardner, P. 'Reconstructing the classroom teacher, 1903–1945', in I. Grosvenor, M. Lawn and K. Rousmaniere (eds), *Silences and Images: The Social History of the Classroom* (New York: Peter Lang, 1999), pp. 123–44.

119

'Getting Gray', letter, *TNS*, May (1921), p.14.

Gilbert R. and Gilbert, P. *Masculinity Goes to School* (London: Routledge, 1998).

Glover, J. *Humanity: A Moral History of the Twentieth Century* (London: Jonathan Cape, 1999).

Griffin, R. *The Nature of Fascism* (London: Routledge, 1994).

— *Fellow Travellers of the Right: British Enthusiasts for Nazi Germany, 1933–1939* (London: Constable, 1980).

Griggs, C. 'The National Union of Teachers in the Eastbourne area 1874–1916: a tale of tact and pragmatism', *History of Education*, 20, 4 (1991) pp. 235–340.

Grundy, T. *Memoir of a Fascist Childhood: A Boy in Mosley's Britain* (London: Heinemann, 1998).

Hall, L. A. 'Impotent ghosts from no man's land, flappers' boyfriends, or crypto-patriarchs? Men, sex and social change in 1920s Britain', *Social History*, 21, 1 (1996), pp. 54–70.

Herzstein, R. E. *When Nazi Dreams Come True* (London: Abacus, 1982).

'HM', 'Conference Viewed by the New Member', *TNS*, May (1924), pp. 28–30.

Holden, K. 'Formations of discipline and manliness: culture, politics and 1930s women's writing', *Journal of Gender Studies*, 8, 2 (1999), pp. 141–57.

Howson, J. 'Men Fail to Get Places', *Times Educational Supplement*, 22 September (2000), p. 23.

Johnson, M. *Failing School, Failing City: The Reality of Inner City Education* (Charlbury: Jon Carpenter, 1999).

Kean, H. *Challenging the State?* (Lewes: Falmer Press, 1990)

Khan, Y. 'Schooling Japan's imperial subjects in the early Shôwa period', *History of Education*, 29, 2 (2000), pp. 213–23.

King, S. 'Feminists in teaching: the National Union of Women Teachers, 1920–1945', in M. Lawn and G. Grace (eds), *Teachers: The Culture and Politics of Work* (Lewes: Falmer Press, 1987).

Lewis, D. S. *Illusions of Grandeur: Mosley, Fascism and British Society, 1931–1981* (Manchester: Manchester University Press, 1987).

Limond, D. '"Only talk in the staffroom": "subversive" teaching in a Scottish school, 1939–1940', *History of Education*, 29, 3 (2000), pp. 239–52.

Littlewood, M. 'Makers of Men', *Trouble and Strife*, 5 (1985), pp. 23–9.

Livingstone, G. 'Teachers' professional organisations', in T. G. K. Bryce and W. M. Humes (eds), *Scottish Education* (Edinburgh: Edinburgh University Press, 1999), pp. 978–82.

Macey, D. 'Michel Foucault: J'Accuse', *New Formations*, 25 (1995), pp. 5–13.

Mansell, W. 'More Male Teachers Needed to Help Boys', *Times Educational Supplement*, 1 September (2000), p. 9.

Messner, M. A. *Politics of Masculinities: Men in Movements* (Thousand Oaks: Sage, 1997), p. 9.

Mitchell, J. L. *The 13th Disciple* (Edinburgh: B and W Publishing, 1995/1931).

Morgan, D. H. J. 'Theater of war: combat, the military, and masculinities', in H. Brod and M. Kaufman (eds), *Theorizing Masculinities* (Thousand Oaks: Sage, 1994), pp. 165–82.

Morton, B. *Action 1919–1969: A Record of the Growth of the National Association of Schoolmasters* (Hemel Hempstead: NAS, 1969).

Mosse, E. L. *Fallen Soldiers: Reshaping the Memory of the World Wars* (Oxford: Oxford University Press, 1990).

Mussolini, B. 'Trincerocrazia', *Il Popolo d'Italia*, 15 December, (1917), in R. Griffin (ed.), *Oxford Readers: Fascism* (Oxford: Oxford University Press, 1995), document 5, pp. 28–9.

National Association of Schoolmasters First Annual Report and Yearbook, (1920), Modern Records Centre, University of Warwick, MSS.38A/4/3/1.

Oram, A. '"Men must be educated and women must do it"; The National Federation (later Union) of Women Teachers and Contemporary Feminism, 1910–1930', *Gender and Education*, 2, 2 (1990), pp. 147–67.

— 'Inequalities in the teaching profession: the effect on teachers and pupils, 1910–1939', in F. Hunt (ed.), *Lessons for Life: The Schooling of Girls and Women, 1850–1950* (Oxford: Basil Blackwell, 1987), pp. 101–23.

— *Women Teachers and Feminist Politics, 1900–1930* (Manchester: Manchester University Press, 1996).

— '"To Cook Dinners With Love in Them"'?: sexuality, marital status and women teachers in England and Wales, 1920–1939', in K. Weiler and S. Middleton (eds), *Telling Women's Lives: Narrative Inquiries in the History of Women's Education* (Milton Keynes: Open University Press, 1999), pp. 96–112.

Orlow, D. 'A difficult relationship of unequal relatives: the Dutch NSB and Nazi Germany, 1933–1940', *European History Quarterly*, 29, 3 (1999), pp. 349–80.

Partington, G. *Women Teachers in the 20th Century in England and Wales* (Windsor: NFER, 1976).

Pierotti, A. M. *The Story of the National Union of Women Teachers* (Southend-on-Sea: NUWT, 1963).

Pumphrey, G. H. 'An Elementary School in Germany', *TNS*, December (1938), pp. 11–12.

Rabinow, P. 'Introduction', in M. Foucault, *The Foucault Reader: An Introduction to Foucault's Thought*, P. Rabinow (ed.), (Harmondsworth: Penguin, 1991), pp. 1–29.

Ralston Saul, J. *The Unconscious Civilization* (Harmondsworth: Penguin, 1997).

Rawnsley, S. 'The membership of the British Union of Fascists', in K. Lunn and R. Thurlow (eds), *British Fascism* (London: Croom Helm, 1980), pp. 150–65.

Renton, D. *Fascism: Theory and Practice* (London: Pluto, 1999).

— 'Was Fascism an Ideology? British Fascism Reconsidered', *Race and Class*, 41, 3 (2000), pp. 72–84.

Ross A. and Thomson, D. 'The Vanishing Male Maths Teacher', *Times Educational Supplement*, 12 November (1999), p. 24.

Ross, I. *Little Grey Partridge: First World War Diary of Isobel Ross Who Served With the Scottish Women's Hospitals Unit in Serbia*, J. Dixon (ed.) (Aberdeen: Aberdeen University Press, 1988).

Roulston K. and Mills, M. 'Male teachers in feminised teaching areas: marching to the beat of the Men's Movement drums?', *Oxford Review of Education*, 26, 2 (2000), pp. 221–37.

Schrag, F. 'Why Foucault Now?', *Journal of Curriculum Studies*, 31, 4 (1999), pp. 375–83.

Simpson, W. B. *In the Highest Degree Odious: Detention Without Trial in Wartime Britain* (Oxford: Oxford University Press, 1994).

Smith, H. L. 'British feminism and the Equal Pay issue in the 1930s', *Women's History Review*, 5, 1 (1996), pp. 97–110.

Sternhell, Z. Sznajder M. and Asheri, M. trans. D. Maisel, *The Birth of Fascist Ideology: From Cultural Rebellion to Political Revolution* (Princeton: Princeton University Press, 1992).

Theweliet, K. *Male Fantasies: Women, Floods, Bodies and History*, trans. E. Carter and C. Turner (Cambridge: Polity Press, 1987).

Tropp, A. *The School Teachers: The Growth of the Teaching Profession in England and Wales from 1800 to the Present Day* (London: Heinemann, 1957).

— *Male Fantasies, Male bodies: Psychoanalyzing the White Terror*, trans. E. Carter, S. Conway and C. Turner (Cambridge: Polity Press, 1988).

Wade, 'The Boy Can't Help It', *Spectator*, 2 September 2000, p. 26.

Wells, H.G. *Travels of a Republic Radical in Search of Hot Water*

(Harmondsworth: Penguin, 1939).

Winston, R. 'A Pleasing Valediction', *TNS*, January (1922), p. 27.

Wollacott, A. 'Sisters and brothers in arms: family, class, and gendering in World War I Britain', in M. Cooke and A. Wollacott (eds), *Gendering War Talk* (Princeton: Princeton University Press, 1995), pp. 128–47.

Young, W. H. 'An Open Letter to the President', *TNS*, December (1932), p. 31.

6

Contesting Knowledge: Mary Bridges Adams and the Workers' Education Movement, 1900–18

JANE MARTIN

Mary Bridges Adams (née Daltry) made a considerable contribution to the spread of independent working class education in Britain at a crucial turning point in the politics of education, 100 years ago. The significance of her work was acknowledged in a rare personal tribute from George Sims, original secretary of the Central Labour College, in 1912, 15 years after she entered public life as a socialist member of the London School Board.[1] In thinking about her life this chapter explores certain central themes that underpinned her political purpose, and assesses her effectiveness and influence in achieving her goals. It begins with a brief account of her family background, schooling and work experiences for clues to her interest in labour politics. A second area of focus is her vision of an education system that would include all students. The final section examines her contribution to the cause of independent working class education. As time went on she rejected the ideals of a non-partisan education in favour of one that had both a class character and a socialist content. Inspiration came from the words of the Socialist League slogan, to 'educate, agitate, organise'. This paved the way for her sustained and intense political commitment. Despite her exclusion from the national power structures, I will argue that the activities of Mary Bridges Adams had significant implications for an intellectual culture rooted in a larger tradition of individual workers' search for knowledge.

In her day, Mary Bridges Adams was a prominent figure in one of Britain's leading socialist organisations, the Social Democratic Federation (SDF). She was a person for whom politics mattered. Yet, she is missing from much of the historiography of British socialism even though she did receive attention in the *Dictionary of Labour Biography*.[2] This oversight stems partly from the fact that the overwhelming majority of published autobiographies are by men who pay little or no attention to women's participation in the development of British socialism. Bridges Adams neither wrote an autobiography, nor left contemporary records describing her political activities, so retrieval of her story requires particular ingenuity. This is a major reason for the partial picture of her struggle to find a place in the male world of organised labour politics. The Marxist SDF has been generally identified (both by contemporaries and labour historians) as 'blatantly misogynist',[3] although June Hannam and Karen Hunt contend that this is an 'unforgiving and inaccurate stereotype'.[4] These authors comment further that the arguments of feminist historians 'have had relatively little impact on the frameworks in which historians continue to narrate socialist politics of this period'.[5] From a different perspective, Stuart Macintyre, in his analysis of Marxism in Britain 1917–33, argues that mainstream scholarship 'suffers from a preoccupation with the successful – successful organisations, leadership and ideologies'.[6] Such a focus diverts attention away from a more considered analysis of peripheral strands in British labour and intellectual history and Macintyre attempts to disentangle the narratives to extrapolate:

> a more general militant and anti-capitalist tradition... which cannot be defined institutionally and finds organised expression only fleetingly in periods of special stress, but is nevertheless rooted in different sections of the British working class. Indeed the tradition might almost seem to define itself against the respectable lineage, the 'moral force' Chartists, the top-hatted leaders of the early T.U.C., the Lib-Lab M.P.s, the men who organised, lobbied, waited on Royal Commissions and finally were admitted to office. The hallmark of our tradition is a certain stubborn intransigence, a rejection of both the mores and the institutions of the existing social order combined with a deep suspicion of the respectable path to social reform.[7]

But I would argue that this is a phenomenon, which cannot be examined without taking women's participation in it into account. Writing Mary Bridges Adams back into the historical record is to challenge the stereotypically male figure of the heroic autodidact. So, this work is in part a project of recovery but it is by no means of purely antiquarian interest.

To contribute to that project I use prosopography, or collective biography, to analyse Mary's educational ideals and their translation into practice. Looking at formal and informal associations of educator activists, prosopography is concerned with small group dynamics and the prosopographer uses the documentation (that has survived) to pay attention to the source of political action. Through a biographical approach we see the effect on her life of having access to education as a developing form of employment and the consequences for her emergent subjectivity (including the struggle and contest over personal identity) and agency. Her story enables us to explore the ways in which activist women are positioned and position themselves as agents of change – for themselves, for others and for society at large. Above all, prosopography and biography bring the thoughts of a less well-known socialist woman more clearly into focus.

Mary Daltry was the youngest of two children born in Maesycwimmer, South Wales, in 1855 to William and Margaret Daltry.[8] As a girl, Mary moved with her family to Newcastle, England, where she attended elementary school. Her socio-economic origins were in the skilled, artisan working class and staying on as a pupil-teacher offered the opportunity for independence and intellectual growth. To qualify, she had to provide a certificate of good health from school managers and (as a female) demonstrate proficiency in needlework. After completing a satisfactory apprenticeship she went on to serve in elementary schools and was not unusual in becoming a head teacher in her twenties, working in the urban centres of Birmingham, London and Newcastle. In addition to her professional teaching qualifications, Mary continued her studies, working part-time towards an inter-BA qualification with the University of London. The acquisition of further academic credentials was accompanied by a growing appreciation of the case for socialism. Her obituary in *The Times* records that she skirted Fabianism under the influence of Peter Kropotkin (the intellectual leader of anarchist communism) and William Morris (founder of the Socialist League). By the mid-1880s she had become an 'uncompromising Socialist'.[9] So, like most of the respondents in Pamela Graves's study of labour women in the inter-war period, Mary was already active in labour organisations when she married Walter Bridges Adams on 22 October 1887.[10] It seems likely that the couple met through their independent political activities since Walter was one of the signatories to the 1885 manifesto of the Socialist League. His father had been a civil engineer and paternalistic employer, pivotal in the radical unitarian network centred on William Johnson Fox's South Place Chapel in Finsbury in the 1830s and 1840s, using journalism to advocate divorce reform and schemes to liberate women from housework. Nothing is known of Walter's education but his sister Hope was sent to Bedford College, the second college in England founded for women, which had Unitarian connections. In the early 1870s Hope and her widowed mother moved to Germany where Hope became a doctor and went on to combine professional status, marriage and motherhood. Demonstrating a commitment to a nominally mass Marxist movement, Hope was very much enmeshed in the political circles of leading European socialists and engaged across a range of social and political reforms. These family and friendship connections helped Mary challenge the educational norms of the day and it may be that Walter tried personally to share domestic responsibility. On 1 March 1889 she gave birth to her only child, William, and by 1893 the young family had settled in Greenwich.

The move to Greenwich was significant because it provided Mary with a means of entry into local labour politics. Although London teachers usually joined the National Union of Elementary Teachers or the Metropolitan Board Teachers Association, she joined the Gasworkers and General Labourers Union, a mixed union that broke the pattern of the craft traditions and moderate politics of the old unionism. This union was strongly represented in Woolwich in the early 1890s (when the movement in London was notably weak) as were the Amalgamated Society of Engineers and the Dockers Union. Unsurprisingly, movement into some form of labour or socialist politics accompanied locality based trade unionism. There were active branches of the Independent Labour Party and the Social Democratic Federation and the symbiotic relationship between the industrial and political sides of the labour movement was satisfied by the Woolwich Trades Council which became the leading labour political force in the borough. The Royal Arsenal Co-operative Society (initially dominated by a small group of Arsenal employees belonging to the Amalgamated Society of Engineers) also came into the political arena at this time. Mary participated in the work of its education committee and its guildswomen and these connections served as leverage for a new public role. Having been a successful professional within the elementary-school world, in 1894 she accepted a request to stand for election for the Greenwich seat on the London School Board. Her political candidature can serve as an example of the continuing networks that were so important to early British socialism. The secretary of the Gasworkers, Will Thorne, was among a circle of trade-unionist colleagues that included George Barnes (secretary of the Amalgamated Society of Engineers) and Gertrude Tuckwell (secretary of the Women's Trade Union League). Other local sponsors included Will Crooks (Liberal-Labour member of the London County Council and Poplar Board of Guardians), Fred Knee (Social Democrat with special interests in education, housing and unemployment), and Mary Lawrenson (ex-teacher and founder of the Woolwich branch of the Women's Co-operative Guild). In her first contest Bridges Adams just failed to win the division for Labour; in 1897 she defeated a serving member to capture the fourth Greenwich seat. This victory was the result of her personality and the unusual vitality of the Woolwich labour movement. Writing in *The Millgate* in the 1930s, W. J. Brown recalled that this was the first 'practical step of the Royal Arsenal Society to wield influence in the realms of local government'.[11] Nonetheless, standard texts on London politics omit or marginalise her contribution.

According to Paul Thompson, several distinctive factors contributed to labour's success in this particular London borough.[12] First, Woolwich had a singular social and occupational structure which can be traced to the position of the Royal Arsenal as the sole major employer. The Arsenal created a large core of skilled artisans whose livelihood was secure and stable enough (as government employees) to give them a degree of independence from local employers and a certain status in local society. Second, the district had a rich range of independent working-class social institutions (including the largest London co-operative society) that enhanced its cultural and political 'tone'. Third, the absence of communication networks (other than the railway) sustained a feeling of independence, reinforced by the relative absence of commuters. Although Thompson acknowledges the importance of the School Board, Bridges Adams has not been absorbed into his story of Woolwich Labour Party. E.T. Fennell's victory at a Borough Council by-election in 1901 is described as the 'first of a series of Labour triumphs'[13] despite her achievement in turning a thin majority into a safe seat in 1900. Against this landscape, the affirmation of her achievements was muted by the personal tragedy of Mary's life, her husband's death. But what does her story tell us about women's participation in public policy?

Created under the terms of the 1870 Education Act, the London Board was a flagship institution and played a vital role in setting the educational standards for others to follow. By the mid-1880s it had 55 members representing 11 educational districts that varied in size from the inner square mile of the City to the vast Greenwich ward covering the parliamentary seats of Deptford, Greenwich, Lewisham and Woolwich. Each district returned a number of candidates and 326 Londoners served during the period of the School Board, including 29 women. This was a key political step for women, and women members were subjected to media speculation, focus and interest, and an expectation that they would make a difference. Nonetheless, space and opportunities were not going to be ceded without a struggle and middle- and upper-class men overwhelmingly dominated the world of educational policy-making. The organisational and procedural structures were modelled on those at

Westminster and the character and social interactions were clearly connected to specific class-based masculinities. In all cases, school-board women were working in uncharted territory and experienced substantial tensions despite differences in perspective and approach.

I have demonstrated elsewhere that school-board women were not a homogenous group, the individual complexities make it necessary to employ a relational understanding of difference, in which the 'other' is not an oppositional category. Here, Mary Bridges Adams was distinctive as the only one to grow up in a labour aristocratic community and lacked the independence of a large unearned income. Second, she did not share a common culture with the others from more middle-class, non-elementary school backgrounds. Third, her story does not show the overlapping membership of women's organisations or party-political affiliation evident in the biographies of most women on the London Board who were generally liberal in politics. Finally, she was exceptional in seeking election as the mother of a young child. A survey of the power positions in the Board reveals that school-board women were concentrated at the lower levels and men at the higher levels. Men always held the top political posts, and only one woman became chair of a permanent standing committee. In addition, the sexual stereotyping of men's work and women's work in the wider society was reflected in the horizontal segregation of educational administration at local government level. Ten of the 12 female office-holders were limited to administering the feminine (managing domestic subjects and dealing with child welfare) and in 1902 Hilda Miall-Smith became chair of the sub-committee that organised the tea! Nonetheless, at a time when women had no direct say in central government, they *had* gained access to what Felicity Hunt terms organisational policy: 'a middle level of decision-making which intervenes between government policy and actual school practice'.[14] As women school-board members they took decisions on the aims and content of elementary education, as well as questions dealing with attendance, the provision of sites and buildings, staff and equipment. Kept outside the main arenas of power and authority, Mary broke into some traditionally male domains such as the committees dealing with sites and buildings, as well as the evening-schools committee, and sub-committees dealing with teaching staff and reformatory institutions. She had the confidence and skills to fight for her constituents even if, as a socialist woman, she did not always influence educational policy-making in the city. In part, her work was reported because she was not afraid to say controversial things. This was vital because it ensured that she got noticed even if the attendant publicity offered mixed rewards since the media coverage was often negative. Her debating profile reveals that she spoke more than the average male member and brought her socialism to bear on the policies she promoted.

In 1897, the Progressives were returned to power after a 12-year period of Moderate rule. The London Board was highly politicised and from the 1880s on a majority of the candidates elected were either Moderates (members of the Anglican clergy and/or the Conservative Party) or Progressives (including independent labour, Liberals, progressive clergymen and socialists). Once elected, Mary joined Stewart Headlam (first elected in 1888, chair of the evening-schools committee) and Lyulph Stanley (first elected in 1876, leader of the Progressive faction) in promoting an extended education for the working classes. She was scathing of class-based provision and consistently argued that education was the prerogative of all. This meant secondary education should not be restricted to fee-paying children from the middle classes and a small minority of working-class children caught by a scholarship ladder. Her vision was of a socially comprehensive educational system to encompass all needs and give working people access to all levels of education. For this programme to be meaningful, however, you had to combat child poverty. Socialists wanted to see collective provision for children's well-being, with a special emphasis on free meals (provided for all children who wanted them, not just those who were starving, as the Independent Labour Party and the Fabians argued) and medical inspection. So, in supporting statist approaches to the care of children, Mary proved an ideal representative of the remarkable ferment of progressive ideas, which was particularly manifest in Woolwich. Giving evidence to the sub-committee dealing with underfed children, she proposed a system of universal provision because charitable societies had failed to meet the need. Here she received support from Honnor Morten (first elected in 1897) who argued from the perspective of her medical training and experience of living in a women's settlement house. Honnor and Mary both campaigned to reduce the physical punishment of children with a third Progressive woman, Ruth Homan (first elected in 1891). In 1899 the three women unsuccessfully proposed the abolition of the cane in truant schools with Morten dubbing the Board 'birch-thirsty' and Bridges Adams going so far as to call it 'blood-thirsty'.[15]

Overall, the policies pursued by Progressive politicians on the London Board antagonised the Conservative governments of 1895 and 1900, but the push to extend the scope of elementary education in the higher-grade schools and evening classes was especially controversial. This development had powerful enemies among some contemporaries such as

Sir John Gorst (Conservative politician, Vice-President of the Board of Education) and Robert Morant (civil servant in the central educational administration) who took a hand in challenging its legal status. In 1899 London's activities were declared illegal by the Cockerton judgment which was subsequently upheld in the High Court and the Court of Appeal (December 1900).

Mary, meanwhile, took the initiative. She was able to instigate the support of the Royal Arsenal Co-operative Society and an initial conference was convened in March 1901 with Stewart Headlam and Lyulph Stanley as the main speakers. Later that month the co-operators petitioned Parliament to reverse the effects of the verdict and pledged £25 towards the cost of an appeal to the House of Lords. Again, at Mary's request, they sent the London Board a copy of the resolution, along with a message of support.[16] In May, the education committee sent delegates in two deputations to the Board of Education, and worked with the Woolwich Trades Council to organise a June protest meeting. The platform speakers were Mary Bridges Adams, Keir Hardie (leader of the Independent Labour Party) and Stewart Headlam who called on the government to legalise the work condemned by Cockerton.[17] Five months later Mary launched the National Labour Education League to offer a substitute to the educational ideology of the Conservative government and its organisational principles. The nearest approach to a labour education programme at this period, the League aimed to publicise trade union views and to challenge the political agenda. The third goal was to build up the educational activity of the labour movement. The fourth was to free state-maintained education from the control of sectarians and political 'wirepullers' (a popular epithet for the technique of feeding facts to anyone who could be persuaded to use them). The final objective was to work towards an education system (organised in age-defined stages) that would include all students, without exceptions. The programme had the support of the first trade unionists to enter Parliament (the Liberal-Labour men Richard Bell, Thomas Burt and Charles Fenwick), three on the Trades Union Congress (TUC) Parliamentary Committee (including Will Thorne), seven Liberal-Labour men on the London County Council, Alex Wilkie (Newcastle School Board), Ben Jones (secretary of the Co-operative Union Parliamentary Committee) and three on the Royal Arsenal Co-operative Society education committee.

By November, the number of affiliated trade unions had grown to 45 and amongst other things Mary was extensively involved in the organisation of demonstrations and campaigns, distributing pamphlets and participating in debates all over the country. In March 1902 Arthur

Balfour introduced legislative proposals to the House of Commons intended to transfer education to council committee administration, to build up a state-supported system of selective secondary schools, and provide further assistance for the religious schools. At the time, the League made a spirited, if unsuccessful, bid to fight the Bill and could only protest with equal impotence at the London Education Bill, 1903.[18]

Mary recognised there was everything to be gained from drawing in a cross-section of support and made a serious effort to appeal to politicised women in the National Union of Women Workers (which worked to implement wide-ranging reforms with its support for women's rights and social welfare provision) and the Women's National Liberal Federation. She was included in a League and later a School Board deputation who put their views to the Education Minister and managed to rally impressive support at a socialist demonstration timed to precede local elections in 1904. On this occasion she shared the platform with Keir Hardie, Henry Hyndman (the leader of the Social Democrats), Harry Quelch (Social Democrat, London Trades Council) and Will Thorne.[19] When the County Council took over, the new education committee was composed of 38 men and 5 co-opted women, but these did not include the only acknowledged representative of organised labour to serve on the Board. Due to the initiative of Fred Knee, moves were made by the London Trades Council to persuade Liberal-Labour councillors to join with them in supporting Mary's co-option but she, like other potential troublemakers, was excluded.[20]

Out of local government, the 1900s saw Mary concentrate her efforts on the need for socialist alternatives to the status quo. She became education spokesperson for the Social Democrats and her son maintained that she consolidated her position as the 'educational mentor' of trade unionism in these years.[21] In the winter of 1904–5 she became Lady Warwick's secretary and collaborator, running a London-based office and discussion centre for the new recruit to the SDF. For a time this flat was to be Mary's home and Will Thorne remembered that it was here Lady Warwick used to 'gather together the advanced thinkers of the Labour Movement'.[22] Mary's speaking talents meant that she was much in demand and like Harry Snell (of Woolwich Labour Party), 'had to undertake much night travelling, to sleep in many strange beds, to speak at noisy street corners, and in many stuffy halls'.[23] Of course, a better understanding of her efficacy requires at least some reference to broader educational and political narratives. As Richard Johnson has shown, it is possible to draw a distinction between 'substitutional' and 'statist' strategies to identify shifts in the nature of popular educational practices and dilemmas from the 1790s.[24] The first of these two tendencies represents at root an expression of independent community control and an implicit rejection of all forms of 'provided' education whether supplied by charity, church or state.

The remedy, to develop a series of educational networks, reached a climax in the 1830s and 1840s within the Owenite socialist movement and the Chartist movement. This education project was characterised by an important internal debate about the content of the educational process and it was characteristic of the 'spearhead knowledge' promulgated by early nineteenth-century radicalism that it connected both education and politics, stressing the educational needs of adults and children alike. On top of that, radical educator activists insisted on the need for workers and citizens to understand the relations of exploitation underpinning existing social, economic and political circumstances. Nonetheless, the 1850s saw the beginning of a broad and enduring popular concession to the need to adopt 'statist' strategies involving agitation for the extension and reform of state-maintained elementary education. This represented a shift in the attempt to carry on independent educational activities, although various examples of substitutional activity remained.

Here the real, lived dilemmas of working-class political activists are demonstrated by the public career of Mary Bridges Adams. On the one hand, her experience of elected office shows a commitment to 'statist' strategies associated with the growth of public education itself. On the other, there is a sense in which her later propaganda records a disillusion with the promise that state intervention carried; and she certainly saw the 1902 Act as a wrong turning. Most important was the diminution of popular involvement and curtailment of educational opportunity as the division between elementary and secondary education became more firmly defined. She travelled into revolutionary socialism in the 1880s when, as Stephen Yeo reminds us, the intensity of aspiration was charged with an almost millennial ethical fervour. Indeed Yeo accentuates the 'religious' elements in what he calls the mass conversion, 'making socialists' phase.[25] It was this political trend that lay behind Mary's adult educational initiatives: at first through the study groups and more informal reading circles established by socialist or labour political parties, then the evening classes of the London Board which were of considerable importance in Woolwich at the turn of the century.

Increasingly, Mary regarded anything standing in the way of independent working-class education with a very particular hostility. Speaking in 1900 about the newly founded Ruskin College (a college for working men, in Oxford) and urging the delegates of the London Trades Council to oppose it, she claimed 'the system of teaching and conditions of that institution was degrading to the name of "Ruskin" '.[26] The whole question of relationship to the labour movement was a real difficulty. Will Thorne was the only one to question the motives of the founders on the TUC Parliamentary Committee, but Social Democrats on the Trades Council shared his concern. Led by Fred Knee and James Macdonald, they were able to work up considerable support in London through delegate meetings. A quarrel developed between Macdonald (the Council's Secretary) and Walter Vrooman, one of Ruskin's three American founders, over false claims of a trade union mandate for a conference of 'English speaking peoples to form an Anglo-Saxon alliance'. Macdonald condemned the jingoism and social patriotism within Vrooman's proposals and urged delegates to boycott the conference, Knee proposed that the Trades Council withdraw its representation from the governing body. This they stopped short of doing but a sub-committee was set up to explain their concerns to British trade unions and the American Federation of Labour. At this point Bridges Adams brought her influence to bear. She received a 'hearty vote of thanks' and a resolution against the action of Ruskin Hall council was supported by the delegates, even though this caused friction in the Trades Council relationship with the TUC Parliamentary Committee.[27] The obstacle was the weakness of the socialist position on the latter, which was dominated by Liberal-Labour men. Bridges Adams, Knee and Macdonald were further isolated in sustaining the anti-imperialist and anti-war strand within the SDF during the Boer War.

Beyond a powerful undercurrent of suspicion and ambivalence at the liberal adult education philosophy offered by Ruskin, Mary instigated a mounting attack on the Workers' Educational Association (WEA), founded in 1903, by Albert Mansbridge. She suspected the WEA on class grounds, as education from above, and criticised its socially reformist ethos and outlook. Mansbridge wanted to open up communication across class lines and was condescending in the intellectual aspirations that he projected, developed and organised through the WEA:

> As an organisation for education it stands unique, because it has united for the purposes of their mutual development Labour and Scholarship in and through their respective associations of Trade Unions and Universities, and because of this unity, so secured, the power of the spirit of wisdom has been increased in the affairs of men, and the building of 'Jerusalem in England's green and pleasant land' has become at least a nearer prospect.[28]

These possibilities sustained the beliefs of Oxford liberals like the classical scholar Alfred Zimmern and William Temple, later Archbishop of Canterbury and first president of the WEA, influenced by the social philosophy of Plato. Jose Harris has noted four aspects of Plato's thought which were especially attractive to idealists: first, the 'emphasis on society as an organic spiritual community'; second, his 'vision of the ethical nature of citizenship'; third, the focus on justice rather than force as the basis of the state' and finally, 'his mysticism and anti-materialism'.[29] Representative of a new type of English intellectual with 'a more developed sense of the linkages between scholarship and politics and of the social responsibilities of privilege',[30] Mansbridge acknowledged the influence of Charles Gore, Richard Burdon Haldane and Robert Morant.[31] Their fundamental belief was that education would sustain and bind together the members of society, to allow them ultimately to recognise their common humanity and the need to co-operate for a common good.

Although independent of each other, Ruskin and the WEA had many supporters in common. These included David Shackleton (Liberal-Labour MP, secretary of the Weavers Union, on the TUC Parliamentary Committee) and C. W. Bowerman of the London Compositors (Liberal-Labour MP, on the TUC Parliamentary Committee) who both attended a joint meeting of University and WEA representatives in 1907. For those wary of the link, their report, *Oxford and Working-Class Education*, which suggested the new (male) working-class voter should be steered down the paths of moderation, heightened any uneasiness and dissatisfaction they felt.[32] Indeed, the special significance attached to the imperative need for wise education was just the sort of thing to fuel the ardour of a revolutionary socialist like Mary, who felt dissatisfied with the performance of the 29 Labour members in Parliament and saw the educational future of the working-class adult as being outside, or against, the state, *not* within it. Typically, the Welsh miner Noah Ablett caricatured the influence and status of 'Gentleman Bowerman' (a loyal supporter of Ruskin and the WEA) at the 1911 Trades Union Congress: 'Black broadcloth, three-quarter tail coat, semi-top-hat to match, with an air of refinement, silky voice, and deprecatory manner'.[33] The class-conciliatory sentiment Bowerman personified had to face the development of a radical critique not only of labour leadership but also of capitalism, among those in the van of the Ruskin College strike of 1909.

So, it was the profound differences between these two quite separate traditions within working-class education that lay behind the confrontation with the Ruskin authorities in 1908–9. The question of working class cultural and political autonomy was key and for dissenting students the choice seemed stark – either endorse the growing links with the University of Oxford or set up a separate institution. After some discussion the counter-proposals were opposed by the trade union governors, Richard Bell (MP for Derby, the Railway Servants secretary, supporter of the National Labour Education League) and David Shackleton, who thought it unfeasible because of the continued dependence on private donations.[34] Rebel students disagreed and in the autumn of 1908 they joined together in the Plebs League to appeal to the ranks in the unions. The academic 'virtues' of detachment and objectivity were not accepted as necessary and neutral, especially in the teaching of economics, and they opposed wider developments that were soon to make adult education dependent on public funds. To disseminate ideas, information and news they launched a monthly magazine, *Plebs*, and in August 1909 Mary Bridges Adams was among the 200 members who attended the first Annual Meeting of the Plebs League of past and present students and sympathisers. Buoyed with hope, the main resolution for the principle of independence in working-class education was moved by Noah Ablett, who went to Ruskin on a miner's scholarship in 1907 and played a big part in the League. Mary seconded the resolution in what the August *Plebs* describes as 'a fighting speech of great power and force, the University being treated to a terrific onslaught in her inimitable style'.[35] This suggests Ablett and the striking students valued her notoriety and eloquence, coupled with her political training in the labour movement. A Provisional Committee of 13, including Ablett and Bridges Adams, was elected to found the new residential college and there was concern to reach working-class women.[36] At the Trades Union Congress of that year Mary was the only woman speaker at a meeting in support of the Central Labour College, with Robert Smillie (Scottish miner's president) in the chair, but no mention of the matter appears in the press report in *Justice*. This refers only to her involvement in the Gasworker's celebration of Children's Sunday. Mary, with characteristic candour, wrote a letter to the editor in which she expressed 'regret that in your note on the new Central Labour College, you do not state that I am a member of the Provisional Committee'.[37]

The later career of Mary Bridges Adams demonstrates that she never abandoned her commitment to a tradition of working-class self-education. She retained a happy optimism that the labour college movement and the Plebs League and magazine were a means to an end – a model of adult education leading directly to political action. From this perspective the WEA was an attempt to contain the rising aspirations and expectations of working-class people in general and organised labour in particular. In her eyes the rival organisation was hopelessly compromised by the acceptance of state aid to finance its work as well as donations from anti-Labour movement sources such as the Duke of Westminster. As for the standpoint of impartiality, to Bridges Adams this was anathema given the refusal to support trade union education policy and the restoration of funds from educational endowments to their proper use (help to the poor).[38] Her tireless propaganda in this early phase earned her the enmity of her protagonists, since her championing of the labour college and Plebs League hindered their drive for support from branches of unions on a grass-roots basis. Albert Mansbridge must have been aware of this when he sent confidential correspondence to organisers of the tutorial classes:

> We beg to inform you that Mrs Bridges Adams, taking advantage of the strike at Ruskin College, is seeking engagements in the country, ostensibly to oppose the Report on Oxford and Working Class Education, but in reality to make bizarre mis-statements concerning the W.E.A. We shall be glad if you will inform us as to any statements she may make in your district, and if you will endeavour to arrange for an answer to be made to the same Organisation which she addresses.[39]

He deplored her politics and in 1910 wrote to Zimmern, 'the Bridges Adams opposition is more furious than ever – lies, misrepresentations, the devilments of the pit – are all brought to bear'.[40] The link with coalfield militants is striking, for the link was a direct one, but this vocabulary of demonology is missing from the public narrative. In his autobiography Mansbridge simply records how the WEA 'excited active opposition on the part of Mrs Bridges Adams, a well-known woman in Labour circles of the times, who, in fact regarded herself as the leader of trade union education policy'.[41] Rather later (1955) another protagonist, Mary Stocks, patronises the ardent advocate of independent working-class education in the conventional history:

> From its earliest days there had been a rumble of thunder on the left, and when the W.E.A. had appeared to make headway in trade-union circles, Mansbridge was able to record the existence of active opposition. It came, to begin with, from the activities of a certain Mrs Bridges Adams, who professed a particular concern for trade-union education. Mrs Adams had a profound distrust of universities. They were in her opinion citadels of class-privilege whose denizens were dedicated to its preservation. If they were

137

prepared to patronise the efforts of Mansbridge and his friends, it could only be because they hoped to divert him from uncontrolled activities which might otherwise subvert the privileged position of the rich, and to inoculate him with economic doctrines likely to render him tolerant, if not appreciative of the status quo.[42]

This all suggests that Mary maintained the fervour of earlier days, finding new forms of expression to champion the Marxist educational initiatives of the Plebs League and harry the alternate model. To her, the flaws within the rhetoric of a classless educational society were blatantly obvious since group-based material inequalities remain in order to serve the interests of capitalism and patriarchy. Unsurprisingly, Stocks does not consider her a labour 'notable' but George Sims (editor of *Plebs*) disagrees. In 1912 he remembered a conversation they had shortly after the strike was declared:

> I was impressed by the stress she laid upon rank-and-file control of any workers' educational institutions, also of her keenness in probing our educational ideals. I laughingly teased her about the latter and her reply has a lasting place in my memory: 'I want to keep pace with the most youthful of you in thought.' She has easily succeeded in doing so, while her wide experience and varied knowledge of educational matters, persons, and movements has been of inestimable service to us all.[43]

Moving on, Sims asked his readers to support Mary's plans for a working women's college. Her model was the School of Social Science maintained by the German Socialist Party and now she devoted her formidable energy to winning support for these proposals.

Her first article was published in the *Railway Review* accompanied by the use of a cartoon to promote a political view.[44] Funds were openly courted from the Engineers, the Gas Workers and the Miners, to meet 'the growing demand of working women for the education necessary to fit them to take their place beside their men comrades in the industrial, political and educational work of the Labour movement'.[45] At the 1912 Central Labour College conference Mary was able to report grounds for optimism. The response from working women and feminists had been encouraging, notably from the Lancashire mill woman Annie Kenney. Virtually the only working-class woman close to the decision-making leadership of the suffragettes, Kenny had joined the Oldham Cardroom Association in her teens. Her brother, Rowland, supported the Plebs League and later 'accused Mansbridge of co-opting workers into "the development of the Servile State"'.[46] Thanks to the anonymous donation from a 'friend of the cause of women and of Labour' it became possible to buy outright the long lease of a house close to the men's college in the Earls Court district of London shortly after and at the age of 57 Mary assumed the role of resident principal.[47] The direction of the college was made clear:

> The activities of Bebel House will be many, and all of a constructive, educational character, and while economics and industrial history will be taught from the Socialist standpoint, opportunities will be given to the students to learn something of the other point of view. Means will also be taken to give students opportunities of learning, under competent direction, something of other educational institutions.[48]

Her dream was short lived. Two resident students, Mary Howarth (Bury Weavers Association) and Alice Smith (Oldham Cardroom Association) attended classes at the men's college for the year 1913–14, but exactly what happened to the scheme is not known. A disagreement had arisen within the Labour College when Bridges Adams refused to loan £200 during the financial crisis in December 1912 and in response the governors set up a women's league with more limited fund-raising aims.[49] W. W. Craik (student, tutor and principal of the Central Labour College) says simply that Bebel House closed; but the wholehearted enthusiasm shown by Rebecca West, a league member, suggests relations remained cordial.[50] There is evidence that education functioned as a transformative force for the students. Mary Howarth became a full time trade union official; Alice Smith returned to Oldham and took over a Plebs League class on philosophic logic there, made contributions to trade union work and published articles in the *Cotton Factory Times* and in *Plebs*.[51] In February 1915 Smith contributed to the debate over women's place in labour politics, identifying the 'cause and cure' of gender differentiation: 'Cause: ignorance of administration and procedure owing to the view that woman's place was in the home, dispelled by practical experience of working women. Cure: knowledge and training via the Working Women's College.'[52]

As the First World War approached, Mary's support for a vision larger than the national one grew stronger. She rested her hopes for international labour on the next generation and consistently advocated the founding of international socialist students' union to press for change, besides calling on the trade unions to consider education questions, including child labour, from an international standpoint. In looking for a way forward she claimed for women a part in world affairs proposing a system of travelling scholarships to enable working women to study at first hand the social and industrial conditions in other countries. Both of these proposals had the backing of the Munich socialists (including her sister-in-law) as well as that of the Irish feminist and pacifist Francis Sheehy-Skeffington, murdered by the British authorities during the Easter rising.[53] In this way Mary projected her national plans for a militant and committed approach to workers' education on to the international arena.

When war broke out in 1914 Mary immediately took up an uncompromising anti-war position. She maintained contacts with the growing émigré groups in Britain and western Europe and as the war developed her internationalism placed her at odds with the leadership of the British Socialist Party (the direct descendant of the SDF). In these critical years she used the columns of the *Cotton Factory Times* to denounce the trial and imprisonment of John Maclean under the Defence of the Realm Act promulgated in 1915. Maclean travelled to the Rhondda Valley during the Cambrian Combine Committee strike in the summer of 1911 where he met Noah Ablett (possibly Mary also) and began to assume a more formal commitment to the systematic development and provision of Marxist education.[54] Afterwards he built up a considerable reputation as a teacher of Marxist economics, poured energy into the campaign to create a Scottish labour college and on the outbreak of hostilities actively engaged in anti-war propaganda. Willie Gallacher, a particularly close associate and fellow member of the anti-war section of the British Socialist Party, claimed 'Maclean had become a figure known to everyone' by 1915,[55] but this is an exaggeration. Only after the sentence of three years penal servitude did he receive a dramatic elevation of status as Britain's most important political prisoner excluding Sinn Feiners.[56] Mary was outraged at the travesty of justice meted out on 'one of the best men' she had known. She denounced the failure of Labour parliamentarians to come forward while castigating erstwhile colleagues like Henry Hyndman and Lady Warwick for their silence. In her opinion there were two distinct elements within the organised labour movement. Those whom she termed the 'servants of the Plutocracy' advocated a respectable path to social reform. Others who, like Maclean, were working to build the movement on strong independent class lines, opposed them.[57] As striking as the substance of her comments is that she made them with assurance and authority, never questioning her right to speak out despite the hostility expressed in conditions of wartime repression. Indeed on 30 June 1916 (shortly after her condemnation of Maclean's trial) she was detained in custody for 26 hours for distributing a leaflet entitled 'The Right of Asylum' in contravention of government regulations. Amid panic about German spies and moral outrage whipped up by establishment newspapers, Mary took up the challenge of the military authorities with alacrity. As she later reported: she was not charged, the Inspector told her, because she was 'not worth powder and shot'.[58]

By the end of the war Mary's health was failing but her story confounds any easy understanding of the left and educational politics in the early years of the twentieth century. She rejected the conventional wisdom of the day to practise labour movement entrism and to work for socialism, feminism and internationalism combined. An outstanding feature is the sheer energy and enthusiasm with which she struggled for the workers' education movement and the right of women to a say in the destiny of the world. The largest group of organised women was in the textile trade and this was why she considered Lancashire crucial and wrote extensively in the *Cotton Factory Times*. Through the biographical approach we see her perceptions, priorities and alliances come full circle – back to the economic and geographical context of the South Wales coalfield where she was born.[59] For Mary's world-view and critique of capitalist culture was not far removed from that of the Ruskin College-product, Noah Ablett. Crossing the borders of gender and generation they shared a cultural identification and political allegiance that exposed the extent and the power of the illusion of the transcendent ideal of upper-class culture. A belief that, despite its claims to the contrary, is tangled among the self-interest and prejudices of the needs of capitalism and those of patriarchy. However, as the years went by, there was a tendency for the 'mainstream' occupied by men to get their version of events accepted, while those positioned in a different way had difficulty gaining acceptance and were less favoured by history. Listening to the voices on the margins, in this case Mary Bridges Adams, enables us to foreground gender in an exploration of the left and educational politics in the early years of the twentieth century. Bridges Adams presented a remarkably consistent record of outspoken advocacy in a succinct and cogent writing style. As for her achievements, the alternate values that she put forward in her writings and actions, are themselves a legacy. In the words of a friend, the 'sweeper-up' of the *Yorkshire Factory Times:*

> [she] is always helping what some call 'forlorn causes', but which to my mind are the causes that make for a better future for the human race... I am with Mrs Bridges Adams heart and soul in her agitation for political freedom and justice.[60]

ENDNOTES

1. G. Sims, 'A Tribute', *Plebs*, June 1912, p. 132.
2. J. Bellamy and J. Saville (eds), *The Dictionary of Labour Biography*, 6 (London: Macmillan), p. 1.
3. C. Steedman, *Childhood, Culture and Class in Britain. Margaret McMillan 1860–1931* (London: Virago), p. 131.
4. J. Hannam and K. Hunt, 'Gendering the stories of socialism: an essay in historical criticism', in M. Walsh (ed.), *Working Out Gender. Perspectives from Labour History* (Aldershot: Aldgate), p. 103.
5. Ibid, p. 102.
6. S. Macintyre, *A Proletarian Science. Marxism in Britain, 1917–1933* (London: Lawrence and Wishart), pp. 1–2.
7. Ibid, p. 3.
8. See J. Martin, '"An Awful Woman"? The life and work of Mrs Bridges Adams, 1855–1939', *Women's History Review*, 8, 1, pp. 139–61.
9. *The Times*, 16 January 1939.
10. P. Graves, *Labour Women. Women in Working-Class Politics* (Cambridge: Cambridge University Press), pp. 57–9.
11. W.J. Brown, 'Open-air recovery schools', reprinted from *The Millgate*, in *Comradeship and Wheatsheaf*, December 1933, p. xvi.
12. P. Thompson, *Socialists, Liberals and Labour, the Struggle for London, 1885–1914* (London: Routledge and Kegan Paul).
13. Ibid, p. 254.
14. F. Hunt, *Gender and Policy in English Education 1902–1944* (London: Harvester Wheatsheaf), p. 11.
15. *Board Teacher*, February 1899. For more detail see J. Martin, *Women and the Politics of Schooling in Victorian and Edwardian England* (London: Leicester University Press); 'Working for the people? Mrs Bridges Adams and the London School Board, 1897–1904', *History of Education*, 29, 1, pp. 49–62.
16. *Comradeship and Wheatsheaf*, December 1901.
17. Ibid.
18. See J. Martin, 'London women and the 1902 Education Act' in J. Goodman and S. Harrop (eds), *Women, Educational Policy-Making and Administration in England: Authoritative Women Since 1800* (London: Routledge), pp. 87–91.
19. *Justice*, 27 February 1904.
20. London Trades Council, Minutes of delegate meeting, 10 March 1904.

21. W. P. McCann, Trade unionist, co-operative and socialist organisations in relation to popular education, 1870–1902 (Unpublished PhD thesis, University of Manchester), p.478.
22. W. Thorne, *My Life's Battles* (London: George Newnes), p. 199.
23. N. Bridges-Adams, 1998, personal communication. I want to express my thanks to Jenifer Bridges-Adams for her help and encouragement with this project. Lord Snell, *Men, Movements and Myself* (London: J. M. Dent), p. 149.
24. R. Johnson, *The State and the Politics of Education*, Unit 1, E353, Society, Education and the State (Milton Keynes: Open University Press), p. 28; R. Johnson, '"Really useful knowledge": radical education and working-class culture, 1790–1848' in R. Dale *et al.* (eds), *Politics, Patriarchy and Practice* (Lewes: Falmer Press), pp. 3–19.
25. S. Yeo, 'A new life: the religion of socialism in Britain, 1883–1896', *History Workshop*, 4, pp. 5–56.
26. London Trades Council, Minutes of delegate meeting, 12 July 1900.
27. Ibid, 26 July 1900. For the position of the TUC Parliamentary Committee see C. Griggs, *The Trades Union Congress and the Struggle for Education 1868–1925* (Lewes: Falmer Press), pp. 175–208.
28. A. Mansbridge, *An Adventure in Working-Class Education* (London: Longmans, Green and Co), p. xi.
29. J. Harris, 'Political thought and the welfare state 1870–1940: an intellectual framework for British social policy', *Past and Present*, 135, p. 128.
30. L. Goldman, 'Intellectuals and the English working class 1870–1945: the case of adult education', *History of Education*, 29, 4, p. 285.
31. A. Mansbridge, *The Trodden Road* (London: J. M. Dent), p. vii.
32. B. Simon, 'The struggle for hegemony, 1920–1926' in B. Simon (ed.), *The Search for Enlightenment: the Working Class and Adult Education in the Twentieth Century* (London: Lawrence and Wishart), pp. 18–19.
33. *Plebs*, November 1911, p. 236.
34. See I. W. Hamilton, 'Education for revolution. The Plebs League and Labour College Movement 1908-1921' (Unpublished MA thesis, University of Warwick); R. Fieldhouse, 'The 1908 Report: antidote to class struggle?' in G. Andrews, H. Kean and J. Thompson (eds), *Ruskin College, Contesting Knowledge, Dissenting Politics* (London: Lawrence and Wishart), pp. 35–57.
35. *Plebs*, August 1909, p. 174.

36. *Plebs*, October 1909, p. 185.
37. *Justice*, 21 August 1909.
38. *Railway Review*, 20 May 1910.
39. A. Mansbridge to 'Dear Sir', 20 April 1910.
40. A. Mansbridge to A. E. Zimmern, n.d. (May 1910) quoted in B. Jennings, *Knowledge is Power. A Short History of the WEA 1903–78* (University of Hull Department of Adult Education, Newland Papers Number One), p. 20.
41. A. Mansbridge, *The Trodden Road* (London: J. M. Dent), p. 63.
42. M. Stocks, *The WEA: The First Fifty Years* (London: George Allen and Unwin), p. 48.
43. *Plebs*, July 1912, pp. 131–2.
44. *Railway Review*, 16 August 1912, p. 9.
45. *Plebs*, August 1912, pp. 161–4.
46. R. Kenney, 'Education for the workers', *New Age*, 26 March 1914, pp. 652–3.
47. *Cotton Factory Times*, 23 April 1913.
48. Ibid.
49. Central Labour College, Board of Management Minutes, 21 June 1913.
50. W. W. Craik, *The Central Labour College* (London: Lawrence and Wishart), pp. 102–3; R. West 'The Working Women's College' *The Clarion*, 14 February 1913.
51. E. Frow and R. Frow, 'The spark of independent working-class education: Lancashire, 1909–1930', in B. Simon (ed.), *Search*, pp. 73–4.
52. *Cotton Factory Times*, 26 February 1915.
53. *Cotton Factory Times*, 5 March 1915, 19 May 1916.
54. B. J. Ripley and J. McHugh, *John Maclean* (Manchester: Manchester University Press), pp. 55–6.
55. W. Gallacher, *Revolt on the Clyde* (London: Lawrence and Wishart), p. 67.
56. Ripley and McHugh, *John Maclean*, pp. 70–1.
57. *Cotton Factory Times*, 21 April 1916, 28 April 1916, 12 May 1916.
58. *Cotton Factory Times*, 14 July 1916.
59. D. Egan, '"A cult of their own": syndicalism and *The Miners' Next Step*', in A. Campbell, N. Fishman, D. Howell (eds), *Miners, Unions and Politics, 1910–1947* (Aldershot: Scolar Press), pp. 13–33.
60. *Yorkshire Factory Times*, 6 January 1916.

REFERENCES

Bellamy, J. and Saville, J. (eds,) *The Dictionary of Labour Biography*, 6 (London: Macmillan, 1982).

Brown, W. J. 'Open-air recovery schools'. Reprinted from *The Millgate* in *Comradeship and Wheatsheaf*, December 1933.

Central Labour College Minutes 1909–1918 (Trades Union Congress library collections, University of North London).

Cotton Factory Times, 1913, 1915, 1916.

Craik, W. W. *The Central Labour College*, (London: Lawrence and Wishart, 1964).

Egan, D. '"A cult of their own": syndicalism, and *The Miners' Next Step'*, in A. Campbell, N. Fishman, and D. Howell (eds), *Miners, Unions and Politics, 1910–1947* (Aldershot: Scolar Press, 1996), pp. 13–33.

Fieldhouse, R. 'The 1908 Report: antidote to class struggle?' in G. Andrews, H. Kean and J. Thompson (eds), *Ruskin College, Contesting Knowledge, Dissenting Politics* (London: Lawrence and Wishart, 1999), pp. 35–57.

Frow, E. and Frow, R. 'The spark of independent working-class education: Lancashire, 1909–1930' in B. Simon (ed.), *The Search for Enlightenment: the Working Class and Adult Education in the Twentieth Century* (London: Lawrence and Wishart, 1990), pp. 71–104.

Gallacher, W. *Revolt on the Clyde* (London: Lawrence and Wishart, 1980).

Goldman, L. 'Intellectuals and the English working class 1870–1945: the case of adult education', *History of Education*, 29, 4 (2000), pp. 281–300.

Graves, P. *Labour Women. Women in British Working-Class Politics, 1918–1939* (Cambridge: Cambridge University Press, 1996).

Griggs, C. *The Trades Union Congress and the Struggle for Education 1968–1925* (Lewes: Falmer Press, 1983).

Hamilton, I. W. 'Education for revolution. The Plebs League and Labour College Movement 1908–1921' (Unpublished MA thesis, University of Warwick).

Hannam, J., and Hunt, K. 'Gendering the stories of socialism: an essay in historical criticism' in M. Walsh (ed.) *Working Out Gender. Perspectives from Labour History* (Aldershot: Ashgate, 2000), pp. 102–18.

Harris, J. 'Political thought and the welfare state 1870–1940: an intellectual framework for British educational thought and practice', *Past and Present*, 135 (1992), pp. 116–41.

Hunt, F. *Gender and Policy in English Education 1902–1944* (London: Harvester Wheatsheaf, 1991).

Jennings, B. *Knowledge is Power. A Short History of the W.E.A. 1903–78* (University of Hull Department of Adult Education: Newland Papers Number One, 1979).

Johnson, R. *The State and the Politics of Education*, Unit 1 E353, Society, Education and the State (Milton Keynes: Open University Press, 1981).

— '"Really useful knowledge": radical education and working-class culture, 1790–1848' in R. Dale, G. Esland, Ferguson and N. MacDonald (eds), *Politics, Patriarchy and Practice* (Lewes: Falmer Press, 1981), pp. 3–19.

Kennedy, R. 'Education for the workers', *New Age*, 26 March 1914.

Justice, 1904, 1909.

London Trades Council, Minute Books 1899–1928 (Trades Union Congress library collections, University of North London).

Macintyre, S. *A Proletarian Science. Marxism in Britain, 1917–1933* (London: Lawrence and Wishart, 1980).

Mansbridge, A. *An Adventure in Working-Class Education* (London: Longmans, Green and Co., 1920).

— *The Trodden Road* (London: J. M. Dent, 1940).

— to 'Dear Sir', 20 April 1910.

Martin, J. 'An "Awful Woman?" The life and work of Mrs Bridges Adams, 1855–1939', *Women's History Review*, 8, 1 (1999), pp. 139–61.

— *Women and the Politics of Schooling in Victorian and Edwardian England* (London: Leicester University Press, 1999).

— 'Working for the people? Mrs Bridges Adams and the London School Board, 1897–1904', *History of Education*, 29, 1 (2000), pp. 49–62.

— '"Women not wanted" the fight to secure political representation on Local Education Authorities, 1870–1907', in J. Goodman and S. Harrop (eds), *Women, Educational Policy-Making and Administration in England: Authoritative Women Since 1800* (London: Routledge, 2000), pp. 78–96.

McCann, W. P. 'Trade unionist, co-operative and socialist organisations in relation to popular education, 1870–1902', (Unpublished PhD thesis, University of Manchester, 1960).

Plebs, 1909, 1911, 1912.

Railway Review, 1910, 1912.

Ripley, B. J. and McHugh, J. *John Maclean* (Manchester: Manchester University Press, 1989).

Simon, B. 'The struggle for hegemony, 1920–1926' in B. Simon (ed.), *The*

Search for Enlightenment: the Working Class and Adult Education in the Twentieth Century (London: Lawrence and Wishart, 1990), pp. 15–70.

Sims, G. 'A Tribute', *Plebs*, June 1912.

Snell, Lord *Men, Movements and Myself* (London: J. M. Dent, 1936).

Steedman, C. *Childhood, Culture and Class in Britain. Margaret McMillan 1860–1931* (London: Virago, 1990).

Stocks, M. O. *The WEA: the First Fifty Years* (London: George Allen and Unwin, 1955).

Thompson, P. *Socialists, Liberals and Labour, the Struggle for London, 1885–1914* (London: Routledge and Kegan Paul, 1967).

Thorne, W. *My Life's Battles* (London: George Newnes, n.d.)

Weiler, K. 'Reflections on writing a history of women teachers' in K. Weiler and S. Middleton (eds), *Telling Women's Lives* (Milton Keynes: Open University Press, 1999).

West, R. 'The Working Women's College', *The Clarion*, 14 February 1913.

Yeo, S. 'A new life: the religion of socialism in Britain, 1833–1896', *History Workshop*, 4 (1997) pp. 5–56.

Yorkshire Factory Times, 1916.

7

Gendering the 'Wisconsin Idea': The Women's Self-Government Association and University Life, c. 1898–1948

CHRISTINE D. MYERS

The gap in time between women's first inclusion in American higher education in 1837, and the Nineteenth Amendment allowing women to vote in 1920 is highlighted by many notable attempts on the part of women to carve a place for themselves in public, as well as political, life. While the most noteworthy of these, such as the Seneca Falls Convention of 1848, have been written about at length by historians, there are a great number of untold stories from women working on a local or institutional level.[1] This chapter will tell one such story by focusing on the work of the Women's Self-Government Association at the University of Wisconsin in Madison. Founded in 1898 by the Dean of Women (Annie C. Emery), this group provided a way for female students to play an active role in the governance of their university.[2] Women had first been admitted to Wisconsin through its Normal College for teacher training in 1860. Complete academic equality was reached in 1875 when women were finally graduated in the same ceremony as men.[3] By looking at a single organisation it becomes possible to ascertain the way women students governed themselves and interacted with their male counterparts as they made their way into larger society.

Prior to the establishment of the Women's Self-Government Association, women had little or no voice in campus affairs at Wisconsin, indicating that the emergence of this group had great significance for the women involved in it. The Women's Self-Government Association also had an amount of wider, national importance due to its involvement in the turn-of-the-century school of progressive thought known as the 'Wisconsin Idea'.

In exploring the Women's Self-Government Association, I will first examine various theories of citizenship, as they were explored by the women students of the University of Wisconsin from 1898 to 1948.[4] Second, I will discuss the concept known as the Wisconsin Idea that emerged at the University of Wisconsin around the same time as the association. The women in question were primarily middle- to upper-class, white students, which, while limiting in some respects, does provide unique insight into the Wisconsin concept of citizenship. The remainder of the chapter will focus on the activities and arguments of the association itself, considering their role prior to the Nineteenth Amendment, and then examining whether there were any shifts in the group's identity through the Second World War. The chapter will also look at the Women's Self-Government Association's Semi-Centennial celebrations in 1948, by which time women's place in the university had solidified. Finally, I will address the question, did women's suffrage bring any great change to gender roles in American universities?

THEORIES OF CITIZENSHIP

Debates over the nature and definition of citizenship, particularly as it pertains to women, are numerous. As postmodern theorists deconstruct the term, both in the political world and in academia, new arguments arise about the validity of the use of the concept generally and in specific historical context. As Ruth Lister discusses at length in her 1997 book, *Citizenship: Feminist Perspectives*, the term 'citizenship' can be contested at every level. For women this questioning is further complicated by a false assumption that citizenship is a gender-neutral term, when clearly men and women in all countries have experienced different types of citizenship at various points in history. Accepting for the moment that citizenship is a valuable word to use in reference to women (and I think it is), how best can it be defined to include them fully and 'not simply append' them?[5] Lister provides one possible answer to this when she notes that 'the social and political dimensions of citizenship are interlinked'.[6] In this way the traditionally female, social side of the community is blended with the traditionally male, political one. Thus the concept of citizenship must be gendered for *both* male *and* female participants.

This conclusion leads directly to the next point to be raised in this chapter – citizenship is an active process. In the first half of the twentieth century, the period covered by this chapter, acceptance of the *status quo* in the United States, as in many other parts of the world, meant acceptance of one's status as a full or partial citizen. Although the key area of consideration in the chapter is women's citizenship, this argument can also

149

be applied on ethnic, racial or religious grounds. Prior to 1920, it might be argued that women in America were not citizens at all as they did not yet have the key ingredient to being an American citizen – the constitutional right to vote. Linda K. Kerber reminds us, however, that though women did not have access to 'the most explicit gesture' of citizenship, voting, they were still, in point of fact, American citizens.[7] As she notes:

> Women have been citizens of the United States as long as the republic has existed. Passports were issued to them. They could be naturalized; they could claim the protection of the courts. They were subject to the laws and were obliged to pay taxes. But from the beginning American women's relationship to the state has been different in substantial and important respects from that of men.[8]

While women's lack of voting rights led to a lesser sense of citizenship in a basic, practical sense, white American women were entitled to many of the other rights of citizenship. In return for these rights, white American women had early on been given a role within the community through the theory of 'Republican Motherhood'; and while this ideology did not have the same immediate power as filling out a ballot paper, the emotional value to women who 'might play a deferential political role through the raising of a patriotic child' should not be underestimated.[9] The decision of women, whether conscious or unconscious, to accept this societal role solidified their place as 'second-class citizens'. When large numbers of women finally began agitating for 'full' citizenship in the nineteenth century, they did so because playing a 'deferential role' was no longer acceptable.

A final point raised by Lister, which is of particular importance in a study of the Wisconsin Idea, is that citizenship is both a process and an outcome.[10] This process, when engaged individually or as a group, provides women with much of the active citizenship they seek. It is difficult to imagine that Susan B. Anthony did not consider herself a 'citizen' of the United States during her work at the Seneca Falls Convention, despite never having a chance to vote herself.[11] In other words, the active pursuit of citizenship often leads to a fuller *sense* of citizenship than that experienced by someone born to the privilege. Men could easily become complacent about their rights in political life, if they did not choose to engage in political debates. The women working for their own franchise, however, were at the centre of the political process, albeit in an unofficial capacity. American women at various points since colonial times had an understanding of these differences in 'citizenship', while many men may not have. Increasingly, near the end of the nineteenth century, however, male politicians also began to re-examine the nature of American politics with an idea of becoming more community-based, and less detached from society.

The turn of the twentieth century brought with it many changes in American university life. In general terms, most of these changes came in the area of extracurricular student activities, which saw a dramatic increase. Sports replaced military drill as a source of physical training for men, and women were finally granted access to sports facilities on most campuses. The other key area of growth was in student social and 'interest' groups. These ranged from departmentally related clubs to fraternities and sororities. All these new organisations highlight another shift in the university experience, as faculty and administrators sought to exercise control over their students outside the classroom. Along with providing a traditional education, universities in the twentieth century became increasingly responsible for producing well-rounded citizens of the nation, who would go on to lead their communities both politically and by moral example. This was a paramount concern at state-funded institutions like Wisconsin, whose primary obligation was to the public itself. Additionally, administrators knew that if men and women were to work together in all areas of society, the co-education provided in universities (as opposed to the experience in a single-sex institution) was good practice for later life. Glen H. Elder's study of 'marriage mobility' in America supports this conclusion, revealing that women in university in the 1920s and 1930s were more apt to marry 'well' due to their higher levels of 'educational attainment'.[12]

In 1900, two years after the establishment of the Women's Self-Government Association, Robert LaFollette was elected Governor of Wisconsin. With a reputation as a practical, no-nonsense politician, LaFollette began to guide the state government towards a series of progressive reforms. These reforms, and the ideals behind them, came to be known as the Wisconsin Idea in national political circles.[13] At the University of Wisconsin, these political initiatives were translated into a civic component of higher education, also referred to as the Wisconsin Idea. In academic terms, this philosophy argues that the borders of the campus are not fixed, and that the work of the institution should embrace the people of the city and state as well.[14] Under the leadership of president Charles R. Van Hise, the university strove to use its resources to help solve the problems of the state. Many noteworthy examples of this exist, though most came in the field of agriculture (for example: in 1924 Professor Harry

Steenbock found a way to enrich food with vitamin D and wipe out infantile rickets). There were, of course, other non-agriculture related contributions, such as the oldest educational radio station in the world, that began transmission in 1917.[15] While it is possible to argue that such research and development was present at all major American universities, the evolution into a defined school of thought that took place at Wisconsin was unique. This was due in large part to the university's connection to Robert LaFollette, who was himself a graduate of the institution. This relationship made the commitment to such a philosophy more impassioned than in other areas of the country, as the faculty and students felt obligated in many ways to make LaFollette's vision of civic consciousness a reality. Thus, close proximity of LaFollette's governorship and the formation of the Wisconsin Idea to the establishment of the Women's Self-Government Association indicates a parallel timeline between men and women at the institution historically, though the divergence of student activities along gender lines remains striking.

The focus of this chapter is on the particular efforts of women to participate in the Wisconsin Idea as it pertained to their lives on campus. Because much of the university's contribution to society associated with the Wisconsin Idea came through scientific fields, in which women still did not take a major part, there was a heightened need for women to assert their own ability to contribute to the Wisconsin Idea through different modes of expression. Issues to consider include the requirements placed on the women by the university to learn how to act as responsible members of society, as well as the need of students to establish their own standards of conduct. There is sufficient evidence from a study of the University of Wisconsin to suggest that most women at co-educational universities were basically conservative and that in the first half of the twentieth century they wanted an amount of 'equality' of educational choice and opportunity with their male counterparts, which they could then pursue in a traditional fashion. A modern definition of feminism cannot be applied to their actions. Certainly radical feminists in the modern sense did exist, but they were few and far between.

AIMS AND STRUCTURE OF THE WOMEN'S SELF-GOVERNMENT ASSOCIATION

In 1898 'The Women of the University... organized themselves into a Self-Government Association.' Emerging in the wake of many other women's clubs in the state of Wisconsin, most of which dealt with issues of educational reform or the enforcement of child labour laws, the student association tried to mimic their adult counterparts' community-minded focus.[16] As noted in the introduction to their constitution: 'This organization exists to further in every way the spirit of women in the University, to increase their sense of responsibility toward each other and to be a medium by which the social standard of the University can be made and kept high.'[17]

Already several components of the *women's* 'Wisconsin Idea' are apparent. The first section of the above statement emphasises two of the main themes – spirit and responsibility. The students felt there was a spirit of community amongst them and they wished to nurture that through mutual responsibility. The second section of the statement illustrates how the women planned to accomplish this increased responsibility – by keeping the social standards of the university high. This control over student social lives began when the association passed their first two bylaws: '1. All girls of the University are required to leave all parties at 12 o'clock. 2. No girls in the University shall attend mid-week parties without the sanction of University authorities.'[18] So, while the idea of a 'self-government association' might lead one to think that female students were experimenting with political issues in the light of the suffrage movement, they were, in fact, working to solidify their proper place in a male-dominated society.

A Commemorative Booklet on the Women's Self-Government Association, entitled *A Half Century of Progress, A Future of Promise*, notes that the 'initial purpose of the [group] was to improve social relations between men and women on the campus and to handle matters of student life which were outside faculty jurisdiction'.[19] While the administration of the university 'smiled' on the new organisation, the male students were not impressed. As one woman student recalled, 'the boys gave their usual disdainful snort at the idea of politics and such for mere women'.[20] The concerns of male students were reinforced by Victorian arguments that giving women the right to self-governance would lead them into taking on the man's role in society.[21] The support of the Board of Regents, however, was based on the idea that self-imposed supervision would be beneficial for the women themselves. This support was tempered, however, as the administration recognised a need to regulate women's presence in student government. At Wisconsin this led to the emergence of a complex structure of student government, with primarily separate male and female halves. The Women's Self-Government Association was established as a parallel to the men's organisation – the Wisconsin Student Organization. The nomenclature of these two 'parallel' groups was meaningful as the men's organisation was designed to govern all university students and the 'gendered' women's association was only to have authority over women. This distinction was intentional, and it provided instant restraints on the possible areas of work for the women. Ruth Lister's separation between the social and political can be seen in action here, as the women's association moved directly into regulation of the social side of campus life.

When the Women's Self-Government Association began, there was only one residence hall for women on campus, with more than 75 per cent of the female students forced to find other accommodations in the city.[22] Madison had long been considered to be 'an expensive and unsafe locality for an educational institution'.[23] In the earliest days of the school's history the all-male student body was encouraged to board with faculty members and their families. The admittance of women in the 1860s duly magnified this concern, as they were felt by the administrators to be more naive in the ways of the world. The Women's Self-Government Association made the issue of housing one of their primary concerns, as they helped the university officials to convince parents of prospective students that their daughters would be well looked after while at Wisconsin. To this end they produced a pamphlet entitled 'How Wisconsin Protects and Helps Your Daughter'.[24] This pamphlet outlined standards by which *all* women students were to live, regardless of whether or not they lived on campus. The first two bylaws of the Women's Self-Government Association began the regulations, followed by restrictions on where women could rent rooms (there could be no men residing on the same premises), along with 'other regulations' which prohibited women from taking part in risky activities such as driving, motoring, canoeing, skating or swimming after 10 o'clock at night (this version of the pamphlet is clearly from the 1920s). The regulations established by the Women's Self-Government Association were enforced through peer pressure, with little or no interference from the university itself. Should there be violations, cases would be dealt with in the first instance by the Executive Committee of the group, with problem cases being forwarded to the Dean of Women. The male university establishment thus had virtually no responsibility in controlling the women students, which was a situation they greatly appreciated. In 1907 President Van Hise commented that he did 'not know of any member of the university faculty who is opposed to the present system of coeducation', of which, by this time, the Women's Self-Government Association was an integral part.[25]

'How Wisconsin Protects and Helps Your Daughter' also provided valuable information to parents about the Women's Self-Government Association's other activities. A list of social and charitable functions included raising money for the Madam Curie Radium Fund, selling

Christmas Seals, and holding an annual Vocational Conference for women. This demonstrated the social consciousness espoused by the Wisconsin Idea as the students took it upon themselves to help the citizens of the state. As noted in a history of the group, their first remit was as 'a disciplinary agency' though they also 'undertook projects to unite the women of the university' that included 'Parties, teas, receptions and picnics'.[26] As with any Women's Self-Government Association activity, the social functions brought with them a series of conduct regulations. Possibly the most notable were the 'dancing rules' which 'specified that there must be a distance of three or four inches between men and women while dancing, and that men must place their hands along the left side of their partner's waist, and not at the back.'[27] Here, then, we find that the organisation was regulating *both* male and female behaviour in social situations. This reinforces the traditional female societal role as the protector of the community's virtues, as women were responsible for not letting men get out of line. J. F. A. Pyre commented in his history of the University of Wisconsin that 'The difficulties of student discipline were rather mitigated than increased by coeducation... Upon the usual peccadilloes of the college student, the presence of women acted as a restraint.'[28] Through this expectation of control over male–female relationships at university, administrators felt they were giving the women valuable practice for life after graduation when they would become the moral guardians of both home and family.

UNIVERSITY WOMEN AND THE FIRST WORLD WAR

The Wisconsin Idea was at its most popular during the First World War. The encouragement of active citizenship in aid of the war effort was apparent from the outset of the conflict. The academic community found numerous outlets for aiding state residents, both in training prospective soldiers, and in the dissemination of information on the progress of the war. The female students began their own War Work Council, to facilitate their service in the community. This group was a new division of the Women's Self-Government Association, and it aimed to encourage awareness of war issues among the women students of the university. This Council was divided into four committees; the County Council of Defense, the Committee on Regulation of Student Activities, the Committee on Emergency War Work and the Committee on the Red Cross. Through the campaigns of these groups, two key themes of women's war work emerge. First, an aggressive, quasi-militaristic thrust of patriotism, used to rally support for the war effort; and second, a gentler focus on women's traditional female duties of education and health care, particularly first aid and nursing.

The first of these themes is best represented by a Patriotic Rally held by the War Work Council in October 1917. In the flyer advertising the rally the group chose to invoke an heroic historical figure – Joan of Arc – to lead them into battle:[29]

Joan of Arc, Joan of Arc,
Do your eyes from the skies see the foe?
Don't you see the drooping Fleur-de-lis?
Can't you hear the tears of Normandy?
Joan of Arc, Joan of Arc,
Let your spirit guide us through:
Come, lead your France to victory,
Joan of Arc, they are calling you.

This event was held in the women's gymnasium on campus, targeting students and faculty in particular. Those in attendance heard talks on work in war camps, conservation and liberty loans, discussed the usual business of the War Work Council, and sang patriotic songs. The choice of Joan of Arc in this instance had numerous implications. Along with being one of history's strongest female characters, she was also a woman who defied her prescribed gender role to participate in war. The significance of this extreme, active form of citizenship would not have been lost on those who saw the flyers for this event, nor on those who attended the rally.

This aggressive approach was also used in mixed-gender rallies. In particular, the school song, 'On Wisconsin' (a military-type march in its standard version), was rewritten to call vigorously for both the 'sons and daughters' of the state to join in the fight.[30] There was also a second, more inflammatory rewriting, entitled 'On America'. In this version, the favoured American topics of freedom and democracy were supported by the line 'Kaiser follow Czar'. The clear implication that an overthrow of the monarchy in Germany is called for echoes many traditional themes from American ideology. This version of the song also appealed to both male and female in the crowd, by including 'Red Cross and Khaki' as two types of 'troops' who will 'win the fight'. The elevating of the Red Cross to the level of 'troops' should not be underestimated either. As Margaret Randolph Higonnet, *et al.* note, 'During total war, the discourse of militarism, with its stress on 'masculine' qualities, permeates the whole fabric of society, touching on both men and women.'[31] This discourse then blurs existing gender roles, allowing women to take on new, more masculine identities for a short period of time. Higonnet, *et al.*, are quick to point out society's need to constantly reinforce the feminine side of women's war-time identity, however, as 'images of femininity, nurturance, and the family can be invoked to restore the balance' in an otherwise chaotic world.[32] Thus, at Wisconsin, the female-centred Red Cross was permitted, for a time, to consider themselves 'troops' engaged on the battlefield in a more masculine role.

The Women's War Work Council also played a key part in the dissemination of information to the campus community. In November 1917 the University of Wisconsin's War Course considered the public awareness issues of 'Sanity in War Time', 'Food and Fuel Laws', and 'Public Information in War Time'. The fourth topic – Florence Nightingale – again emphasised the common propagandist tool in war-time America, providing examples of heroic women as role models for the women of a new generation.[33] In addition, the Women's Self-Government Association worked closely with the Committee of Woman's Service for War, established by wives of University of Wisconsin faculty and staff. This group acted as a role model for the female students, whose activities often paralleled those of their older counterparts.

Women felt it was their duty to raise awareness of service that was 'not strictly speaking military in nature', such as nursing and food conservation. In this way, women did not threaten the social status quo of gender relations.[34] The Committee of Woman's Service for War, with the aid of the Women's Self-Government Association, worked in the wider community by organizing lectures on health, home gardening, conservation of food and clothing, Red Cross service and other topics of interest to the women of Wisconsin.[35] When possible, they acted as interpreters for those new residents of the state from parts of Europe who did not yet speak English. These efforts, though indicating an amount of social consciousness in helping marginalised members of the community, were primarily undertaken as a way to Americanise immigrants at the earliest possible opportunity. In taking this role upon themselves, women revived old notions of 'Republican Motherhood', with women continuing to educate future citizens of America. Other typically 'womanly' activities undertaken by the group included providing a list of books and bulletins available at the Wisconsin Library on canning, preserving and dehydrating fruits and vegetables, used again as a way to educate state residents.[36] Another objective was the completion of a survey of the alumnae and students of the university 'to aid the State Council of Defense, the Council of National Defense, and other authorised bodies'

157

in finding experienced women to help in the war effort.[37]

This mobilisation of the female 'troops' in the state also reinforced the active citizenship encouraged by the Wisconsin Idea. In reaching out to the people of the state of Wisconsin, the members of the Women's Self-Government Association were doing their civic duty at a time of national crisis. As former President Theodore Roosevelt noted on a visit to Wisconsin, the First World War provided an opportunity to 'see the degree to which the university had put the right spirit into the soul of its students.'[38] The spirit of the students brought considerable pride to the University of Wisconsin during this conflict, especially that of the women students. War has traditionally been a male domain, although the American Civil War did provide a beginning for female front-line participation through Clara Barton's nursing work (she later established the American Red Cross in 1881).[39] The First World War continued this re-gendering of the experience of war through an increase in nursing by women. Home Nursing courses were developed by the university extension division at Wisconsin as a programme to educate local Red Cross chapters 'in their efforts to relieve the families of soldiers'.[40] They were later used by women nurses who had enlisted in the National Red Cross for service overseas. The campus-based support activities also included bulletins, addresses and correspondence to the general public in order to 'stimulate an interest in nursing as a patriotic duty'. As a result of these efforts there was an increasingly dominant presence of women's functions on the campus, despite the male-centred focus of the war itself. Although these courses were sponsored by the university as a whole, they were clearly intended for a female audience, indicating a heightened importance attributed to women during the war. Meetings or rallies hosted by the Women's Self-Government Association were not limited to women. Male students and faculty also attended to lend their support to both the women and the greater cause.

The lack of a peace movement on campus is particularly significant. Since peace movements are traditionally classified as feminine, one would expect to find a group like the Women's Self-Government Association involved in pacifist activities as well as, or instead of, war-work.[41] While this may have been the case on other American university campuses, the history of the University of Wisconsin is, in this instance, unique. The State of Wisconsin, as a largely German-settled area, felt a strong need to assert its American-ness during the war, as did several other communities in the country. Wisconsin's support for the war, because of its German heritage, was brought into question on a number of occasions. Much of this was due to the vocal opposition to the military conflict in a congressional filibuster by then Wisconsin Senator Robert LaFollette. This opened the door for disparaging remarks about his home state and the university.[42] So, although there were undoubtedly students or faculty who opposed the war, they remained silent rather than giving opportunities for further attacks against the institution or state.

As a result of this xenophobia, the Wisconsin Idea became a more than usually valuable tool enabling the university and the state as a whole to exhibit their American-ness. Since the state's philosophy reflected many of the key ingredients of America's national identity – mutual assistance, pride in your work, contributions to the greater good – the university and state officials used this rhetoric to maintain Wisconsin's dignity in the country, despite its 'suspicious' German heritage. Following the war the Committee of Woman's Service for War and the Women's Self-Government Association helped organise a Western Wisconsin Re-Adjustment Convention. This meeting included talks on Americanisation, governing readjusted nations, and included gender specific luncheons to discuss general issues of readjustment.[43]

UNIVERSITY WOMEN AND THE SUFFRAGE MOVEMENT

Following the First World War, the next major national concern faced by the women of the Women's Self-Government Association was that of suffrage. The question of women's suffrage had been actively on the political agenda in Wisconsin since the 1870s when reconstruction politics after the Civil War raised the question of why uneducated black men could legally vote and educated women could not. In 1886, a School Suffrage Bill was passed in Wisconsin giving women the right to vote in elections for school board members.[44] The concept of school suffrage developed out of the progressive movement in the state, which increasingly led to the view that education, health, safety and welfare were central political issues. As these newly politicised topics had long been part of women's traditional sphere in society, the extension of a political voice to women seemed natural to many male politicians at the time. Once women were able to exercise their new voting rights successfully, the men of the state were more amenable to the idea of women attaining full suffrage on a state, and later national, level.[45] The entrance to suffrage through the side door by Wisconsin women then led to a lesser degree of struggle as the national campaign came to a head early in the twentieth century, because the transition had been undertaken more gradually, giving the men a chance to adjust.[46]

On campus, Wisconsin students established their own Equal Suffrage League under the auspices of the Women's Self-Government Association by 1912, before the passing of the constitutional amendment in 1920. This organisation then became a chapter of the national Collegiate League of Women Voters in 1921.[47] Lynn D. Gordon notes that student activism in suffrage campaigns was limited and that 'college students, the nation's female intellectual and preprofessional élite [had] only a minimal impact on the suffrage movement before the formation of the College Equal Suffrage League.'[48] Barbara Miller Solomon supports this conclusion when she discusses the very limited 'pockets of opposition and advocacy' on university campuses, which while active, did not indicate an overwhelming concern for the issues of suffrage.[49] The education received by women in co-educational universities was designed to reinforce traditional gender roles, and although university women did appreciate the desire by more militant activists for increased rights for women, they were largely satisfied with the position they were able to maintain in society. As part of the intellectual élite, co-educated university women typically had good lives and marriages following graduation, resulting in fewer concerns among students that equality with men was essential to lead a fulfilling life.[50]

Wisconsin's Equal Suffrage League was at its most visible in 1915 and 1916 when membership numbered just over 500.[51] The group worked to raise funds to send to national suffrage groups by hosting a Suffrage Tea Dance and the collection of donations. Once again, a thoroughly traditional female activity was chosen by the students, even if the cause was one that questioned traditional female roles. The organisation also did a house-to-house canvass to assess the amount of support for women's suffrage in Madison. The group found that 95 per cent of the university faculty were in favour of the new amendment, along with a significant portion of the male students who were targeted by the group in surveys.[52] In 1917, petitions were sent to Wisconsin's senators and congressmen in favour of the federal suffrage amendment, backed up by the statistical evidence gathered by the students in the League. This active exercise of citizenship is a good example of female students using their place in society to further the democratic process, while remaining non-threatening to the men around them. Canvassing, such as that done in 1916, brought awareness to the community of a particular political issue. In this way the women were acting out their traditional female role as teachers, while at the same time forwarding their wider political status.

Regardless of this distance between university women and feminist advocates, the entrance of women to universities, and their successful participation in courses and extracurricular debate, did help to show the general population that women were capable of participating in public government. In Wisconsin, for example, the most vocal support for women's suffrage can be seen in Madison, Whitewater, Kenosha, Ripon, Milton and other towns that were the homes of co-educational institutions of higher education. This acceptance of women in non-traditional, more public roles translated into support for their enfranchisement. The increase of women's education then, was crucial to the passage of women's suffrage legislation. Along with this, university women were looked to as leaders of a newly politicised role for women in society.

Once women were granted the vote, the Collegiate League of Women Voters worked to raise political awareness among women in the community. Current political questions were discussed, both informally and when speakers were brought to campus. Informal topics of discussion included conditions in juvenile courts, women in politics, and women's positions in other countries. During the academic year 1923–24, four speakers were brought in to address the League. One of the speakers, Belle Case LaFollette, was herself a graduate of the university, and was the wife of Robert LaFollette. Mrs LaFollette had been the first female graduate of the University's Law School, and was known in governmental circles for her 'political sagacity' and as a source of inspiration for her husband's career.[53] The very model of an educated wife, she was a gracious hostess as well as a leader in women's reform movements. On this particular occasion she spoke on 'Women and War'. On a practical level, Mrs LaFollette's talk would have recalled the efforts of American and European women during the First World War. On a more symbolic level, however, her presence as the speaker would have shown the young university women in the audience what they were expected to do upon graduation. First and foremost, they were to be supportive wives to their husband's careers, but additionally they could use their education to further educate other women. Mrs LaFollette's speech was scheduled with a lecture on 'Legislative Procedure', aimed at giving those present a detailed understanding of the process of government and their role within it.[54] As new voting members of the population, it was especially important to train women in the basics of government, which they may have had little or no grasp of previously.

Another main project of the League was following selected bills through the Wisconsin Legislature. Members of the League attended committee hearings and utilised lobbyists on their behalf. The bills selected were generally of interest to women in the community, often appealing to traditional female roles in the family. In 1923–24 the League selected two bills to support – the National Guard Bill and the Military Drill Bill. The second of these bills made military drill on campus for men optional, while the National Guard Bill established this organisation in the state as a whole.[55] The women, as well as most of the male members of the university, felt that the military drill, which had been compulsory for male students since the American Civil War, was beneficial to the moral fabric of the institution.[56] The elimination of this requirement (which was primarily replaced with the increasing importance of organised sporting events) brought questions about the lack of discipline amongst male students, something that concerned the women of the League greatly.

Aside from working with legislation which dealt with the women's cultural ideals, they also had many practical goals to work towards. The League tried to encourage female student participation in government by urging them to vote in elections throughout the year. Often this work was done in conjunction with the Dane County League of Women Voters, as the combined resources of the two groups could draw larger audiences to meetings and speeches. Each Monday the Collegiate League posted a list of all their activities for the following week on their bulletin board in Lathrop Hall, the women's recreational centre, to help organise student political events.[57] A final undertaking of the Collegiate League was to bring the work of their group to the notice of national organisations. To this end, their president travelled to the national convention in Buffalo where she 'made three speeches on the conditions of coeds in Wisconsin and their attitudes toward voting'.[58] Clearly the students were making every attempt to put themselves forward as female representatives of the Wisconsin Idea as they widened their sphere of influence beyond the boundaries of the university.

THE WOMEN'S SELF-GOVERNMENT ASSOCIATION IN THE 1930S AND 1940S

Following the First World War and Suffrage Campaigns, the Women's Self-Government Association was left to deal with primarily on-campus issues. They reverted to their pre-war disciplinary role, setting up regulations for interaction between students. As seen in gender relations throughout the nation, the men and women of the university had to re-establish a balance of power, after the war which acknowledged women's new place within the public sphere.[59] The Women's Self-Government Association once again took a leading role, though they now made bolder statements on the life of university students. The most notable of these was a booklet entitled *Wiscetiquette*.[60] First published in the mid-1920s, and then annually through the 1930s and 1940s, this booklet amounted to a form of prescriptive literature and was subtitled: 'A Brief Guide to Wisconsin Student Social Customs and Activities'.[61] Designed to educate both male and female students, the 27-page booklet was divided into four main categories, 'On the Hill', 'Dating', 'Fraternities and Sororities', and 'Traditions'. *Wiscetiquette*'s writers realised that as women their sphere of influence was that of social life, and they left academic concerns (other than the occasional reference) to the faculty of the university. The booklet offered many practical suggestions, including urging students not to cut class and to do homework assignments as they came in, rather than letting them pile up. This later point, it was suggested, would allow for far more free time to socialise as the term progressed. This emphasis on the social aspects of campus life again illustrates the desire of the women of the association to assert their influence over the traditionally female areas.

Another topic in *Wiscetiquette* is entitled with the question 'A Coed Yet?' The term "coed" was historically used in American universities to refer specifically to women students. The term was initially intended to be derogatory, or more precisely as a slight on an institution, often made by Eastern men's colleges. For example, a New York book entitled *Wisconsin Wickedness* used the 'coed' of Wisconsin to illustrate the distraction women would inevitably cause if they were allowed to enter universities, by preventing men from concentrating on their studies.[62] At Wisconsin, however, the members of the Women's Self-Government Association who wrote *Wiscetiquette* did not challenge the stereotypes of this term on any level. Instead they embraced the term, and added their own chapter to the cliché of the coed:

> It isn't enough to have just paid your fees at Wisconsin to become a true, dyed-in-the-wool coed. No siree. But get yourself firmly kissed under the clock in Music Hall at 12 o'clock (midnight, that is) and you will graduate cum laude into the Wisconsin tribe of true coeds. Or if Music Hall is occupied, the ski slide will do. Or the Carillon. Or Observatory Hill. Or even Picnic Point. You'll find your coed degree the easiest one to obtain at the University.[63]

This extracurricular inauguration into university life had implications for both male and female students, though it particularly refers to female 'coeds'. Additionally, the distinction made between a degree and a 'coed degree' is of particular significance. While a man was expected to go to university to learn something academic, a woman was expected to go to learn how to get a man (or, more specifically, a husband), and this gender division in higher education, as seen through the Women's Self-Government Association, appeared in the 1930s and 1940s to be widening, rather than becoming more equal after the inclusion of women in the American political process. Indeed, women's position in control of social interactions at the University of Wisconsin is illustrative of a key phenomenon in a gendered society. The inter-war period and depression era provoked an increased desire amongst the students actively to seek social entertainment.[64] As extracurricular life expanded, so too female influence on campus continued to expand, and as this non-academic interaction increased in importance, handbooks like *Wiscetiquette* were also of considerable value to students wishing not to find themselves on the peripheries of campus social life. In other words, the more complex the gender roles became, the more guidance was seen to be needed to navigate relationships.

This increased complexity of gender roles brought on by the Nineteenth Amendment in 1920 reached its height at Wisconsin by the end of the 1930s. When campus issues again took a backseat to national conflict after the United States entered the Second World War, another reassessment of the gender dynamic in society took place. Women's activities during the Second World War focused on support for the Red Cross and Nurses' Training programmes, along with organising food drives for widows, orphans, and refugees. Similar to their campaigns during the First World War, the women of the university engaged in outreach programmes for the community and state as a whole, helping the public to better understand and cope with the military conflict.[65] Unlike the First World War, however, the conclusion of the Second World War did not lead to continued social upheaval along gender lines. Instead the United States worked to provide women with solid domestic roles, intended to re-establish a complementary relationship between the sexes. The Women's Self-Government Association is once again a good example of this campaign as they continued their fundraising efforts for the community through the 1940s.

Local press coverage of the Women's Self-Government Association's 50th anniversary in 1948 focused on their annual fashion show, with only a small article reporting on their 35th annual 'conference on co-ed careers'.[66] This disparity may have simply been the result of the newspaper editor's preference, but the association's own anniversary publication, *A Half Century of Progress, A Future of Promise*, maintains a remarkably consistent emphasis in the group's self-history on the evolution of women's fashions. Indeed, their only direct reference to the state's progressive movement came in their summary of events in 1915 when 'Wisconsin's progressive women were among the first to adopt the full skirt, whose hemline was raised six inches from the ground.'[67] The fashions on display in 1948 were conservative and matronly, while still being the height of femininity at the time. Though far from academic, and having little to do with social reform, the annual Women's Self-Government Association fashion show did contribute in a small way to the perpetuation of a female version of the Wisconsin Idea. The association used the event to collect donations for local charities, and did so in a way that called attention to both their social consciousness *and* womanhood. This final blend of active citizenship and gender signifies a return, in many ways, to the starting point of the Women's Self-Government Association in 1898. The Association was established 'to further in every way the spirit of women in the University, to increase their sense of responsibility toward each other and to be a medium by which the social standard of the University can be made and kept high.'[68] It can be argued that the women of the Association never strayed from this basic tenant during their first 50 years. Rather, what changed was the 'social standard' itself. In the final analysis, however, what remained was a group of educated women who valued their place in a socially conscious community, both as individuals, and as role models for future generations.

CONCLUSION

The Wisconsin Idea itself ties directly into twenty-first-century arguments about active citizenship. In fact, some scholars might argue that it provided the twentieth-century definitions in the American democratic context. The ideas of social progressivism and the belief that citizenship has both 'social and political dimensions' are closely related.[69] Social issues that affect people's daily lives, education being the primary example, can no longer be separated from political debates. Therefore, in trying to establish a greater civic consciousness for government on the whole, the Wisconsin Idea also opened a door for women to engage in the political life of the state. Furthermore, as the women students at the University of Wisconsin witnessed this political transformation in their state, and learned about it in their classrooms, their desire to become a part of it was undeniable. How did they choose to become a part of it? And did the male Wisconsin progressives truly appreciate the implications of opening philosophical floodgates? Edward Doan defines Robert LaFollette as someone who wanted to 'translate ideals into reality' and his personal life with his politically minded wife, Belle Case LaFollette, certainly seems to bear this out on gender lines.[70] However, as evidenced by the experience of the Women's Self-Government Association on campus, not all men were open to the idea of politically active women and this at times directly and indirectly led the female students to pursue less threatening modes of expression of their women's Wisconsin Idea.

To an extent, the history of the Women's Self-Government Association does not do justice to the new opportunities open to women in the first half of the twentieth century. It does, however, embody the key elements of the Wisconsin Idea that were taught to all students of the university. The idea that the borders of the campus are not fixed, and that the work of the institution should embrace the people of the city and state as well, found resonance within the female student population. The expansion of the traditionally female social sphere on campus allowed women to assert their own identities, separate from those of men. Despite surges of social awareness during national crises, the Women's Self-Government Association was really at its strongest during peace time. This strength came primarily from the fact that the female students did not feel obligated to remain in the shadows of male, wartime achievements. Additionally, during peacetime the university campus had much more time to devote to extracurricular activities, the woman's sphere on campus. As Barbara Miller Solomon points out, this increased 'involvement in myriad activities kept students constantly aware of their responsibilities as liberally educated women, giving them additional purpose as a result of their position in society'.[71] As educated women, they were in a position to transmit their knowledge and understanding to the wider community in which they lived, and, strengthened by the philosophy of the Wisconsin Idea, they strove to do just that.

ENDNOTES

1. K. Barry, *Susan B. Anthony: A Biography of a Singular Feminist* (New York: New York University Press), pp. 61, 367.
2. M. Curti and V. Carstensen, *The University of Wisconsin: A History, 1848–1925* (2 vols) (Madison, WI: University of Wisconsin Press), p. 78.
3. University of Wisconsin Archives (UWA), *Minutes of the Board of Regents*, pp. 114, 147.
4. UWA, Women's Self-Government Association General Subject Files, S.G.A. Semi-Centennial, 1898–1948.
5. R. Lister, *Citizenship: Feminist Perspectives* (New York: New York University Press), p. 3.

6. Ibid., p. 10.
7. L. K. Kerber, *No Constitutional Right to be Ladies: Women and the Obligations of Citizenship* (New York: Hill and Wang), p. 305.
8. Ibid., pp. xx–xxi.
9. L. Kerber, 'The Republican Mother: women and the Enlightenment – an American perspective,' *American Quarterly* 28, p. 205 and *No Constitutional Right to be Ladies*, p. 305.
10. Lister, *Citizenship*, p. 5.
11. Barry, *Susan B. Anthony*, pp. 61, 367.
12. G. H. Elder, 'Appearance and education in marriage mobility', *American Sociological Review* 34, pp. 531–32. For more see C. D. Myers, '"Give her the apple and see what comes of it": University Coeducation in Britain and America, c. 1860–1940' (PhD Thesis, University of Strathclyde), chapter 9: 'Outcomes'.
13. E. N. Doan, *The LaFollettes and the Wisconsin Idea* (New York: Rinehart), pp. 11–13.
14. Wisconsin Idea Sesquicentennial Exhibit: Commemorating the University of Wisconsin-Madison's 150th Anniversary (Madison, WI).
15. Ibid., See also J. W. Gooch, *Transplanting Extension: A New Look at the 'Wisconsin Idea'* (Madison, WI: Office of Outreach Development and Extension Liaison), pp. 6–7.
16. D. P. Thelen, *The New Citizenship: Origins of Progressivism in Wisconsin, 1885–1900* (Columbia, MO: University of Missouri Press), chapter 5.
17. UWA 1901 Constitution of the Women's Self-Government Association, General Subject Files, S.G.A. Semi-Centennial, 1898–1948.
18. Ibid.
19. UWA, WSGA Commemorative Booklet, *A Half Century of Progress, A Future of Promise* (Madison, WI), p. 5.
20. UWA, H. Voight, 'While We Grew Up' (sketch written February 1948 for the 50th Anniversary WSGA banquet). In archives with cover letter from University Chancellor Donna Shalala, dated 5 February 1992.
21. H. L. Horowitz, *Alma Mater: Design and Experience in the Women's Colleges from their Nineteenth-Century Beginnings to the 1930s* (Amherst, MA: University of Massachusetts Press), p. 58.
22. UWA, *A Half Century of Progress, A Future of Promise*, p. 5.
23. D. Mollenhoff, *Madison: A History of the Formative Years* (Dubuque, IA: Kendall/Hunt Publishing Company), p. 193 and Horowitz, *Alma Mater*, p. 32.

24. UWA, Women's Self-Government Association General Subject Files, S.G.A. Semi-Centennial, 1898–1948.
25. UWA, *A Half Century of Progress, A Future of Promise*, p. 12.
26. Ibid., p. 8.
27. Ibid., p. 14.
28. J. F. A. Pyre, *Wisconsin* (New York: Oxford University Press), p. 227.
29. UWA, Patriotic Rally of S.G.A. Called by The Women Students' War Work Council, 18 October 1917. It is unclear if these lines, entitled 'Joan of Arc, They are Calling You' are simply a poem, or if they were song lyrics.
30. UWA, Songs for the Wisconsin Student Army.
31. M. R. Higonnet, J. Jenson, S. Michel, and M. Collins Weitz (eds), *Behind the Lines: Gender and the Two World Wars* (New Haven and London: Yale University Press), p. 4.
32. Ibid., p. 1.
33. UWA, November War Course, 1917.
34. Higonnet, *et al.*, *Behind the Lines*, pp. 3, 8.
35. UWA, Letter from the Committee on Woman's Service for War, 5 May 1917 and Report of the Sub-Committee on Woman's Service, n.d.
36. UWA, *Preservation of Fruits and Vegetables*, compiled by Ada E. Hunt.
37. UWA, Letter from the Committee on Woman's Service for War, 5 May 1917 and Report of the Sub-Committee on Woman's Service, n.d.
38. UWA, 'What Roosevelt Says About Wisconsin,' Address given 28 May 1918.
39. N. O. Berry, *War and the Red Cross: the Unspoken Mission* (New York: St Martin's Press), p. 9.
40. UWA, Record of Patriotic Addresses Delivered in the State by University of Wisconsin Faculty Members, 1 December 1917 to 14 April 1918.
41. Higonnet, *et al.*, *Behind the Lines*, pp. 43, 286.
42. M. M. Vance, *Charles Richard Van Hise: Scientist Progressive* (Madison, WI: University of Wisconsin Press), pp. 178–9.
43. UWA, Western Wisconsin Re-Adjustment Convention, La Crosse, Wisconsin, 27–28 March 1919.
44. Thelen, *The New Citizenship*, p. 20.
45. T. J. Mertz, '"A Peculiar Public Matter": school politics, policy and Wisconsin women, 1885–1921', paper presented at the History of Education Society Annual Conference, Chicago, October 1998.

46. Thelen, *The New Citizenship*, chapter 5.
47. UWA, 'Bulletin of the Self-Government Association of the University of Wisconsin, 1912', p. 18. See also UWA, Report of the Collegiate League of Women Voters, Women's Self-Government Association General Subject Files.
48. L. D. Gordon, *Gender and Higher Education in the Progressive Era* (New Haven and London: Yale University Press), p. 194. The College Equal Suffrage League began in 1900 at Radcliffe, and became a national force in 1906. See also B. Miller Solomon, *In the Company of Educated Women* (New Haven and London: Yale University Press), pp. 111–14.
49. Solomon, *In the Company of Educated Women*, pp. 111–12. The author is only referring to the United States in her statement, but she includes the influence of 'English' suffragettes in the American movement after 1870. See also Horowitz, *Alma Mater*, p. 193.
50. C. D. Myers, ' "Give her the apple and see what comes of it" ': chapter 9: 'Outcomes'.
51. UWA, Women's Self Government Association, General Subject Files, 1889–1957.
52. Ibid.
53. Doan, *The LaFollettes*, pp. 18–19.
54. UWA, Report of the Collegiate League of Women Voters with a History of the Suffrage Organization, 1923–24.
55. Curti and Carstensen, *The University of Wisconsin*, p. 221.
56. For more see M. Pearlman, 'To make the university safe for morality: higher education, football and military training from the 1890s through the 1920s', *The Canadian Review of American Studies* 12 1 (Spring), pp. 37–56.
57. UWA, *A Half Century of Progress*, p. 9.
58. UWA, Report of the Collegiate League of Women Voters with a history of the Suffrage Organization, 1923–24.
59. Higonnet, *et al.*, *Behind the Lines*, pp. 1–5.
60. UWA, *A Half Century of Progress, A Future of Promise*, p. 18.
61. UWA, Women's Self-Government Association, *Wiscetiquette: A Brief Guide to Wisconsin Student Social Customs and Activities* (Madison, WI).
62. UWA, *Wisconsin Wickedness* (New York).
63. UWA, *Wiscetiquette*, p. 25.
64. UWA, *A Half Century of Progress, A Future of Promise*, p. 21.
65. Ibid., pp. 23–4.
66. *The Wisconsin State Journal*, 22 February 1948.

67. UWA, *A Half Century of Progress, A Future of Promise*, p. 14.
68. UWA 1901 Constitution of the Women's Self-Government Association, General Subject Files, S.G.A. Semi-Centennial, 1898–1948.
69. Lister, *Citizenship: Feminist Perspectives*, p. 10.
70. Doan, *The LaFollettes*, p. 13.
71. Gordon, *Gender and Higher Education in the Progressive Era*, pp. 95, 107.

REFERENCES

Barry, K. *Susan B. Anthony: A Biography of a Singular Feminist* (New York: New York University Press, 1988).
Berry, N. O. *War and the Red Cross: The Unspoken Mission* (New York: St Martin's Press, 1997).
Curti, M. and Carstensen, V. *The University of Wisconsin: A History, 1848–1925* (2 vols). (Madison, WI: University of Wisconsin Press, 1949).
Doan, E. N. *The LaFollettes and the Wisconsin Idea* (New York: Rinehart, 1947).
Elder, G. H. 'Appearance and education in marriage mobility', *American Sociological Review* 34 (1969), pp. 519–33.
Gooch, J. W. *Transplanting Extension: A New Look at the 'Wisconsin Idea'* (Madison, WI: Office of Outreach Development and Extension Liaison, 1995).
Gordon, L. D. *Gender and Higher Education in the Progressive Era* (New Haven and London: Yale University Press, 1990).
Higonnet, M. R., Jenson, J., Michel, S. and Collins Weitz, M. (eds), *Behind the Lines: Gender and the Two World Wars* (New Haven and London: Yale University Press, 1987).
Horowitz, H. L. *Alma Mater: Design and Experience in the Women's Colleges from their Nineteenth-Century Beginnings to the 1930s* (Amherst, MA: University of Massachusetts Press, 1993).
Kerber, L. K. 'The Republican Mother: women and the Enlightenment: an American perspective', *American Quarterly*, 28 (1976), pp. 187–205.
— *No constitutional right to be ladies: women and the obligations of citizenship* (New York: Hill and Wang, 1998).
Lister, R. *Citizenship: Feminist Perspectives* (New York: New York University Press, 1997).
Mertz, T. J. '"A Peculiar Public Matter": school politics, policy and

Wisconsin women, 1885–1921,' paper presented at the History of Education Society Annual Conference, Chicago, October 1998.

Mollenhoff, D. *Madison: A History of the Formative Years* (Dubuque, IA: Kendall/Hunt Publishing Company, 1982).

Myers, C. D. '"Give her the apple and see what comes of it": University Coeducation in Britain and America, c.1860–1940' (PhD Thesis, University of Strathclyde, 1999).

Pearlman, M. 'To Make the University Safe for Morality: Higher Education, Football and Military Training from the 1890s through the 1920s', *The Canadian Review of American Studies* 12, 1, Spring (1981), pp. 37–56.

Pyre, J. F. A. *Wisconsin* (New York: Oxford University Press, 1920).

Miller Solomon, B. *In the Company of Educated Women* (New Haven and London: Yale University Press, 1985).

Thelen, D. P. *The New Citizenship: Origins of Progressivism in Wisconsin, 1885–1900* (Columbia, MO: University of Missouri Press, 1972).

Vance, M. M. *Charles Richard Van Hise: Scientist Progressive* (Madison, WI: University of Wisconsin Press, 1960).

University of Wisconsin Archives (UWA)

'Bulletin of the Self-Government Association of the University of Wisconsin, 1912' (Series No. 20/2/3/1—2 Box No. 7).

Document 90: Resolution Submitted by the War Committee in Regard to the McElroy Matter, 24 April 1918 (Series No. 19/12/1–7, Box No. 1).

'How Wisconsin Protects and Helps Your Daughter' (Series No. 20/2/3/1–2 Box No. 7).

Hunt, Ada E. *Preservation of Fruits and Vegetables* (Series No. 5/114, Box No. 1).

Letter from the Committee on Woman's Service for War, 5 May 1917 (Series No. I-4/13, Box No. 1).

Minutes of the Board of Regents (Series No. 1/1/1, Vol. No. 3, 1866 through 1876).

November War Course, 1917 (Series No. I-4/13, Box No. 7, Folder 2–1917).

Patriotic Rally of S.G.A. Called by The Women Students' War Work Council, 18 October 1917 (Series No. I-4/13, Box No. 1).

Record of Patriotic Addresses Delivered in the State by University of Wisconsin Faculty Members, 1 December 1917 to 14 April 1918 (Series No. 5/114, Box No. 1).

Report of the Collegiate League of Women Voters, Women's Self-

Government Association General Subject Files (Series No. 20/2/3/1–2, Box No. 7, Folder on Associated Women Students Files, 1921–1923).

Report of the Sub-Committee on Woman's Service, n.d. (Series No. 5/114, Box No. 1).

Songs for the Wisconsin Student Army (Series No. 19/12/1–7, Box No. 1).

Voight, Helga. 'While We Grew Up' (sketch written February 1948 for the 50th Anniversary WSGA banquet). In archives with cover letter from University Chancellor Donna Shalala, dated 5 February 1992. (Series No. 20/2/3/1–2, Box No. 7, Folder on W.S.G.A. Semi Centennial).

Western Wisconsin Re-Adjustment Convention, La Crosse, Wisconsin, 27-28 March 1919 (Series No. I–4/13, Box No. 7, Folder 4–1919).

'What Roosevelt Says About Wisconsin,' extract from Address given 28 May 1918 (Series No. 19/12/1–7, Box. No. 1).

Wisconsin Idea Sesquicentennial Exhibit: Commemorating the University of Wisconsin-Madison's 150th Anniversary (Madison, WI: 1998).

The Wisconsin State Journal (22 February 1948).

Wisconsin Wickedness (New York: 1900) located in Memorabilia, 1895–1900 (Series No. I–4/13 Box No. 3 Folder 6).

Women's Self-Government Association General Subject Files, S.G.A. Semi-Centennial, 1898–1948 (Series No. 20/2/3/1–2, Box No. 7).

Women's Self Government Association, General Subject Files, 1889–1957 (Series No. 20/2/3/1–2 Box No. 1).

Women's Self-Government Association, *Wiscetiquette: A Brief Guide to Wisconsin Student Social Customs and Activities* (Madison, WI: 1947) (Series No. 20/2/3/1–2 Box No. 7).

WSGA Commemorative Booklet, *A Half Century of Progress, A Future of Promise* (Madison, WI: 1947) (Series No. 20/2/3/1–2, Box No. 7).

SECTION 3

GENDER, COLONIALISM AND THE EXPERIENCE OF EDUCATION

8

'Their Market Value must be Greater for the Experience they had Gained': Secondary School Headmistresses and Empire, 1897–1914

JOYCE GOODMAN

In November 1914 Annie Watt Whitelaw, Headmistress of Wycombe Abbey School, chaired a meeting in London of the Overseas Committee of the Association of Head Mistresses (AHM). She was one of five headmistresses assembled that day who had worked abroad. Also present to meet with members of the committee was Miss Irving, head of Lauriston Girls School, Melbourne.[1] The gathering of women illustrated the geographical mobility that had begun to characterise the careers of a growing number of highly educated women teachers by the late nineteenth and early twentieth centuries.

The career of Annie Whitelaw exemplified this mobility. Born in Scotland, Whitelaw moved with her family to Auckland, Aotearoa/New Zealand when she was three-and-a-half. She attended a primary public school, Auckland Girls' High School and then Auckland Grammar School before studying for the mathematical tripos in England at Girton College, Cambridge, between 1894 and 1897. After Girton, she taught under Frances Dove at Wycombe Abbey, travelling in 1905 with Dove to collect her MA from Trinity College, Dublin. When her old school, Auckland Girls' Grammar, formally separated from the boys' school, she was invited to become its first Head, a post she filled from 1906 until 1910. On Francis Dove's retirement, Whitelaw became Head of Wycombe Abbey, where she remained until 1925. After Wycombe Abbey she was a Lecturer and Director of Women's Education at Selly Oak, a training college in Birmingham, England, which prepared many missionaries for service overseas. She also served as a member of the British Colonial Office Committee on Native Education, travelling in 1926 throughout South and Central Africa with Dr J. H. Oldham on his official tour of inspection of schools and colleges. From 1932–37 she lived in London as Warden of the

Talbot Settlement in Camberwell, before retiring to Aotearoa/New Zealand, where in 1941 she became a member of a commission inquiring into the Church of England's provision for Maori Education and a committee member of Auckland YWCA.[2]

Alison Mackinnon, Kay Morris Matthews, Marjorie Theobald and Wendy Robinson have all demonstrated that willingness to emigrate was characteristic of highly motivated women career teachers.[3] Marjorie Theobald cites many examples of Girton and Newnham educated women taking up posts in the new girls' secondary schools in Australia.[4] Wendy Robinson shows that some ambitious, highly motivated woman teachers working in pupil-teacher centres were also taking up posts overseas by the start of the twentieth century.[5] These women formed part of what Marjorie Theobald terms 'a diaspora of highly educated and independent British women on the move across international boundaries at a time when migration for unaccompanied women was considered ill-advised or downright dangerous'.[6]

These re-locations were often supported by extensive networking. Many of the women had studied at the Cambridge women's colleges, where the Principals encouraged students to take posts as teachers overseas. As Theobald demonstrates for Australia, this drew overseas schools into the network of Cambridge women, 'sustained through their alumni and professional associations and through personal correspondence with their heads of college'.[7] Cheltenham College also provided a network of past pupils and staff who became overseas headmistresses: Miss Knox of Havergal College, Toronto; Miss Warburton of the British Syrian Institute at Beyrut (*sic*) and of Cairo; Miss Blanche Lefroy of Edgehill, Nova Scotia; Miss Hamilton-Meade, Principal of the Saniel Training College Cairo and Miss Pulling of Auckland Diocesan School Aotearoa/New Zealand.[8] Some GPDSC (Girls' Public Day School Company) schools developed overseas networks. Former staff of Nottingham High School included Miss Aitken, of the High School, Pretoria; Miss Headland, of Mussoorie Girls School; and Miss Cromarti and Miss Owen, who both went as head teachers to Grahamstown, South Africa.[9] Some women travelled with, or appointed to their staffs, other English women with whom they were colleagues or close friends. Mary Pulling travelled to Auckland with Beatrice Anna Ward. Both had been pupils at Cheltenham Ladies College and had taught together under Agnes Body at Lincoln High School.[10] Others, including Annie Whitelaw, took sisters with them to teach, or to help with the more domestic arrangements of the school.

Like Annie Whitelaw, some returned to the metropolis to posts of considerable prestige. Miss Strong worked more or less alternately at Cheltenham Ladies College, sometimes at the High School in Grahamstown, South Africa, and sometimes at the school of the Community of St Michael and All Angels at Bloemfontein. In 1891 she was appointed headmistress of the Francis Holland School for Girls in Baker Street, London, England, before going in 1905 to Simla as head of Auckland House, the Diocesan School.[11] The Scottish born Isabel Dickson, a contemporary of Annie Whitelaw at Girton, was Acting Principal of Sydney Women's College from 1901 to early 1902. From 1902–3 she reorganised the work of Sydney's prestigious Ascham School, before returning to London as Acting Principal of Bedford College. She became one of the first three women appointed Inspector of Schools under the Board of Education, first woman Inspector of Training Colleges in England and the first woman to hold a post of assistant secretary to the Board of Education.[12]

The career trajectories of women like Whitelaw, Strong and Dickson suggest that colonial experience held the potential to enhance female careers in the metropolis. In announcing Annie Whitelaw's appointment to Wycombe Abbey, Dr Burge, Headmaster of Winchester College and chair of the Abbey's Council, noted that alongside her 'fine intellectual abilities and strength of character, courage...charming personality and her knowledge of the "ideals and manner of life" of Wycombe Abbey', her time as Head in Auckland meant that she also brought to the post 'the experience of organisation and responsibility of a particularly searching kind' which, he concluded, had 'brought out most conspicuously her splendid capabilities'.[13] In 1913, as chair of the Overseas Committee of the AHM, Annie Whitelaw reiterated the view that overseas experience was beneficial and could enhance professional careers. She wished, she said to:[14]

> emphasise the advantage...to the Mother Country of having someone with not perhaps a wider but a different outlook who had something in her training that England could not give. Mistresses were deterred from going abroad by the fear of getting out of touch with the educational world at home and being at a disadvantage on their return. But their market value must be greater for the experience they had gained.[15]

Descriptions of teachers who returned to England with different outlooks acquired through their overseas experience drew on an Edwardian trope of travel 'concerned with self-realization in the spaces of the Other'.[16] According to Inderpal Grewal, this was a particularly

European understanding of 'travel' as 'freedom', which erased or conflated mobilities that were not part of Eurocentric imperialist formations and 'became an ontological discourse ... by which knowledge of a Self, society and nation was, within European and North American culture, to be understood and obtained'.[17] These descriptions of returning women (head)teachers also reflected contemporary views of an Englishness that could remain supposedly 'inviolate' in conditions abroad, which were depicted as the antithesis of 'home' – an 'overcoming' thought to require extra effort on the part of women.[18]

This chapter explores some of the links between diaspora, empire, gender, professional identities and professionalisation, which are demonstrated by such geographically mobile teaching careers. It examines the strategies adopted to facilitate the overseas movement of women teachers and heads by the AHM. The chapter is informed by Linda Eisenmann's argument that institution-building was used by women for a variety of purposes: to provide education (in both formal and informal settings), to create leadership opportunities, to challenge the mainstream, to attack problems within their 'sphere', to connect similar people, to accredit their efforts, to provide jobs, to advance professionalism, to negotiate with the state, and to organise nationally and internationally.[19] The chapter begins by outlining the developing interest of the AHM in empire and traces the shifting views of the headmistresses towards metropole and colony as well as their constructions of Englishness. It considers how headmistresses' professional identities and their strategies of professionalisation related to nation, citizenship and empire. It concludes by briefly reflecting on new approaches to analysis within which such careers might be understood.

THE AHM AND EMPIRE

The AHM was founded in 1874 by Frances Mary Buss as a professional organisation for headmistresses working in the new public secondary schools for girls.[20] The association held an annual conference for its members, established a number of sub-committees to investigate educational issues and published a range of pamphlets and books on educational subjects. As Dina Copelman and Alison Oram illustrate, the AHM worked as a professional organisation to improve the working conditions, pay and prospects of its members, and the participation of women in the public sphere. Neo-Weberians have depicted professionalisation as a process of closure, effected through the construction of boundaries of belonging and Otherness, which were both symbolic and material and implicated in class and state formation.[21] The AHM adopted the liberal and outwardly gender-neutral, meritocratic arguments associated with professionalisation and also argued for improved status for women teachers and heads in terms of the interests of the pupils. Like male professional educational organisations, the AHM espoused a view of professionalism which stressed service combined with expertise, both of which enabled women to claim a 'special' role as educators of girls alongside gender-neutral notions of professionalism.[22]

From 1897 the AHM began to consider educational issues related to empire. The executive discussed the paper delivered to the National Union of Women Workers by Ellen Joyce, President of the British Women's Emigration Association (BWEA)[23] and the 1897 annual report carried a paper from Miss M. E. Pope, headmistress of the Caineville School Mussoorie, India.[24] Imperial activities developed more systematically when formal links were forged with the League of Empire and the Victoria League.[25] The AHM sent representatives to the committees of these organisations, both of which were keen to involve the girls' high schools in spreading ideals of empire. The AHM representatives kept the AHM executive informed of the latest imperial initiatives for education, which were publicised in AHM annual reports.[26]

The League of Empire proved the more influential in fostering the growth of imperial activity in the AHM. The League's greatest successes were its imperial education conferences in 1907 and 1911 and its organisation of the first conference for imperial teachers' associations in 1912.[27] The League's objectives were congruent with those of the AHM: 'to provide facilities for intercourse and exchange of ideas'. The League's 1907 congress, attended by AHM delegates Sophie Bryant[28] and Miss Mowbray, drew together 'those engaged in the work of education in the various parts of the empire', including colonial ministers of education and heads of education departments as well as those running universities and colleges throughout the British Empire.[29] In the same year, the AHM established their Colonial Committee, with Sara Burstall[30] as first chair[31] and Miss Mowbray as permanent chair from 1908.[32] The latter also attended several committee meetings of the Victoria League, which aimed 'to stimulate the interest of the children of our schools in their comrades in other parts of the Empire'.[33] Like the League of Empire, the Victoria League held special educational conferences in London, although it had less success in promoting its activities within the high schools.[34]

The establishment of the AHM Colonial Committee coincided with preparations for the Pan-Anglican Congress held in 1908.[35] Ann Laura

Stoler points to the importance of international congresses for constructing and affirming shared notions of 'civility' and as sites for consolidating a 'formal pan-European imperial moral and legal order'.[36] Miss Wolseley Lewis, attending the AHM executive to describe the work of the congress, suggested that it would provide an opportunity for the AHM to get in touch with overseas headmistresses visiting England.[37] Like the Girls' Friendly Society and the Mothers' Union, who organised their own imperial meetings alongside the main congress,[38] the AHM held its Annual Conference in the same week[39] and organised an 'At Home' at Clapham High School to meet the headmistresses from overseas who were attending the congress.[40] This networking with overseas headmistresses set the pattern for much of the subsequent imperial activity of the AHM.

A further strand of imperial activity within the AHM grew from headmistresses' concern to provide information for their pupils on future employment prospects, both at home and in the British colonies. At the time when the executive was developing formal relationships with the League of Empire and the Victoria League, it was also building links with the Central Bureau for the Employment of Women (CBEW). As part of its remit to raise the salaries for women's work, the CBEW aimed to provide information about new employment opportunities for women all over the world.[41] Like the imperial organisations, it was keen to involve high school headmistresses.[42] In 1910, the AHM set up a sub-committee 'to enquire into the openings for educated girls and women in the colonies'[43] and commissioned the CBEW to provide them with 'expert' information on women's employment. The difficulties the CBEW experienced in obtaining information on employment opportunities for educated women in the British colonies and dependencies[44] led to a formal relationship between the CBEW, the AHM and Committee of Colonial Intelligence for Educated Women.

The Committee of Colonial Intelligence was established in 1910 by members of the BWEA and the South African Colonisation Society, who thought more 'expert' knowledge about employment opportunities was necessary to 'successfully' emigrate the 'educated' woman.[45] The Committee of Colonial Intelligence shared the view of the AHM that women needed to emigrate for careers rather than to marry. It set itself up as an 'Intelligence Office' and aimed to establish paid agents in the British colonies and dependencies to investigate and report on local demands for women's work.[46] The Committee of Colonial Intelligence was keen to: 'bring before women and girls of the educated classes the opportunities for useful work in the Dominions, to help them to avail themselves of such opportunities, and to impress upon them the necessity for suitable training'.[47]

The President of the Committee of Colonial Intelligence, the Honourable Mrs Norman Grosvenor, explained the objects of the Committee to the AHM executive and urged the AHM to accept representation on the Committee of Colonial Intelligence, rather than establish any separate emigration agency of its own.[48] Key figures belonging to the Committee of Colonial Intelligence, the Honourable Mrs Norman Grosvenor, Mrs Arthur Grenfell and Miss Bonham Carter, were already active in the educational circles of middle-class girls' education. The Committee of Colonial Intelligence re-formed under the name of the Colonial Intelligence League (CIL), with half the seats on the executive taken by members of the AHM, who agreed to promote the work of the League in their schools.[49] The CIL was convinced of 'the imperial importance' of its work, which, it claimed, would 'help to keep the British Empire for the British race'.[50] It had a very clear view of the 'right' sort of woman to emigrate, which did not include women who had attended municipal secondary schools and polytechnics.[51] Headmistresses acted as gatekeepers for the CIL, enabling the CIL to promote its ideas to the 'right' sort of women and girls in the high schools and the women's colleges.[52] The CIL worked with a range of teachers' professional organisations[53] and forged links with overseas educationists, who provided information about the openings for women's work,[54] who sent to the committee particulars of vacancies at schools of 'good standing' in Eastern and Western Canada.[55] This networking reflected both CIL policy and the AHM's stress on the exchange of professional ideas and information.

BUILDING A PROFESSIONAL NETWORK

The AHM's emphasis on the 'valuable exchange of experience' located headmistresses in the AHM within a web of relationships in which headmistresses in Britain together built expertise and wove the threads which constituted professional identities. The headmistress overseas, on the other hand, was represented in terms of her isolation.

> It is hoped that the proposed link with schools of a public character in the Colonies, India and the Dependencies will provide a helpful bond of union between headmistresses at home and those who, in many cases are working in a somewhat isolated or limited educational sphere.[56]

181

To alleviate this 'isolation' the AHM built a network of headmistresses which expanded geographically, while effecting the closures characteristic of professionalisation.

In discussing the possibility of headmistresses overseas joining the AHM, Miss Latham referred to headmistresses overseas as 'the English women who might belong to the Head Mistresses' Association' and insisted that 'those admitted to the Head Mistresses' Association ... should be British subjects'.[57] Miss Douglas saw the AHM in terms of bringing together 'fellow-countrywomen'.

> She felt strongly that our fellow-countrywomen wherever they might be, should be included in this privilege. They were in many cases girls who had been in their schools and at the women's colleges, who would value being in touch with the Head Mistresses' Association.[58]

As Dina Copelman argues, the forms of knowledge and values propagated by the women's colleges constructed the work and professional ethos of teachers in the girls' secondary schools by barring both the 'inadequately educated' and the 'inadequately socialised'.[59] Some overseas correspondents between 1909 and 1914 had attended Girton or Newnham Colleges, with others having attended London University or the provincial co-educational Universities. The desire to build a network of headmistresses based on the type of women educated in the English women's colleges represented the closures characteristic of professionalisation.[60]

The depiction of the 'isolated' headmistress underpinning AHM networking drew on longer-standing representations used to legitimate the need for teachers' professional organisations.[61] The representation of the 'isolated' headmistress was contradictory, not least because it built upon, sustained and masked an 'isolation' deployed in other situations as a strategy of professionalisation. Mike Savage argues that within the rise of professional society, professionals retained their distance from the particular organisations which employed them by claiming that only they had the expertise to apply professional knowledge in specific contexts by virtue of an independent cognitive base within institutions of higher education.[62] Being a professional, therefore, pre-supposed the distance and marking of boundaries between the 'expert' and the 'amateur', a practice which underpinned the philosophy and work of the AHM.[63] The view of the headmistress overseas as 'isolated' was a mis-recognition of the membership of some correspondents within Coteries of professional women in the British colonies.[64] It also downplayed the expertise of overseas headmistresses, which caused their schools to prosper.

The desire to build a network of headmistresses based on the type of women educated in the English women's colleges, taken together with the binary representation of the 'isolated' overseas headmistress and her professionally networked counterpart, the headmistress in Britain, demonstrates the boundary maintenance characteristic of constructions of ethnicity ('whiteness').[65] Stuart Hall argues that a culturally constructed sense of Englishness has worked by constructing symbolic boundaries, which naturalised the differences of belonging and Otherness through its binary system of representation. He maintains that a distinctive and dominant English ethnicity was constructed around nationalism, imperialism, racism and the state, which operated as 'points of attachment' for the construction of Englishness.[66] Because closures of professionalisation were also symbolic and material and effected through the construction of boundaries of belonging and Otherness,[67] professionalisation within the AHM also acted as a 'point of attachment' around which dominant but gendered notions of Englishness were (re)constructed.

Debates about membership 'worked' to 'recognise' Englishness by drawing on understandings of belonging which related to conceptions of nation and empire.[68] The network of headmistresses was formally restricted to what Miss Latham referred to as headmistresses of 'approved secondary schools, i.e. schools approved by the executive committee of the headmistresses'.[69] Miss Mowbray, as chair of the Colonial Committee, had been distressed by the 'interference' from 'headquarters' with the right of some overseas headmistresses to decide on the curricula and timetables of their schools. Florence Gadesden of the AHM Colonial Committee served on a selection committee to appoint headmistresses to schools in South Africa, and was 'astonished at the way in which they were dictated to regarding the appointment of their assistant mistresses'. Miss Latham thought 'those in England had not the smallest idea of the amount of red tape to which schools in the colonies were subject'.[70] The AHM altered the regulation excluding heads of private schools in Britain to admit headmistresses of private schools overseas because members of the colonial committee felt that the freedom to develop girls' education was being fostered in the private schools, where headmistresses 'were not fast bound by government rule'.[71] This relaxation of membership rules reflected the importance the AHM attached to professional autonomy.[72]

Admittance to the AHM for headmistresses overseas was, nonetheless, tightly regulated. Professional closure was effected through the 'invitation' to individual overseas headmistresses.[73] Miss Mowbray, as chair of the colonial committee initially wrote to 30 overseas headmistresses inviting them to join[74] and to a further 22 in 1909.[75] Alison Oram argues that being encouraged to join a professional organisation as a 'fellow' professional, validated and enhanced teachers' professional identities.[76] Both Dina Copelman and Alison McKinnon illustrate that the success of middle-class women's professions often rested upon the development of communities of like-minded women, who offered each other support, companionship, respectability and contact.[77] As Marjorie Theobald and Kay Morris Matthews have shown, the AHM helped strengthen the network of Cambridge women which spread through Australia and Aotearoa/New Zealand.[78] Yet, overseas headmistresses in the early days of overseas links were admitted to the AHM as correspondents, rather than as full members, despite British nationality and in many cases an English university education. While on furlough in England they were eligible to join temporarily as members and were entitled to vote at the annual meeting. Voting, full membership and hence professional authority had a spatial dimension and was located geographically 'at home' in England.

Inderpal Grewal demonstrates that the imagery of 'home' acted as a crucial category in European thinking as 'the space of return and of consolidation of the Self enabled by the encounter with the "Other"'.[79] As Ian Grosvenor notes, 'home' in imperial Britain linked to ideas of nation and belonging and to the nation as 'home'... 'If "home" represented the nation, women (and girls) were allocated a different place in discourses of national identity from men.'[80] Full members of the AHM occupied a different place in discourses of nation and national identity from those of their English-born and educated counterparts working overseas in the British colonies and dominions. Within the AHM, debates about who might belong to the association and in what ways, and who had the right to vote and participate in its governance, drew on and strengthened boundaries and hierarchies of 'subject and citizen', 'mother country, colony, nation and empire'. As Catherine Hall notes, 'metropolitan society, white settler societies, societies with non-white majority populations, each provided sites for the articulation of different relations of power, different subject position, different cultural identities'.[81] Debates in the AHM invoked political definitions in which there were 'particular and differentiated forms of cultural belonging'.[82] This raises questions: first, about the simultaneous distinguishing and positioning of groups of women within the AHM in relation to membership; and second, about the meaning of such positioning for the professional and cultural identities of its members. This may well have been particularly problematic for the woman from overseas, educated in the English women's colleges who returned to her country of origin to teach, who was caught, as Alison Mackinnon and Kay Morris Matthews argue, in the trap of both 'colonised and colonizing'.[83]

The following section identifies a shift from a relatively straightforward exporting of English expertise to support 'isolated' headmistresses, to a more dynamic model in which colonial experience was thought to enhance metropolitan professional identities.

'A VALUABLE INTERCHANGE OF EXPERIENCE'[84]

In the early days of their colonial encounter, the AHM saw sharing professional expertise with headmistresses overseas as a process in which headmistresses in England gave advice to 'isolated' headmistresses deemed to be working in more 'limited' educational spheres overseas. The AHM told overseas correspondents that 'as schools of various types are represented on the association, the executive is able to take counsel of headmistresses who have personal experience of problems and difficulties which often vary with locality and aim'.[85] This assumed that English solutions were universally applicable.

Much of the overseas work of the AHM was based on individual contact with headmistresses working overseas.[86] Miss Mowbray, as chair of the Colonial Committee, noted:

> During the year a number of letters have been received from overseas mistresses travelling in England, and recommended by Correspondents asking for introductions to various schools and in some cases for help in getting temporary work. It is in giving this kind of individual help that the work of the committee seems mainly to consist.[87]

Annie Whitelaw told the AHM that it had been 'a great help and encouragement to her when in Aotearoa/New Zealand to receive letters from the chairman of the sub-committee, Miss Mowbray, and the association's literature'.[88]

To alleviate the 'isolation', of the headmistress overseas, the AHM encouraged correspondents who happened to be in England at the time of the conference to attend the annual meeting and meetings of the executive.[89] Overseas headmistresses were also encouraged to meet personally with members of the association and visit their schools. Epitomising this individual approach, six correspondents visited Miss

Mowbray at Winchester High School.[90] Some sent pupils to take up Winchester High School's 'overseas' scholarship, set up in 1912 at the instigation of Miss Mowbray. One of the two to hold the scholarship in 1913, Marjorie Hallett, nominated by Miss Gosling, correspondent in Bermuda, returned to become headmistress of her old school.[91] Individual assistance of this type drew upon, as well as built up, the personal knowledge headmistresses had of each other and of their schools. Penny Summerfield argues that this individual knowledge enabled head-mistresses to act as gatekeepers to the profession. Much of this activity, therefore, supported the closures of professionalisation.

Miss Fowler of the Diocesan School, Grahamstown, South Africa met with the executive committee and told them of the difficulties of obtaining first-class assistant mistresses from Oxford and Cambridge for work in the colonies.[92] In her correspondence, Miss Badham, of Sydney Church of England Grammar School, asked the AHM to find assistant mistresses for schools overseas.[93] In response, the AHM were pro-active during 1912 and 1913 in canvassing its overseas correspondents about the availability of posts abroad for mistresses from England. The AHM solicited information from them about conditions of work in girls' secondary schools abroad, salaries, costs of living and the academic and professional qualifications required. They also enquired about the number of girls' schools which were employing teachers from England, whether overseas headmistresses preferred to employ mistresses from England, or teachers educated in their 'own part of the Empire', and whether there was 'any strong feeling on the part of colonial mistresses that it is desirable for them to gain experience in England'.[94]

Many headmistresses overseas stated that they preferred teachers from England, although they felt it would be better 'to employ mistresses from their own colonies who had either trained in England or gained experience in English schools'. Headmistresses overseas wanted the AHM to arrange for mistresses from overseas to visit schools in England to see the equipment, organisation and teaching; to send out mistresses to posts abroad; to interview applicants for posts abroad; and to recommend literature, class books etc.,[95] all of which held consequences for the exporting of Englishness. A key issue for headmistresses overseas was the difficulty that teachers experienced in finding employment when they returned to England, which often meant they were wary of emigrating in the first place. The AHM responded by urging heads in England to employ teachers who had experience overseas. This encouraged the two-way traffic in teachers and headteachers between girls' schools in England and girls' schools abroad, which the career profiles of some (head) teachers exemplifies.

This personal contact led to shifts in the thinking and practice within the AHM itself. Some headmistresses from overseas challenged the assumptions that underpinned the view of the 'isolated' headmistress overseas. When Miss Aitken of the Girls' High School, Pretoria, told the annual meeting of 1913 that isolation in the colonies brought about serious ignorance of mutual points of view and ideas, Miss Jacob of Tormore House, Australia, immediately responded that this did not mean their standard of teaching was low.[96] From the early days of the colonial encounter, some English headmistresses had seen the 'valuable interchange of experience' in terms of the benefits to the association itself.[97] In an early discussion about overseas correspondents, Miss Latham said that 'by admitting correspondents the Association would gain fuller knowledge of the great educational issues going on in the world'. This was, she thought, 'worth a great deal to those at home, where it is easy to become too deeply absorbed in daily work'.[98]

Other headmistresses and teachers travelled to widen their perspective on education. Sara Burstall, first chair of the Colonial Committee, visited Canada and the USA in 1908, where she held discussions with a number of headmistresses.[99] As assistant mistress at the North London Collegiate School, she had earlier visited American High Schools on a study-tour funded by a Gilchrist scholarship.[100] Miss M. E. Roberts[101] made an extended visit to India.[102] She subsequently acted as chair of the AHM's Committee for the Education of the Women in India and the East.[103] In this capacity, she co-ordinated AHM contacts with missionary societies and their teachers, as well as with the Association for Promoting the Christian Education of Women in the East; and organised the lobbying of the Secretary of State for India to urge the necessity of appointing women inspectors of Indian secondary schools for girls.[104] By 1914, the feeling was that the association gained a wider view of education from its overseas correspondents had become prevalent. By now, the Association was seeing experience in an overseas school as a positive professional accomplishment for work in England. It was within this context that Miss Whitelaw, as chair of the Overseas Committee, noted that the market value of teachers returning to England 'must be greater for the experience they had gained'.[105]

CONCLUSION

Within the AHM, exporting Englishness operated at several levels. Headmistresses worked openly with the CIL to 'keep the British Empire for the British race' by emigrating the 'right' sort of Englishwoman to the British colonies. The AHM exported advice and expertise to overseas headmistresses based on experience of English education. The association supported a two-way traffic in teachers between Britain and the British colonies. Professionalism and professionalisation within AHM may also have worked in more subtle ways to export English identities as professional identities. The encounter with headmistresses overseas rendered visible some of the hidden processes by which dominant notions of Englishness have been maintained as professional identities.

As Stuart Hall argues, ethnicity is not a static concept. More culturally diverse ethnicities and identities were continuously woven within frameworks of power. The career patterns of the overseas correspondents who attended the Cambridge women's colleges illustrate that experience at the 'periphery' did have the potential to enhance metropolitan professional identities and careers in the eyes of their co-professionals. Women like Miss Whitelaw, Miss Strong and Miss Dickson capitalised on both their English and overseas experience and brought the latter to the exercise of authority within English education. In the context of professionalisation, they were able to turn their experience of travel and the 'different' outlook(s) it engendered into material reward.

The experience of the women returning to the metropole supports the view that historical relations between colony and metropole were dynamic, rather than a simple one-way transmission from metropole to colony.[106] Returning to (or entering) the metropole to positions of (enhanced) professional prestige was made possible within a professional network that included both (head)teachers who participated in the two-way international traffic of highly educated women and those who remained as 'armchair imperialists'.[107] Understanding this two-way traffic requires an interactive approach to histories of women in metropole and colony. As Nym Mayall *et al.* argue, the British Empire can be seen as a set of relations, rather than a series of discrete nation-states and colonies. In this view, Empire constitutes 'a framework structuring political, economic and cultural exchanges between metropole and colonies in a web of interactions that include relationships between colonies as well as between the so-called centre and periphery'.[108] This points to the need for a transnational, rather than a comparative, or an international methodology.[109] While international methodologies are based on a view of 'a system of sovereign nation-states that enjoy formal relations among themselves and the political and organisational ties that can develop between women on that basis', a transnational approach 'denotes a broader field of interactions between peoples and movements'.[110] Grewal argues that a transnational methodology involves an approach in terms of gender that looks 'at the ways in which women in different locations speak to, across, and against each other'.[111] This approach is particularly apposite for researching an international professional network based on the sharing of professional experience. When the focus of attention on the AHM moves to 'the intertwining of the genealogies of dispersion with those of staying put'[112] 'relationships with old stories'[113] about the constitution of gendered professional identities and the processes of professionalisation begin to take on new hues.

ENDNOTES

1. Members of the committee for the year included Misses Broome, Mowbray, Powell, Spurling, Windsor. AHM, *Annual Report* (AR)1914, p. 48. Records of the AHM are at the Modern Records Centre, Warwick University, Mss 188.

2. H. Northey, *Auckland Girls' Grammar School: the First Hundred Years 1888–1988* (Auckland: Auckland Grammar School Old Girls' Association), p. 43. Thanks to Kay Morris Matthews for this reference; E. Bowerman, *Stands There a School: Memories of Dame Frances Dove* (Sussex: Dolphin Press), p. 72; Anon *In Grateful Remembrance AW Headmistress, Supplement to Wycombe Abbey School Gazette July 1967* (Sussex: Dolphin Press), pp. 19, 30.

3. A. MacKinnon, *Love and Freedom: Professional Women and the Reshaping of Personal Life* (Cambridge: Cambridge University Press); M. Theobald, *Knowing Women: Origins of Women's Education in Nineteenth-Century Australia* (Cambridge: Cambridge University Press), pp. 48, 105; K. Morris Matthews, 'For and About Women: Women's Studies in New Zealand Universities, 1973–1990', Unpublished PhD thesis, University of Waikato), p. 71; W. Robinson, 'Women and teacher training: women and pupil-teacher centres, 1880–1914', in J. Goodman and S. Harrop (eds), *Women, Educational Policy-Making and Administration in England: Authoritative Women Since 1800* (London: Routledge), p. 106.

4. Theobald, *Knowing Women*, pp. 48, 105.

5. Robinson, 'Women and teacher training', p. 106.

6. Theobald, *Knowing Women*, p.48.

7. Ibid. p. 105.

8. C. Steadman, *In the Days of Miss Beale: a Study of her Work and Influence* (London: Burrow), pp. 20, 89.

9. L. Magnus, *The Jubilee Book of the GPDST 1873–1923*

(Cambridge: Cambridge University Press), pp. 84, 85.

10. V. Johnson and H. Jensen, *A History of Diocesan High School for Girls Auckland 1903–1953* (Auckland: Whitcombe and Tombs Ltd., 1953), p. 17. Thanks to Kay Morris Matthews for this reference.

11. She eventually became a missionary. Steadman, *Miss Beale*, pp. 20, 90.

12. R. Annable, *Biographical Register: the Women's College within the University of Sydney*, vol. 1 1892–1939 (Sydney: Council of the Women's College), p. 28.

13. Anon., *Remembrance AW*, p. 24.

14. AHM, *AR*, 1911, pp. 40, 41.

15. Ibid., 1913, p. 13.

16. Quoted in I. Grewal, *Home and Harem: Nation, Gender Empire and the Cultures of Travel* (Leicester: Leicester University Press), p. 2.

17. Grewal, *Home and Harem*, p. 4.

18. Ibid, p. 65.

19. L. Eisenmann, 'Creating a framework for interpreting US women's educational history: lessons from historical lexicography', *History of Education*, 30, 5, pp. 453–70. Oram defines 'professionalism' as 'understanding oneself as a professional' and 'professionalisation' as 'the process of deliberately seeking the status of a professional'. A. Oram, *Women Teachers and Feminist Politics, 1900–1939* (Manchester: Manchester University Press), p. 132.

20. M. Price and N. Glenday, *Reluctant Revolutionaries: a Century of Headmistresses 1874–1974* (Bath: Pitman).

21. A. Witz, *Professions and Patriarchy* (London: Routledge), chapter 2; M. Savage, J. Barlow, P. Dickens and T. Fielding, *Property, Bureaucracy and Culture: Middle-Class Formation in Contemporary Britain*, (London: Routledge), chapters 2, 3.

22. Oram, *Women Teachers*, pp. 101, 103, 132; D.Copelman, *London's Women Teachers: Gender, Class and Feminism, 1870–1930*, (London: Routledge), pp. 25, 26.

23. AHM, executive, 11 May 1897.

24. AHM, *AR* 1897, p. 10.

25. AHM, executive, 9 July 1904.

26. AHM executive 24 February 1906. AHM representatives on the League of Empire included Miss Gardiner, St Felix, Southwold and Miss Dove and on the Victoria League Miss Mowbray, St Swithun's, Winchester and Miss Harris, Berkhampstead High School.

27. J. Bush, *Edwardian Ladies and Imperial Power* (Leicester: Leicester University Press, 2000), p. 144.

28. North London Collegiate School, AHM 1909, p. 37. Serving headmistresses on the Colonial Committee in its early days included Misses Burstall, Gavin, Julian, Mowbray, Bryant, Benger, Hewett, Major, McCroben, Day, Douglas, Burns, Gadesden, Julian, Latham, Haig-Brown, Harris, AHM, *AR* 1908, pp. 8, 78; 1909, p. 6.
29. AHM, *AR* 1909, p. 37; executive 11 November, 1912.
30. Manchester High School.
31. AHM, *AR*, 1909, p. 37.
32. AHM, executive, 10 October 1908.
33. AHM, *AR*, 1910, pp. 50, 64.
34. Ibid., 1913, p. 58.
35. Pan-Anglican Congress of 1908, *Report of the Women's Meetings*, London, 1908.
36. A. L. Stoler and F. Cooper, 'Between metropole and colony: rethinking a research agenda', in A. L. Stoler and F. Cooper, *Tensions of Empire: Colonial Cultures in a Bourgeois World* (Berkeley CA: University of California Press), pp. 13, 28.
37. AHM, executive 12 October 1907.
38. Bush, *Edwardian Ladies*, p. 78.
39. AHM, executive, 12 October 1907.
40. AHM, 'Notes of Discussion at the At Home given by the President at the Clapham High School on June 30, 1908'.
41. AHM, executive, 1 February 1910.
42. Ibid., 20 November 1909.
43. Members included Misses Gadesden, Faithful, Oldham and Walker. AHM executive, 12 November 1910.
44. CIL, Minutes, 23 February 1910. Records of the CIL are at the National Library of Women.
45. CIL calendar, p.4, CIL *AR*, 1910–11, pp. 7–14.
46. CIL, *AR*, 1910–11, frontispiece.
47. Ibid.,1912, frontispiece.
48. Both organisations claim to have approached the other; CIL calendar; AHM executive, 8 October 1910.
49. Ibid; AHM, *AR*, 1911, report of the executive, p. 42. Headmistresses on the CIL executive included: Misses Oldham, Douglas, Faithful, Gadesden, Leahy, plus Miss Shove of the Assistant Mistresses. Mrs Bryant was on the CIL Council. CIL, Minutes 4 July 1912.
50. CIL, *AR*, 1910–11, p. 12.
51. CIL, County Organisation Sub-Committee, Minutes, 23 October 1913; 14 December, no year.
52. CIL, *AR*, 1913–14, p. 13.

53. Ibid., pp. 13, 14.
54. For Ethel Hurlbatt see A. Prentice, 'Laying siege to the history professoriate, in B. Boutilier and A. Prentice (eds), *Creating Historical Memory; English Canadian Women and the Work of History* (Toronto: University of Toronto Press), p. 214.
55. CIL, Minutes, 6 July 1910, 7 December 1911.
56. AHM, executive, 9 November 1907.
57. AHM, *AR*, 1909, pp. 16, 17.
58. Ibid., p. 16.
59. Copelman, *London's Women Teachers*, pp. 18, 20.
60. See Savage, *Property*, pp. 22, 23.
61. R. Willis, 'W. B. Hodgson and educational interest groups in Victorian Britain', *History of Education Society Bulletin*, 67, pp. 41–50.
62. Savage, *Property*, pp. 22, 23.
63. J. Goodman and S. Harrop, 'Governing ladies: women governors of middle-class girls' schools, 1870–1925', in Goodman, J. and Harrop, S. (eds), *Women, Policy-Making*.
64. Illustrated in Theobold, *Knowing Women* and Morris Matthews, *For and About Women*.
65. For whiteness see: V. Ware, 'Defining forces: 'race', gender and memories of Empire', in I. Chambers and L. Curti (eds), *The Post-Colonial Question: Common Skies, Divided Horizons* (London: Routledge).
66. S. Hall, 'New ethnicities', in J. Donald and A. Rattansi (eds), *'Race', Culture and Difference* (Milton Keynes: Open University Press), pp. 255–7.
67. Witz, *Professions*, chapter 2; Savage, *Property*, chapters 2, 3.
68. An argument based on C. Hall, 'Missionary stories: gender and ethnicity in England in the 1830s and 1840s', in C. Hall, *White Male and Middle Class: Explorations in Feminism and History*, (London: Polity), p. 209; C. Hall, 'Introduction: thinking the postcolonial, thinking the empire', in C. Hall (ed.) *Cultures of Empire: Colonisers in Britain and the Empire in the Nineteenth and Twentieth Centuries. A Reader* (Manchester: Manchester University Press); C. Hall, 'The rule of difference: gender, class and empire in the making of the 1832 Reform Act', in I. Blom, K. Hagemann, C. Hall (eds), *Gendered Nations: Nationalisms and Gender Order in the Long Nineteenth Century* (Oxford: Berg). The relation between nation and empire remains, as Stoler demonstrates, both contested and problematic. Stoler and Cooper, 'Between metropole and colony', p. 22.
69. AHM, executive, 9 May 1908.

70. AHM, *AR*, 1908, pp. 24, 29.
71. Ibid., 1911, p. 17.
72. Goodman and Harrop, Governing ladies, p. 47ff.
73. AHM, *AR*, 1909, p. 38.
74. AHM, executive, 13 February 1909.
75. AHM, *AR*, 1909, p. 37.
76. Oram, *Women Teachers*, p. 103.
77. Copelman, *London's Women Teachers*, p. 26; MacKinnon, *Love and Freedom*.
78. Theobold, *Knowing Women*, p. 105; Morris Matthews, *For and About Women*, p. 71.
79. Grewal, *Home and Harem*, p. 6.
80. I. Grosvenor, 'There's no place like home': education and the making of national identity', *History of Education*, 28, 3, p. 242.
81. C. Hall, 'Histories, Empires and the post-colonial moment', in I. Chambers and L. Curti (eds), *The Post-Colonial Question: Common Skies, Divided Horizons* (London: Routledge, 1996), p. 72.
82. Hall, 'The rule of difference', p. 111.
83. A. MacKinnon and K. Morris Matthews, 'Colonized and colonizers: early Australian graduate women at home and abroad', Unpublished paper, ISCHE Conference, Education and Ethnicity, Sydney, 1999.
84. AHM, Leaflet, printed by the Colonial Committee, 1907.
85. AHM, executive, 9 November 1907.
86. P. Summerfield, 'Women and the professional labour market 1900–1950: the case of secondary schoolmistresses', in P. Summerfield (ed.), *Women, Education and the Professions* (Leicester: History of Education Society, Occasional Publication no. 8,), pp. 43, 44.
87. AHM, *AR*, 1913, p. 45.
88. Ibid., p. 13.
89. Ibid., 1911, pp. 40–41; 1913, p. 14; 1914, p. 10. Annual meeting Miss Irving, Melbourne; Miss Raymond, Calcutta; Miss Pulling, Auckland; Miss Aitken, Pretoria; Miss Jacob, Australia; Miss Knox Canada; executive Miss Irving, Miss Fowler, Grahamstown; Examination Committee Miss Lambert, Foochow.
90. Miss Gosling, Bermuda; Miss Meade, Cairo; Miss Welsh, William's Town Cape Colony; Miss Rammell, Lahore; Miss Borrows, Jamaica; and Miss Irving, Melbourne. AHM, *AR*, 1910, p. 51.
91. P. Bain, *St. Swithun's. A Centenary History* (Chichester: Phillimore, 1984), pp. 20, 21; R. Zuill, *In Pursuit of Excellence, 1894–1994. The Bermuda High School for Girls* (Canada: University of Toronto Press, 1995), pp. 46, 71. In later years Miss Tothill, first

Headmistresses of Bermuda High School, became a housemistress at Winchester High School, Zuill, *In Pursuit of Excellence*, p.31.

92. AHM, *AR*, 1911, pp. 40–1.
93. AHM, executive, 11 November 1911.
94. AHM, *AR*, 1913, p. 45.
95. Ibid.
96. Ibid., p. 14.
97. AHM, 'Notes of Discussion'.
98. AHM, *AR*, 1909, pp. 16, 17.
99. Ibid., p. 42.
100. S. Burstall, *Retrospect and Prospect: Sixty Years of Women's Education* (London: Longman's Green and Co, 1933), p. 109; J. C. Albisetti, 'Un-learned lessons from the New World? English views of American coeducation and women's colleges, c.1865–1910', in J. Goodman and J. Martin (eds), *Breaking Boundaries: Gender Politics and the Experience of Education, History of Education Special Edition*, 29, 5 (London: Longman's Green and Co.), pp. 482 and 484.
101. Bradford Girls' Grammar School.
102. AHM, *AR*, 1913, p. 21.
103. AHM, executive , 11 October 1913.
104. AHM, *AR*, 1913, p. 50.
105. Ibid., p. 13.
106. A. L. Stoler, 'Carnal knowledge and imperial power: gender, race and morality in colonial Asia, in J. Wallach Scott, *Feminism and History* (Oxford: Oxford University Press), p. 210; Stoler and Cooper, 'Between metropole and periphery'; L. Mani, *Contentious Traditions: the Debate on Sati in Colonial India* (Berkeley: University of California Press), p. 3; Grewal, *Home and Harem*, p. 9; M. L. Pratt, *Imperial Eyes: Travel Writing and Transculturation* (London: Routledge), p. 5.
107. With thanks to Debbie Gaitskell for pointing out the differences in the experience of missionaries returning to the metropolis and the headmistresses who form the focus of the chapter.
108. L. A.E. Nym Mayhall, P. Levine and I. C. Fletcher, 'Introduction' in E. C. Fletcher, L. E. Nym Mayhall and P. Levine (eds), *Women's Suffrage in the British Empire: Citizenship, Nation and Race* (London: Routledge), pp. xiii, xvi.
109. Grewal, *Home and Harem*, p. 117; Nym Mayall, 'Introduction', p. xvii.
110 Nym Mayall, 'Introduction', p. xviii.

111. Grewal, *Home and Harem*, p. 18; C. Kaplan and I. Grewal, 'Transnational feminist cultural studies: beyond the marxism/poststructuralism/feminism divides', *positions*, Fall (1994), pp. 430–45.
112. Brah, A. *Cartographies of Diaspora: Contesting Identities* (London: Routledge), p. 209.
113. An argument Antoinette Burton makes in relation to suffrage. A. Burton, *Burdens of History. British Feminists, Indian Women and Imperial Culture 1865–1915* (Chapel Hill: University of North Carolina Press), p. 23.

REFERENCES

Albisetti, J. C. 'Un-learned lessons from the New World? English views of American coeducation and women's colleges, c.1865–1910', in J. Goodman and J. Martin (eds), *Breaking Boundaries: Gender Politics and the Experience of Education, History of Education*, 29, 5 (2000), pp. 473–90.

Annable, R. *Biographical Register: the Women's College within the University of Sydney, vol. 1 1892–1939* (Sydney: Council of the Women's College, 1995).

Anon., *In Grateful Remembrance AW Headmistress, Supplement to Wycombe Abbey School Gazette July 1967*, (Sussex: Dolphin Press, 1967).

Association of Head Mistresses, Records 1890–1914 (Modern Records Centre, Warwick, Mss 188).

Bain, P. *St. Swithun's. A Centenary History* (Chichester: Phillimore, 1984).

Bowerman, E. *Stands There a School: Memories of Dame Frances Dove* (Sussex: Dolphin Press, n.d.).

Brah, A. *Cartographies of Diaspora: Contesting Identities* (London: Routledge, 1996).

Burstall, S. *Retrospect and Prospect: Sixty Years of Women's Education* (London: Longman's Green and Co., 1933).

Burton, A. *Burdens of History. British Feminists, Indian Women and Imperial Culture 1865–1915* (Chapel Hill, NC: University of North Carolina Press, 1994).

Bush, J. *Edwardian Ladies and Imperial Power* (Leicester: Leicester University Press, 2000).

Butler, J. T. and McMorran, H. L. *Girton College Register, 1869–1946*

(Cambridge: privately printed for Girton College, 1948).

Colonial Intelligence League, *Annual Reports*, 1910–1914 (National Library of Women).

— County Organisation Sub-Committee, Minutes (no year).

— Minutes, 1910–1914.

Copelman, D. *London's Women Teachers: Gender, Class and Feminism, 1870–1930*, (London: Routledge, 1996).

Eisenmann, L. 'Creating a framework for interpreting US women's educational history: lessons from historical lexicography', *History of Education*, 30, 5 (2001), pp. 453–70.

Goodman, J. and Harrop, S. 'Governing ladies: women governors of middle-class girls' schools, 1870–1925', in J. Goodman and S. Harrop (eds), *Women, Educational Policy-Making and Administration in England: Authoritative Women Since 1800* (London: Routledge, 2000), pp. 37–55.

Grewal, I. *Home and Harem: Nation, Gender Empire and the Cultures of Travel* (Leicester: Leicester University Press, 1996).

Grimshaw, M. E. *Newnham College Register, 1871–1971* (Cambridge: privately printed for Newnham College, 1979).

Grosvenor, I. 'There's no place like home': education and the making of national identity', *History of Education*, 28, 3 (1998), pp. 237–50.

Hall, C. 'Histories, Empires and the post-colonial moment', in I. Chambers and L. Curti (eds), *The Post-Colonial Question: Common Skies, Divided Horizons* (London: Routledge, 1996), pp. 65–77.

Hall, C. 'Missionary stories: gender and ethnicity in England in the 1830s and 1840s', in C. Hall, *White Male and Middle Class: Explorations in Feminism and History*, (London: Polity, 1996), pp. 205–51.

— 'Introduction: thinking the postcolonial, thinking the empire', in C. Hall, (ed.) *Cultures of Empire: Colonizers in Britain and the Empire in the Nineteenth and Twentieth Centuries. A Reader* (Manchester: Manchester University Press, 2000), pp. 1–33.

— 'The rule of difference: gender, class and empire in the making of the 1832 Reform Act' in I. Blom, K. Hagerman and C. Hall (eds), *Gendered Nations: Nationalisms and Gender Order in the Long Nineteenth Century* (Oxford: Berg, 2000), pp. 107–36.

Hall, S. 'New ethnicities', in J. Donald and A. Rattansi (eds), *'Race', Culture and Difference*, (Milton Keynes: Open University Press, 1992), pp. 252–9.

Johnson V. and Jensen, H. *A History of Diocesan High School for Girls Auckland 1903–1953* (Auckland: Whitcombe and Tombs Ltd., 1953).

Kaplan, C. and Grewal, I. 'Transnational feminist cultural studies: beyond the marxism/poststructuralism/feminism divides', *positions*, Fall (1994), pp. 430–45.

MacKinnon, A. *Love and Freedom: Professional Women and the Reshaping of Personal Life* (Cambridge: Cambridge University Press, 1997).

— and Morris Matthews, K. 'Colonized and colonizers: early Australian graduate women at home and abroad', Unpublished paper, ISCHE Conference, Education and Ethnicity, Sydney, 1999.

Magnus L. *The Jubilee Book of the GPDST 1873–1923* (Cambridge: Cambridge University Press, 1923).

Mani, L. *Contentious Traditions: the Debate on Sati in Colonial India* (Berkeley CA: University of California Press, 1998).

Mayhall, L. A. E. Nym, Levine, P. and Fletcher, I. C. 'Introduction', in E. C. Fletcher, L.A.E. Nym Mayhall and P. Levine (eds), *Women's Suffrage in the British Empire: Citizenship, Nation and Race* (London: Routledge, 2000), pp. viii–xxii.

Morris Matthews, K. 'For and About Women: Women's Studies in New Zealand Universities, 1973–1990', Unpublished PhD thesis, University of Waikato, 1993,

Northey, H. *Auckland Girls' Grammar School: the first hundred years 1888–1988* (Auckland: Auckland Grammar School Old Girls' Association).

Oram, A. *Women Teachers and Feminist Politics, 1900–1939*, (Manchester: Manchester University Press, 1996).

Pan-Anglican Congress of 1908, *Report of the Women's Meetings*, London, 1908.

Pratt, M. L. *Imperial Eyes: Travel Writing and Transculturation* (London: Routledge, 1992).

Prentice, A. 'Laying siege to the history professoriate', in B. Boutilier and A. Prentice (eds), *Creating Historical Memory; English Canadian Women and the Work of History* (Toronto: University of Toronto Press, 2000), pp. 197–232.

Price M. and Glenday, N. *Reluctant Revolutionaries: a Century of Headmistresses 1874–1974* (Bath: Pitman, 1974).

Robinson, W. 'Women and teacher training: women and pupil-teacher centres, 1880–1914', in J. Goodman and S. Harrop (eds), *Women, Educational Policy-Making and Administration in England: Authoritative Women Since 1800* (London: Routledge, 2000), pp. 99–115.

Savage, M., Barlow, J., Dickens. P. and Fielding, T. *Property, Bureaucracy and Culture: Middle-Class Formation in Contemporary Britain* (London: Routledge, 1992).

Steadman, C. *In the Days of Miss Beale: a Study of her Work and Influence* (London: Burrow, 1931).

Stoler, A. L. 'Carnal knowledge and imperial power: gender, race and morality in colonial Asia', in J. Wallach Scott, *Feminism and History* (Oxford: Oxford University Press, 1997), pp. 209-66.

— and Cooper, F. 'Between metropole and colony: rethinking a research agenda', in A. L. Stoler and F. Cooper (eds), *Tensions of Empire: Colonial Cultures in a Bourgeois World* (Berkeley, CA: University of California Press, 1997), pp. 1-58.

Summerfield, P. 'Women and the professional labour market 1900–1950: the case of secondary schoolmistresses', in P. Summerfield (ed.), *Women, Education and the Professions*, (Leicester: History of Education Society, Occasional Publication no. 8, 1987), pp. 37–52.

Theobald, M. *Knowing Women: Origins of Women's Education in Nineteenth-Century Australia* (Cambridge: Cambridge University Press, 1996).

Ware, V. 'Defining forces: 'race', gender and memories of Empire', in I. Chambers and L. Curti (eds), *The Post-Colonial Question: Common Skies, Divided Horizons* (London: Routledge, 1996), pp. 142–56.

Willis, R. 'W. B. Hodgson and educational interest groups in Victorian Britain', *History of Education Society Bulletin*, 67 (2001), pp. 41–50.

Witz, A. *Professions and Patriarchy* (London: Routledge, 1992).

Zuill, R. *In Pursuit of Excellence, 1894–1994. The Bermuda High School for Girls* (Canada: University of Toronto Press, 1995).

9

Raden Ajeng Kartini: The Experience and Politics of Colonial Education

JOOST COTÉ

In recent years considerable attention has been given to the nature of women's writing and how women have managed to give public voice to their experience. In particular, this question has been posed with regard to the doubly marginalised, women of the working class, and of colonised and enslaved nations. Research into the provenance of women-authored texts and analysis of how women have appropriated or subverted dominant discourses in their effort to be heard, have suggested that for women, particularly colonised women, to speak publicly is rarely unproblematical. This chapter draws on such approaches in examining the writing of a 'well-known' figure in Indonesian history, Raden Ajeng Kartini. It is concerned to explore the constructed layers of gender and politics in which Kartini's voice is entangled and which governed her experience of education in her particular colonial context. It then proceeds to examine her responses to that experience.

While known to a small circle of colonial and colonially connected metropolitan correspondents during her lifetime, Kartini's posthumous fame ultimately derives from a reading of her own account of her life described in many hundreds of pages of letters written in Dutch between 1899 and 1904. In 1911 an edited collection of 105 of these letters was published in the Netherlands under the title of *Door Duisternis Tot Licht*. Kartini had been a protégé of the letter's editor, a former director of native education, and the bulk of the letters had been written to his wife. According to the preface, the purpose of the publication was to publicise the writer's views on her people's development under colonial rule and to use the proceeds of the sale of the book to fund schools for Javanese girls in her memory and to fulfil her aims posthumously. Later published in English translation as *Through Darkness to Light* (1920), Raden Ajeng

Kartini soon became one of the best-known Majority World women of the twentieth century.[1]

The biographical narrative and accompanying commentary which developed over a century were disturbed in 1987, 76 years after the first publication, by the release of a further set of letters and the original editorial deletions.[2] Comfortable assumptions that the letters represented the 'real' Kartini were suddenly challenged. The newly available letters revealed the extent of editorial intervention in the archive and at the same time made apparent the political construction that framed the original publication.[3] They revealed an even richer emotional and intellectual subject than the original, one more politically active in a struggle against colonialism and Javanese feudalism but also underscored the process of self-censorship and conscious self-representation. It might be said that, unedited, Kartini once more took command of her life story.

Kartini was born in 1879, in a small sugar milling town on the north coast of East Java. She was the fourth of eight children of Ibu Ngasirah, one of two official wives of the Bupati (regent) of Jepara, Raden Mas Adipati Aria Sosroningrat, a Javanese aristocrat. Typical of his class, Kartini's father also had an official first wife of aristocratic birth, his *Raden Ayu*. Whereas Kartini's natural mother was a villager, the Raden Ayu came from a royal lineage in Madura, an island off the north-east coast of Java well known for its strict adherence to Islamic teaching. Ibu Ngasirah, the regent's chronologically first wife was the granddaughter of a well-known local teacher of *kebatinan* (Javanese traditional philosophy) and a teacher at a *pesantren* (Islamic scriptural school). Kartini's maternal grandmother, Njai Haji Siti Aminah, had, as her title implies, undertaken the haj, the pilgrimage to Mecca.[4] Pre-colonial Jepara had itself had a noble tradition as a centre of Islamic teaching, and was once the seat of Queen Shema, a warrior queen who had led the Javanese Islamic states of the Pasisir (coastal region) against the early encroachments of the Europeans in the sixteenth century. However, by the beginning of the nineteenth century the region had been incorporated into the Dutch colonial state.

Kartini's father was a member of a prominent and large family whose male members had been co-opted into the expanding colonial administration. By the end of the nineteenth century they occupied many of the highest indigenous administrative positions in eastern Java. Family members were well known to the colonial government for their progressive attitudes and interest in modernisation and Western education. Kartini's grandfather had been amongst the first of his peers to have introduced his children, both male and female, to a formal Western education, a practice which Kartini's father continued by engaging a Dutch governess for his children.

When Kartini's father was promoted to the Jepara regency, Kartini, as a member of the privileged Javanese class – but unusually as a female – attended the local European elementary school. She was withdrawn from school at the onset of puberty when, according to Islamic tradition, she was secluded in the parental residence. Refused permission by her parents to attend a European secondary school like her brother, Sosrokartono, she nevertheless continued her studies at home. These were combined after some time with what amounted to a European 'young ladies education'. This was provided by Mrs Marie Ovink-Soeur, a feminist author and the wife of the local colonial official who lived nearby. Subsequently she was also coached privately by local school teachers Annie Glasser and Mr Both, to prepare her for the teacher training certificate examination. Together with the extensive reading she reports having undertaken, it can be concluded that Kartini had an unusually extended, and an unusually public, Western education for a woman of her position and times.

The extant correspondence commences in 1899, at the point when her European mentor, Marie Ovink-Soeur, transferred from Jepara. By that year, the 20-year-old Kartini had read what can be considered to have been the core of a contemporary Dutch progressive library and, as her correspondence shows, was able to converse knowledgeably on the latest metropolitan liberal progressive, socialist, feminist, as well as colonial reformist, discourses. That this well-read, unusually outspoken and highly articulate woman caught the attention of leading colonial bureaucrats was in part due to the prominence of her family, in particular her uncle and her brother, Kartono. One of the very few Indonesians to have undertaken studies in the Netherlands, Kartono had been fêted in the Netherlands in 1899 for his outspoken demands to allow the Javanese élite access to Western education, a cause his uncle and father had previously taken up.

However, Kartini's entrance on to a public stage was to a large extent due to her own efforts. A significant influence on Kartini's life after Marie Ovink-Soeur was the friendship she formed with Rosa Manuela Abendanon-Mandri, the young Spanish wife of Jacques Abendanon, the progressive Colonial Director of Education. Begun in August 1900, it was this relationship which elicited the substantial correspondence that forms the bulk of the Kartini archive. This relationship provided Kartini with a link to one of the centres of colonial power. Two years previously Kartini had taken the initiative of involving herself in the Dutch feminists movement's National Exhibition of Women's Work through which she became known in the Dutch imperial capital. Subsequently she advertised in a Dutch women's magazine for a penfriend. This led to a second important stream of correspondence, with Stella Zeehandelaar, a young Jewish girl from Amsterdam, and a self-styled feminist and socialist. A third important contact was the Dutch feminist, children's author and evangelical, Nellie van Kol with whom Kartini commenced corresponding in 1902.

Between the ages of 21 and 23 then, linked by letter to a number of European feminists and progressives, Kartini was set on a course aimed at improving her own formal education and attempting to define her goals in life. To this end, her friends encouraged her to take up teaching and to establish a school, but, in fact, little was achieved in that regard. She was probably more influential in helping to develop the local woodcraft industry by acting as a link between local craftsmen and a burgeoning European consumer demand for 'native artefacts'. Be that as it may, Kartini's efforts to gain financial support and approval to undertake further education was thwarted and, after briefly conducting a small school for the children of her father's subordinates, she was forced reluctantly to agree to marry a twice-widowed and polygamously married, Western-educated and colonially well-favoured, Javanese regent of a neighbouring region, Raden Mas Djojoadiningrat Dirdjoparwiro. It was a marriage which most accounts have interpreted as being the result of a bureaucratic conspiracy on the part of European and Javanese officials to shut off the aspirations of this outspoken and determined woman. It contributed to her death soon thereafter, in September 1904, following the birth of her child.

Kartini's letters form the major and almost the sole basis of any biographical sketch of her short life. It is to the letters one must turn to gain an insight into how Kartini responded to her educational experience, how she saw herself in the awkward space between colonial and traditional Javanese society and how she attempted to reconcile the conflicting influences in her life. Collections of 'literary letters' and letters of the famous represent a not insignificant literary genre and have performed as an important repository of autobiographical expression. Indeed, as personal representations, letters may be regarded as the 'ultimate' form of autobiography. Written in disjointed moments, as still 'raw' private communications, each subsequent reader is left free, it may be assumed, to respond anew to the freshness of the communication as if it arrived yesterday. Unlike the polished narrative form of the conventional autobiography, one might suppose private correspondence is free from the artifice of the public autobiographical text which, as Gillian Whitlock has recently reminded us, sets out to ensnare the reader.[5] It may then be expected that this extensive collection of letters will provide a quite unique insight into the nature of the educational experience of this colonised élite indigenous woman in the Dutch East Indies at the beginning of the twentieth century.

Recent post-colonial feminist writing, however, would suggest that a too literal reading of such letters would be misleading. Two kinds of questions central to the task of reading Kartini's experience of education have been posed. First, in as far as the published text accurately represented Kartini in an autobiographical sense, how does the writing of this colonised female 'engage in an on-going process of authorisation in order to capture its object: the [colonial] reader'?[6] This question is linked to a broader issue concerning the nature of the text as autobiography. For if Kartini's letters conform to a traditional Western sense of auto-biographic writing, then, as Smith and Watson suggest, several important 'adjustments' would necessarily be implicated in terms of how a non-Western author presents 'a specific notion of "selfhood"' and the extent to which traditionally accepted 'communicative and aesthetic purposes' of Western autobiographical texts are incorporated.[7] The second question, given that the 'private' letters are turned into a public document in 1911, is how it was that, in Claudine Raynaud's terms, this colonised female was authorised to speak to her imperial audience?[8]

For Kartini, confined as she was within the feudal culture of a colonised nation, letter writing represented a strategic act. It was the means that enabled her to break out of what she perceived as her isolation from a modern world. Letters enabled her to make contact with the colonising Other via an appropriation of their own discursive channels. Despite their apparent intimacy the political context in which the letters are written remains paramount in a post-colonial and feminist reading of them. In writing to her audience of mainly prominent colonial and imperial figures, she acknowledged that her thoughts would be read as public and permanent utterances on colonialism and the colonial experience.[9] Here, any attempt to make a sharp distinction between 'pure' private writing and 'constructed' public presentation of self in an autobiographical sense is largely illusory. Moreover, the editorialisation to which Kartini's original letters were subject introduced other intentions, structures and efforts to influence other readings sometimes confirming but at other times subverting the attempt of the colonial voice to speak.

An acquaintance with Kartini through her letters may be approached by considering the following two extracts which effectively open and close the autobiographical trajectory in the letter collection.

I have so longed to make the acquaintance of a 'modern girl', the proud independent girl whom I so much admire; who confidently steps through life, cheerfully and in high spirits, full of enthusiasm and commitment, working not for her own benefit and happiness alone but also offering herself to the wider society, working for the good of her fellow human beings. I am burning with excitement about this new era and yes, I can say that, even though I will not experience it in the Indies, as regards my thinking and attitudes, I completely share the feelings of my progressive white sisters in the far-off West. (25 May 1899 to Stella Zeehandelaar)[10]

My crown has fallen from my head. My golden illusions of purity and chastity lie shattered in the dust. It was my pride, my glory, that I was a pure, proud girl loved by my moedertje [the recipient] as if I were her own child. Now I am nothing more than all the rest, I am like thousands of others who I had wanted to help but whose number I have now merely come to increase. O God, my God have pity on me! Give me the strength to carry my cross. Can I still be your daughter, without a crown, without golden illusions? (14 July 1903 to Mrs Rosa Abendanon-Mandri)

The first paragraph is from the first extant letter in the Kartini archive, written at the end of Kartini's extensive Western education to the young Amsterdam penfriend. It exudes the sense of the powerful attraction Western progressive thought had for this woman who had been deeply engrossed in its literature in the isolation of her walled *kabupaten*, the formal residence of Javanese rulers. Here Kartini presents herself to an unknown Dutch contemporary as a woman committed to the agenda of First Wave feminism. This was no mere rhetorical flourish since, as she goes on to reveal, she had participated the previous year in the Dutch National Exhibition of Women's Work in the Hague, and was thoroughly conversant with the same feminist and progressivist literature her penfriend was reading in Amsterdam.[11] The second extract is from a letter to Rosa Abendanon-Mandri in which she announces her impending marriage arranged by her parents to a polygamous Javanese aristocrat. It was written a little over a year before her premature death. It is one of a number of letters excluded from the original publication and suppressed until 1987. Both extracts are undoubtedly emotion-charged exclamations torn directly from the heart but in fact both can be read as discursive constructs that Kartini herself establishes in her correspondence. Are we, however, to doubt the authenticity of their evident exuberance and the astonishing expression of misery?

In terms of its contemporary reception, the first extract effectively confirms native support for progressivism while the deletion of the second, no doubt partly out of respect for its intimacy, elides the disillusionment of the colonised. In the first extract, both the author and the editor who selected the paragraph as the opening of the published collection, can be seen to be joining forces in presenting an unambiguously Western persona, for a moment stripped of all the self-doubt and cultural and nationalist reservations that later letters reveal. The deletion of the second extract is perhaps the most extreme example of the way editorialisation covers over the nuances of Kartini's integration with, and subsequent disentanglement from, a colonial project. This is not to say that Kartini's struggle for emancipation as a whole is disguised in the publication – indeed it is that struggle which produces the narrative of a journey 'through darkness to light'. It underscores the sense of the pathos produced by contrasting circumstances suggested by the two extracts quoted and generates much of the persuasive power of the writing as text. Editorial intervention, however, shapes the way the text had to be read, simplified her biographical path as martyrdom, while disguising the complexities of the intense colonial struggle at the heart of the biography.

However, Kartini herself is, clearly, complicit in arranging the reception of her self-presentation. Having presented herself as 'a thoroughly modern woman' initially, her admission four years later that she has had to accept a polygamous marriage is now presented as a violation of body and mind that would leave her 'no better than the rest', an ordinary native, a suppressed woman, a co-wife. Her confession of a sense of an impending loss of 'purity and chastity' is at once a sexual allusion and a reference to the loss of the 'purity' of a European modernity her European friendships and her education had bestowed by retrieving her from unreflective tradition. The high drama Kartini brings to this moment in her writing accurately gauges the sensitivities of her refined European reader. For Kartini, the agony lies in having to recognise how conditional her acceptance by progressive colonialism in fact had been, how her mentor was instrumental in creating the circumstances which ultimately lead to this situation. Her letter is designed to assist her reader make sense of the situation by presenting herself as martyr in a Western narrative construction.

THE EDUCATION OF A JAVANESE WOMAN

Taken as a whole, Kartini's Western education equalled and in many ways exceeded that received by the majority of her male contemporaries of similar social status. Apart from a brief formal Dutch language elementary education, she had undergone an extensive informal 'tutorship' which had introduced her to a broad spectrum of progressive thinking, in particular contemporary socialist and feminist literature. Her library, as reported in her correspondence, included most of the volumes one might have expected in the library of a contemporary Dutch person of progressive leanings. As well, she had access to a range of metropolitan and colonial periodicals and dailies through which, as she reports, she kept abreast of current political developments in the colony and abroad.

Consumption of Western education, if not adherence to Western ideology, had become increasingly desired amongst Kartini's social class as 'successful' indigenous rulers were co-opted into the colonial administrative structure. The trappings of colonial modernity proved an added resource in securing advantage within an increasingly colonially dominated political environment. For Javanese women, as Kartini observes, it had become somewhat of a fashion and Western 'social etiquette' provided added allure to the prospective bride. Within Kartini's family an exemplary tradition in providing Western-style education, for both males and females, had been established over several generations. The use of Dutch language by Javanese in formal interaction with Europeans, however, remained a politically loaded matter in the hierarchal relations of colonialism.[12] Yet for all members of this late nineteenth-century generation of indigenous officials' children who undertook some European schooling in preparation for future careers (or marriage), such schooling was considered only part of a total education required of an élite Javanese.[13]

In her initial presentation of self to her Western correspondents, Stella and Rosa, Kartini emphasised her Western education and the physical and cultural constraints that Javanese traditions imposed on her attempts to conduct her life in accordance with more progressive Western ideals. Having substantially completed her formal and broader Western cultural education by the time she commenced her correspondence, Kartini introduced herself to her Dutch acquaintances via an autobiographical account in which she describes her journey to modernity. It is an obviously selective account in which her Javanese life is presented in European forms. Javanese cultural traditions are transformed into the domestic tensions of a modern family; 'mother fought my liberal tendencies tooth and nail', 'father, dear father, understood me'. In defining her own responses to events in emotional and psychological terms, Kartini creates a universal persona etched in terms recognisable by her contemporary readers since they borrow heavily from contemporary

European women's writing. It is this sense of a universal rebellion and idealism that resonated with the American post-war rediscovery of Kartini and is sensitively articulated by Hildred Geertz in the first post-colonial English introduction to the letters.[14]

Kartini's early correspondence, indeed, confirms that she was a 'thoroughly modern young woman' by 1899, and if largely home- and self-educated this did not differ greatly from the education of many contemporary European women of an equivalent class. She could sprinkle her letters with both trivial and deeply meaningful references from a range of reading materials to which she had access. What the published letters *do not* reveal, however, is the extensive traditional Islamic education and her training in what may be described as cultural gender roles, which were also an essential element in Kartini's education.[15] This omission begins to reveal something of the way in which Kartini herself shaped the public persona presented in her correspondence. It also helps situate the significance of Western educational experience, since in correspondence which otherwise appears so intimate in its detail, the suppression of her 'native self' suggests that Kartini had 'conspired' with influential Dutch colonialists to present her (self) to history as a thoroughly modern person.

It is only in a much later biography by her younger sister, Raden Ayu Reksonegoro (Kardinah), written in post-colonial Indonesia, that her 'other' education is revealed in a positive light.[16] A post-colonial Kardinah presents her sister as a refined young Javanese woman, trained in the arts that were expected to have been well honed by the time of marriage, typically at the age of 15 or 16, but often younger. In a period Kartini describes as her imprisonment in 'Native society... that took no account of youth and refinement', Kardinah describes her as learning the arts of 'sitting on a mat in the family circle, *laku duduk*, [offering food to one's elders while shuffling forward in a crouching position], [learning how] to serve, [and how] to associate with those of lower birth as if social equals'. In letters to the young Dutch Amsterdam feminist, Stella Zeehandelaar, Kartini bitterly lampoons such examples of traditional Javanese etiquette but Kartini's letters *do* reveal her skills and interest in 'native arts'. The celebration of music (gamelan), batik (decorative painting of cloth) and wood-carving crafts all form a major fabric in her correspondence and are important reference points in her interaction with colonial woman. Significantly, these latter activities precisely reflect the newly discovered interest in 'traditional native society' on the part of a growing number of colonials – the progressive administrator, the amateur ethnographer, the curious tourist and the studious missionary.

Kardinah further recounts that Kartini also undertook a more formal

207

traditional education: 'besides learning Dutch [at the elementary school] we also studied Javanese each afternoon from two o'clock to four in our own home . . . As for the reading and study of the Qur'an, we were taught by a woman teacher of religion.'[17] Javanese was taught by a male teacher, Danoe, whose severe traditional methods led to some girlish rebellion.[18] He was subsequently exchanged for a relative, their father's nephew. While Mas Soemarisman was 'very clever in teaching . . . he was also extremely hard' on the girls and as a result they were often:

> reprimanded and punished by having our ears pulled. Often too, we would burst into tears even though we had not been hurt at all. At times, when we were reluctant to study, we would hide ourselves and make the teacher hunt for us all over the place.[19]

Kartini summarised her response to traditional education in her correspondence with Stella and Rosa as a struggle against oppressive forces attempting to suppress her self-expression but the only direct reference occurs with regard to Qur'anic education. Deleted from the 1911 publication – criticism of Islamic practice would have been offensive and politically sensitive – she describes her religious education to a missionary acquaintance, the prominent linguist and Bible translator, Nicholas Adriani. Qur'an classes clearly followed a similar pattern to Javanese lessons, and the rigid methodology of the Islamic school brought out a similar rebellious spirit and a distaste for rote learning of unassimilated normative values.[20] She recalled:

> As young children we learned to read the Koran, recite prayers, aphorisms which we did not understand and nor probably did our religious teachers [*sic*] since these were in Arabic. We fasted, experienced hunger, we did everything required of us. Then a time came when we asked ourselves, why, for what reason, to what end? This question, first silently became increasingly louder in us. And then we expressed it, out loud. We wanted to know, we asked the meaning of prayers and aphorisms that we had to learn and recite. We sinned – wanting to make the book comprehensible to wicked people. People were desperate, we were desperate, we wanted to know and no one told us. And then we refused everything; what we once did without reflection along with everyone else we could no longer do unreflectively. We no longer wanted to read the Book written in a language incomprehensible to us; we no longer wanted to fast; nothing, to the great desperation of Moeder [Ibu Ngasirah]

who had had a strict upbringing. [Kartini to Adriani, 24 September, 1902].[21]

This extract makes quite clear that Kartini found herself torn between a spontaneous self-expression and unquestioning submission, between self-assertion and subjection to tradition valued by competing cultures. This rebellion may well have had deeper psychological foundations. As her sisters, Kardinah and Roekmini both recall, Kartini was considered a precocious, clever child and 'something of a nuisance', an assessment that concurs with Kartini's own self-description.[22] A rebellious nature, a sense of righteous indignation and personal worth rebelled against religious and traditional prescriptions, where passivity and self-deprecation were conventionally prized. Kartini clearly found support in the process and discourse of progressive liberal Western education that prized emancipation from orthodoxies demanding a stoical submission to social, gender and age status.

Powerful forces lay behind the tensions that reverberated in Kartini's household. Emotionally she experienced the widely conflicting pressures: the opposition of her natural mother and stepmother whom she 'fought tooth and nail' as they insisted on her conformity to religious, but more especially, traditional custom (although later she achieved a degree of reconciliation); the constant comfort provided by the support from her father and younger sisters; and her rejection by older siblings and relatives.[23] While her father's family may have epitomised the new class of modern Javanese nobility, cosmopolitan in outlook and reputedly 'relaxed' about their Islamic faith, her maternal lineage rooted her in Islamic and feudal Javanese traditions, and her household was painfully split between the domains of her biological mother and maternal parent.[24] Beyond her family, she felt the reverberations of an ancient aristocratic world at once sensitive to its humiliating imprisonment while simultaneously manipulating its colonised condition to maintain its position against challenges from populist and religious leaders.[25]

Kartini thus inherited a complex web of conflicting traditions derived from feudalism, Islam and colonialism that were manifested in the contrasting educations she received. Western studies provided her with a new language and conceptual repertoire with which to express new normative values that conflicted sharply with traditional *priyayi* (aristocratic Javanese) social conventions. Access both to foreigners and a foreign language provided a medium of expression to 'say' such thoughts and to develop them. New social discourses, in particular those of European feminism, provided a model of a new private/public interface that enabled Kartini to locate herself in a new social context and provide her with an agenda of social responsibility through which to express her ideas and resolve her inner conflicts.

THE ARTICULATION OF FREEDOM

Kartini is remembered as a teacher, for her advocacy of women's education and for her ideas about education for motherhood. It was, in fact, Jacques Abendanon and his wife Rosa and their circle in Batavia who initially encouraged Kartini to become a teacher and to give up her own aspirations to study in the Netherlands. On their return to the Netherlands the Abendanons used Kartini's letters to organise a fund to both establish colonial schools in her name and, arguably, to advocate their own unrealised colonial education policies.

Colonial progressives indeed shaped the Kartini of historiography in terms of her role as a teacher and advocate of reform of the position of women in Javanese society. However, the long, drawn-out story in the correspondence concerning the 'teaching' plan, originally formulated by her European friends is contradicted by a second theme: Kartini's own expressed desire to go to the Netherlands to study and her formulation of a broader discourse of femininist and national emancipation. Kartini's own ambition to go to the Netherlands to study, ('To go to Europe! Until my dying breath that will remain my ideal'),[26] was linked to a higher order of idealism than that recognised by colonial progressives. If at times her resolve to study in the Netherlands appeared to waver, this was in part because of a reluctance to focus in her correspondence on a project of which she recognised the Abendanon's did not approve. It was a project that, even more than the plan to commence teaching, aroused intense opposition when news of it became public in the colony for the first time in 1902. It was a plan, also, which in a sense represented a solution to the uncertainties and moral dilemmas with which she had been grappling since it would have taken her out of her ambiguous 'in between' position.[27] It would have provided an opportunity to vault over the layers of colonial obstructionism and taken her directly to the heart of the empire where, like her brother, she could have presented her message directly.[28] However, it would also have taken her out of 'the struggle', an argument she herself eventually recognised when conditionally accepting the proposal for marriage.[29]

The idea of studying in Europe and writing, together with a preoccupation to be 'socially useful', emerged from Kartini's reading of

210

radical feminist literature. Initially Kartini claimed to Stella she had no idea how her life, now disturbed by Western education, would proceed: 'the only effective solution that I know is that we three fly into the air'.[30] A year later, in a letter of 21 December 1900, she canvassed three alternative suggestions for work: teaching at Abendanon's proposed Native School for Girls (proposed in August 1900 but first raised with her father in November of that year); being lady-in-waiting at the palace of the governor-general (an idea suggested by a European female acquaintance in the capital but quickly dismissed); and training in a mission hospital as a midwife. Her chief concern with each of these had been the extent to which each could provide an opportunity for her to extend her education and participate usefully in a public world. While parental support was the first and essential prerequisite in realising any such ambition, it was the necessity of finding financial assistance that created the dependence on colonial approval. Study in the Netherlands would have taken her out of this colonial dependency but it also entailed a greater initial dependence on it. It was Kartini who first suggested a government scholarship as a way of instituting her claims to financial support (already available to native men) to free her of any dependence on the capricious favours of males in authority. The formal application for funding became a three-year saga sabotaged, subverted and postponed by several layers of male officials in whose hands Kartini's future lay: her family, the native administration, the regional colonial administration and the central colonial government.

By early 1903 the correspondence reveals the various conflicting strands of this saga were coming together in an increasing crescendo. By June of that year the two separate plans with which Kartini and her sister Roekmini had been wrestling for years had come to nothing. All that was left was the small *kabupaten* classroom and, briefly, the hope of continuing her work as a teacher as a married woman. Kartini died the following year, fours days after givinge birth to her child.

What then had Kartini gained from her educational experience and what expression was she able to give to this? Acquaintance with an extensive European literature defined for Kartini a sense of freedom and a realisation that fate could be transcended by rational action. She had learned she said, '3 things from Europeans: love, sympathy and the concept of justice and I want to live according to these'.[31] Kartini referred regularly in her correspondence to these learned ideals that essentially represent the emancipationary slogans of the Enlightenment – liberty, justice and love (fraternity).

For her, liberty was defined both in an intellectual sense and in social progressive terms as freedom from the constraints of tradition. For Kartini it was a notion with extensive personal resonance; it came to represent freedom to be a 'real Javanese'. Linked with her plan to study in the Netherlands, its initial impetus is reflected in her passionate cry to Stella against tradition as impersonated by the Javanese *priyayi* male, 'Oh God! Oh God! I shudder and shiver at the thought that one day it will and must happen that I will be bound to such a person.'[32] Liberty was a concept opposed to those colonised Javanese social forms which constrained the development of modern social relations, horizontally between genders and vertically between classes, and thus freed individual expression.[33] In particular, liberty was a concept she applied to the condition of Javanese women for whom the institution of marriage, polygamous and arranged, meant the denial of genuine communication between husband and wife and between mother and children. This emphatically did not mean the Europeanisation of modern Javanese life but the transformation of traditional forms. It also meant freedom from the colonial claims to universal truths.

Kartini's sense of justice can be most explicitly inferred from her criticism of colonial rule and the actions of colonial officials. Injustice, mistreatment and hypocritical behaviour she saw as the hallmarks of European and Javanese civilisation in their colonial manifestation. Much of the power of her rhetoric derives from her perceptive distinction between the ideals of Javanese and European civilisation and the petty pretensions of their colonial forms in Java. 'What value', she asks, 'have the people had from their revered nobles who the government uses to rule them? To date nothing, or very little.'[34] Against this she held up the virtues of the 'real' Javanese, regularly returning to an image of the idealised Javanese of high moral calibre and artistic sensibility in whose spirit, if not in whose technical skill, the future of an uncolonised people would be grounded. It is in this sense that she defined a modern Javanese motherhood and transformed a liberal maternalist discourse into a radical political discourse. Modern education she saw was a purifier of the national character:

> We definitely do not want to make of them half-Europeans or European Javanese; ... we aim above all to make of the Javanese real Javanese, a Javanese inspired by a love and a passion for their land and people, with an eye and a heart to its beautiful qualities – and needs. We want to give them the finer things of the European civilisation not to force out or replace the finer things of their own but to enrich it.[35]

Most significant for Kartini was the Enlightenment's celebration of humanity that she applied as a universal precept. For her it implied a need to develop relations between well-intentioned Europeans and like-minded individuals of her generation as a way to achieve the transformation of Java and the islands beyond. While this part of her correspondence has been lost, there is some evidence that Kartini maintained contact with a number of her contemporaries.[36] Her sisters maintained this network and in 1908 joined the first student-initiated Javanese nationalist organisation, *Budi Utomo*.[37] While Kartini had no illusions about the colonial situation, she held to the progressive ideal of a co-operative association but believed emphatically that this did not imply assimilation. As reported in her correspondence, for her the core of a distinct modern Javanese national identity was to be found in Javanese culture freed from a ritualised and colonised tradition and self-consciously performed and displayed. Like other early nationalists, Kartini regarded European language and education as a means to modernisation, to assist in the becoming of a 'real Javanese' in a modern world. Within this the vision of women's emancipation, for women to become 'real' women, formed a significant element. As Partha Chatterjee suggests for other nationalisms, it is precisely within such a process of recovering cultural authenticity and often, Chatterjee suggests, through the work of women in ways Kartini demonstrates, that the sense of community, of nation, finds the wellsprings that drive the emancipationary struggle and the rediscovery of the roots of a modern ethnic identity.[38]

Western feminism offered Kartini a radical political vocabulary that she transposed to the Javanese world. This transposition she undertook herself, since Dutch feminists had shown little interest in colonial, let alone indigenous, women's affairs while colonial women and male moral reformers were not prepared to breach indigenous political and gender institutions which might undermine colonial rule.[39] The broad social reformist project expressed in the contemporary feminist novel, *Hilda van Suylenberg* (which Kartini says she had read three times) confirmed for Kartini her own views on Javanese socio-political relations since the implicit feminist critique conveyed by the novel was essentially political. While contemporary Dutch feminist literature was limited to and by its upper-class settings, it nevertheless held the revolutionary message that moral conscience legitimated protest against the state and the conventional social order. It suggested that the forms and institutions governing gender and class relations (in the Netherlands) had become emptied of meaning, corrupting the individual.

Kartini's letters to Stella in 1899 and 1900 were written under the influence of her reading of this novel and a range of other Dutch and English feminist writings and by the momentum generated by her involvement in the Dutch National Exhibition of Women's Work. As her correspondence with Stella in particular reveals, Kartini transposed this radical feminist thematic to her own world through her own reflections on the experience of gender relations within her own society and culture. Access to Western education, contemporary European progressive discourse and an enlightened European audience provided the language, the focus and the occasion for expressing a confidence in a rediscovered tradition. Regardless of the failure of her own educational aspirations, this celebration of tradition amounted to a confident assertion of a modern national identity that, in the historical context, had revolutionary implications. Even her marriage in 1903, against which her 'modern-ness' is often measured, can be seen as a renegotiation of formal 'tradition' in terms of a new radicalised sense of agency whose outcome unfortunately remained unknown.[40]

Kartini claimed in her brief autobiography, written initially for Stella and substantially repeated to Rosa Abendanon, that her ideas regarding female oppression in Javanese society emerged as a pre-pubescent child at elementary school and preceded her reading on the subject in Dutch feminist literature.[41] Nevertheless, access to Western knowledge and the experience of participation in European society were essential prerequisites, she believed, for shaking off the influence of patriarchal traditions that would prevent the expression of her 'national' and gender identity in the public domain:

> We want to free ourselves completely from the stifling bonds of our deeply rooted habits, whose influence we cannot escape, to thrust from us all prejudice that has stayed with us and restricts us so that our spirit, frank and free, can spread its wings more widely – so that more good can and will come from the work we want to undertake . . . Europe will teach us truly *to be free*.[42]

This expression of defiance in the face of opposition from the colonial establishment was not in any sense a rejection of her Javanese identity; rather it was based on her passionate belief that the only way to resuscitate a colonised Java was through modernity. Like the radical Dutch feminists of her day, Kartini argued that the democratisation of relations within both the domestic and public sphere would bring about the moral and intellectual regeneration of traditional society. Radical in the context of contemporary colonial politics, increasingly in the course of her correspondence motivation shifted from its roots in foreign literature to a maturing self-conscious awareness of her own deep-rooted psychological involvement with Javanese tradition. As Benedict Anderson has noted in relation to the autobiographical account of a near contemporary of Kartini, the Javanese nationalist, Soetomo, one can ultimately read into Kartini's appeal for education and improvement in the position of women, a strong register of a traditional Javanese sense of *keadilan* (justice) and *darma* (duty) reinforced by her social position as a member of the *priyayi* caste.[43] In her trajectory towards emancipation which eventually ended in her return to Javanese tradition as a married woman, Kartini's sense of justice and duty had challenged, although not defeated, colonial and Javanese patriarchies and provided Javanese women with a framework for a reconstruction of gender beyond its traditional Javanese and colonial settings.

Read in this context, the two memorials on education which Kartini wrote in 1903 set out specific principles for a political nationalism and explicitly called for a transformation of contemporary government, including Javanese leadership. The first, written at the end of January 1903, addressed to the Dutch government and people, the second, written in April 1903, directed at the colonial bureaucracy, set out a case specifically for government financial support for her education but more broadly for a new colonial responsibility. In both, Kartini attempted to advance her argument for her nation's emancipation by re-presenting colonial and Dutch reformist rhetoric back to the colonial and Dutch authorities. In the memorandum directed to the Dutch parliament, Kartini outlined a radical colonial agenda that presupposed the participation of an educated Javanese professional and civil service corps and the incorporation of indigenous knowledge in the governance of the people.[44] Kartini had turned her back on Dutch progressives' proposition of a concept of 'association'. A cultural association of a modernised Java with Europe would only form, she suggested, where an equivalent education of the Netherlands population for understanding Javanese took place. And Javanese 'enlightenment' was an exemplar of a broader 'Indies' awakening not an exclusive Javanese project.[45]

Pointedly, her memorial to the colonial government in April 1903 begins by asserting a view of 'the Indies as the land of the Javanese, who has a right to the riches of his fatherland'; and later demands recognition 'of the aspirations of the Indies today, which is not the Indies of ten years ago, no, not even that of five years ago'.[46] This was not yet a national revolution but it was an argument against colonialism, a clear distinction was maintained between 'the Government' and 'the nation' and between 'the people' and their 'rulers'.[47] Dutch language education she emphasised, pre-empting her more famous male compatriot Soewardi Soeryanigrat, represented only a means towards the *modernisation* of Java, not its *Europeanisation*, a way of creating broad social change, not a means to individual prestige.[48] Her demand for access to 'the treasure houses of European civilisation' surpassed appeals made by the male members of her family, her uncle, father and brother for greater access to Dutch education.[49] For Kartini, Dutch language education would initially form a:

> goodly number of people...cultivated in mind and spirit, people thoroughly conversant with their own language and affairs and alongside this also in Dutch and European knowledge [who] must process the New on behalf of their countrymen so that the latter may appropriate it later for themselves.[50]

This was the role Kartini envisaged for herself, not as a teacher, but as an educator whose sphere of action was not the classroom, as her colonial mentors had envisaged, but the nation.

None of the emerging generation of male nationalists yet questioned the traditional position of women, since this constituted for them a fundamental element of cultural power, of what it was to be Javanese.[51] Kartini's radicalism, on the other hand, posited self-determination for Javanese women as well as for Java. Here was a feminism which, in a direct borrowing of Dutch feminists' demands for the reconstruction of a modern Dutch state, bypassed colonialist paternalism and preceded Indonesian male nationalist's closure of the gender question by seeking the modernisation of social relations simultaneously with political emancipation. Like contemporary Dutch feminists, the immediate focus of Kartini's perspective was limited to her class but, as in their case, the radical nature of her feminism held implications for all social relations.

CONCLUSION

Kartini did not need to read colonial progressive tracts to be aware of the corruption, vainglory and conservatism of colonialism and of the colonised Javanese elite. She shared the criticism of colonial practices held by self-styled colonial and Javanese progressives. Criticism of colonial practice voiced to her Amsterdam friend could even be recycled in her correspondence to the wife of one of the highest-ranking bureaucrats in the colony. Such frankness and openness had, nevertheless, to be tempered by a clear appreciation – on both sides – of the limits to which colonialism was prepared to go. On other issues as well a significant degree of congruence between the subject of Kartini's correspondence and progressive colonial discourse existed, such as on the need for 'native education', on the beauty of 'native culture and tradition', the direction of 'native development' and the education of 'native women'. But this is not to say she was the 'product' of some Western educational project. Nor, on the other hand, did Kartini merely write to please, to provide a mirror for colonial progressives. Kartini did, however, write to inform, to seek a point of deep communication with her correspondents and to educate them.

Through her extensive reading, Kartini was fully engaged with the reformist discourse being widely disseminated through books, newspapers and periodicals at the time. An important element of this discourse emanated from the contemporary women's movement and it is specifically here that Kartini discovered the language and the models necessary to undertake her own revolutionary project. Her correspondence, especially that to Stella Zeehandelaar, expresses a proto-nationalism that claimed the right to emancipation on the basis of a moral authority bestowed on it by the discourse she shared with colonial progressives. As Mary Louise Pratt has argued in the case of early Latino Creole nationalism, European texts were taken as points of *departure*, not of imitation. The 'expressive power' of emergent national self-consciousness, as in the case of Kartini, was in Pratt's view 'anchored in the intercultural dynamics of the contact zone', or what Whitlock and others have referred to as the 'in between' location of the subject.[52] In her actions and in her correspondence it is evident that Kartini dramatically extended the scope of colonial progressive thinking by transposing the radical emancipatory rhetoric of metropolitan European reformist discourse to express her own distinctly nationalist identity. For Kartini – as it was for her generation, male and female – the experience of education is to be found in the interplay and tensions within and between a modernising Java and a modernising colonialism. Ultimately, Anderson suggests, speaking of another Javanese modernist, 'there [is] no simple evolutionary development from the traditional to the modern'.[53]

European education represented not an end but a point of departure for Kartini. Her writing gave form to the process of transposition she was undertaking. Subjected to Kartini's own attempts at trying on the personas recognisable by her correspondents, restrained by the conventions of colonial etiquette and prefigured by the designs of editorialisation and external discourses, the letters which have survived nevertheless represent a record of that process as much as they are a repository of biography and of ideas. Switching between correspondents, between letters, between different moments and in response to different prompts, the letters reveal their subject attempting to create a new order.

ENDNOTES

1. Until recently Ibu Kartini Day was celebrated annually on 21 April.
2. A listing of the major translations is provided in J. Coté (ed. and trans.), *Letters from Kartini, Indonesian Feminist, 1900–1904*, (Clayton: Hyland House/Monash University, 1992). The 1920 English translation, subsequently adopted in all other English republications, reduced the total number of letter extracts to 79 and is marred by poor translation. The 1922/1938 Indonesian translation, *Habis Gelap,Terbitlah Terang* contains 83 letters. There are also later French, Russian and Japanese translations. The new unexpurgated collection of letters to Rosa Abendanon-Mandri was first published in the Netherlands in 1987 (F. Jaquet, *Brieven*, Leiden: KITLV Press) and subsequently translated into Indonesian (1989) and English (1992). This also contained a further 45 letters to the same correspondent by Kartini's sister, Roekmini. The 14 letters to Stella Zeehandelaar have been retranslated and republished separately in J. Coté (ed. and trans.) *On Feminism and Nationalism: Kartini's Letters to Stella Zeehandelaar* (Clayton: Monash Asia Institute). A further collection of letters by Kartini's sisters has been reviewed in J. Coté, 'The correspondence of Kartini's sisters, annotations on the Indonesian Nationalist Movement 1905–1925', *Archipel*, 55, 1998, pp. 61–82.
3. J. Taylor, 'Once more Kartini,' in L. Sears (ed.) *Autonomous Histories, Particular Truths: Essays in Honour of John Smail*, (Madison: University of Wisconsin-Madison).
4. A. S. Tjitrosomo, 'Dr Sosro Kartono, Sebagai sarjana, nasionalis, patriot, pelopor, pantjasila dan pengemban amanat penderitaan rakjat,' (Typescript, KITLV Archive, H.897) p. 3.
5. G. Whitlock, *The Intimate Empire: Reading Women's Autobiography* (London and New York: Cassell), 'Introduction'. Whitlock's interlinking of autobiography, gender and colonialism in her discussion of anglophone colonial contexts provides an illuminating perspective on the intricacies of 'reading' texts such as that of Kartini.
6. Whitlock, *The Intimate Empire*, p. 6.

7. S. Smith and J. Watson (eds), *De/Colonising the Subject: The Politics of Gender in Women's Autobiography* (Minneapolis: University of Minnesota Press), p. xvii.
8. C. Raynaud, ' "Rubbing the paragraph with a soft cloth"? Muted voices and editorial constraints in *Dust Tracks on a Road*' in Smith and Watson (eds), *De/Colonising the Subject*, pp. 34–64.
9. This is confirmed by the fact that contemporary Dutch feminists were keen to publish individual letters and articles and approached Kartini's father to ask if she could contribute regularly to feminist and other journals.
10. All quotations from letters by Kartini to Rosa Abendanon are from J. Coté (ed. and trans.) *Letters from Kartini*. Letters by Kartini to Stella Zeehandelaar are from J. Coté, (ed. and trans.) *On Feminism and Nationalism*. References to letters from *Door Duisternis Tot Licht* are from the edition edited by E. Allard, 1976.
11. For an account of Kartini's involvement see J. Coté, 'Celebrating women's labour: Raden Ajeng Kartini and the Dutch Women's Exhibition, 1898' in M. Grever and F. Dieteren (eds), *Een Vaderland voor Vrouwen/A Fatherland for Women* (Amsterdam: IISG/VVG), pp. 119–35.
12. Kartini discusses this in detail in Kartini to Stella, 13 January 1900. Using official statistics, Groeneboer estimates that in 1870 there were no more than 100 indigenous speakers of Dutch. In 1900 that number was around 5,000. At the same time he estimates that only 30 per cent of the population legally recognised as European spoke Dutch in 1876 and in 1900 only about 40 per cent did so. K. Groeneboer, *Weg Naar het Westen: Het Nederlands voor Indië, 1600–1950*, (Leiden: KITLV Press).
13. See J. Taylor, 'Kartini in her historical context', *Bijdragen*, vol. 145, pp. 295–307.
14. H. Geertz, Introduction, *Letters of a Javanese Princess* (trans. A. L. Symmers) (New York: Norton).
15. A posthumous biographical account by her sister, Roekmini reiterates Kartini's own self-representation. It is contained in a letter to Hilda Boissevain, 20 March 1913. KITLV Archive, Kartini Archive H.897. This was intended to provide information for a lecture to raise funds for the Kartini Fund, intended to support a girls' school in Java. For a translation see J. Coté, 'Kartini: A personal memoir', *Journal of the Australia–Indonesia Association*, 1994, pp. 16–22.
16. Mrs Kardinah Reksonegoro, 'The Three Sisters', typescript, translated by Mrs A. King, Satya Wacana Christian University,

Salatiga, 1958. Kardinah would have been conscious of having to frame Kartini in a nationalist context.

17. Kardinah, 'The Three Sisters', p. 3.
18. 'We would urge Mr Danoe...to buy us some *petjel semanggi* [Javanese vegetable dish with peanuts]. Then, sitting on the verandah of the *kabupaten*, we would eat the *petjel semanggi*, joking and laughing together because we could not stand its hot peppery taste. Finally father would hear us and give us all a good scolding.' When replaced he was put in charge of 'instructing our younger brothers and sisters who were still small'. Kardinah, 'The Three Sisters', p. 3.
19. Ibid.
20. Descriptions of Kartini as headstrong, rebellious and constantly flouting Javanese etiquette are repeated in each of three biographical reminiscences, 1904, 1913 and 1958 written by her sisters.
21. The quotation is from a deletion by the editor from a letter by Kartini to Adriani of 24 September 1902. The substance of this point is also referred to in a letter to E. C. Abdendanon, 15 August 1902 (*Door Duisternis Tot Licht*). In another deleted extract (filed in the Kartini archive) Kartini informs Adriani that she had a Dutch translation of the Qur'an which she notes 'in the view of the strict orthodox...is sacrilege – God's word translated into a Kaffir language'. She goes on: 'But how can we love, be convinced, if we do not know. Rather despised unbelievers than self-deceivers.' Kartini had criticised Islamic traditions in one of her earliest letters to Stella (6 November 1899).
22. Roekmini to Hilda de Booy-Boissevain, 20 March 1913. Roekmini recounts Kartini's nick-name, Trinil or Nil, the name of a small bird noted for its quick movements, derived from the fact that already at nine months she was walking and exploring the inner rooms of the *kabupaten*.
23. The impact of Kartini's position in the family as the eldest daughter of the 'secondary wife' on her self-perception and on her treatment by others has been debated. Cora Vreede-de Steurs argues that Kartini's biological mother was not socially ostracised, C. Vreede-de Steurs 'Kartini: feiten en ficties', *Bijdragen*, vol. 121, 1965, pp. 213–44.
24. The distinction is normally drawn, following Clifford Geertz, as a distinction between *abangan* (not strict) and *santri* (strict) Muslims.
25. J. Pemberton, *On the subject "Java"*, (Ithaca and London: Cornell University Press).
26. Kartini to Stella, 13 January 1900. The first Indonesian woman to undertake tertiary studies in the Netherlands arrived in 1921. (H.

Poeze, *In het Land der Overheersers: Indonesiërs, 1600–1950*, vol. 1, p. 222.

27. Whitlock suggests that autobiographic writing 'can suggest the multiplicity of histories, the ground 'in between' where differences complicate, both across and within individual subjects.' Whitlock, *The Intimate Empire*, p. 5.

28. Her brother, Sosrokartono, was one of the earliest Indonesians to study in the Netherlands. He had demanded better education for Javanese in a public lecture in 1899, see J. Coté, *On Feminism and Nationalism*, appendix two.

29. That her acceptance was conditional on recognition of her right to continue her project was emphasised by her sister Roekmini in her 1913 biographical sketch.

30. Kartini to Stella, 6 November 1899.

31. 20 November 1901.

32. Kartini to Stella Zeehandelaar, November 1988.

33. This is noted regularly as an essential ingredient for progress to allow the *kaum muda* [young-progressive generation] to communicate.

34. 'Give the Javanese Education!' January 1903. J. Coté, *Letters from Kartini*, appendix one.

35. Kartini to Rosa Abendanon-Mandri, 10 June 1902.

36. Kartini repeatedly speaks of links with the up-coming generation. 'One dream of ours is to be able to communicate with all educated progressive men in the Indies. As a single person alone I am powerless, but if the young generation united and co-operated, we could with our combined efforts bring to life something fine. We burn with emotion when we read cleverly written articles by our countrymen. How shall we be able to get into contact with them?' Kartini to Rosa Abendanon-Mandri, 3 January 1902. After the publication of one of her letters, she reports receiving a letter from 'a student at the native Doctor School' (Kartini to Rosa, March 1903) where her cousin Hassim was studying, and where she hoped her younger brother would also be able to study (Kartini to E. C. Abendanon, 31 January 1903, *Door Duisternis Tot Licht*).

37. J. Coté, 'The correspondence of Kartini's sisters'.

38. P. Chatterjee, 'Women and the Nation', in P. Chatterjee, *The Nation and its Fragments: Colonial and Postcolonial Histories* (Princeton, NJ: Princeton University Press).

39. J Coté, 'Our Indies Colony'.

40. While Kartini in letters to Rosa Abendanon-Mandri described her marriage as enveloped in a series of mystical events (and also

considerable pain), Roekmini later described it as in essence a negotiated arrangement. Her conditions for marrying Djojoadinigrat were that he had to agree to her conception of a modern future. 'Her terms were that he would permit her to continue her work at Rembang, to continue her studies, and her teaching of the daughters of native officials as she had done at home. If he refused these conditions, she would refuse his proposal. He responded that he was entirely in accord with her ideas and that he had known of her and her beliefs for a long time. He added that he had never wanted anything other than that she is at his side so that they could work together for the development of the people, and that it would be a great pleasure for him and other native parents if she would continue her work at Rembang.' Roekmini to Hilda Boissevain, 20 March 1913.

41. Kartini to Stella, 25 May 1899; Kartini to Rosa Abendanon-Mandri, August 1900.

42. Kartini to Rosa Abendanon-Mandri, 6 June 1902. For two months she had delayed detailing to the Abendanons her conversation with van Kol, the first person to listen sympathetically to this proposal in person. A month later she heard via Annie Glasser of the Abendanon's reaction to her 'secret plan' and was forced to write a lengthy defence in the face of the Abendanon opposition. Kartini to Rosa Abendanon-Mandri, 15 July 1902.

43. B. Anderson, 'A time of darkness, a time of light' in B. Anderson (ed.), *Language and Power: Exploring Political Cultures in Indonesia*, (Ithaca and London: Cornell University Press), p. 245.

44. She emphasises the preparation of a sufficient number of Javanese doctors, lawyers and administrators whose education was to include Javanese knowledge and cultural conventions.

45. This is clear from Kartini's references to other members of the progressive younger generation, the *kaum muda*.

46. 'Give the Javanese education!', *Letters*, appendix one.

47. Ibid.

48. Ibid. Prior to this she notes: 'it is only a knowledge of a European language, and in the first instance of course Dutch, which will in the foreseeable future be able to develop [*ontwikkeling*] and bring spiritual freedom to, the upper classes of native society' (p. 534).

49. Kartini to Stella, 13 January 1900.

50. 'Give the Javanese education!', *Letters*, appendix one. In the same vein she continues: 'All significant works of European literature should be translated into Javanese and presented to the Javanese people; then see what the people think of it!'

51. Partha Chatterjee argues this in relation to Indian nationalism and the role of women. P. Chatterjee, *The Nation and its Fragments.*
52. M. L. Pratt, *Imperial Eyes: Travel Writing and Transculturation,* (London: Routledge), p. 195.
53. B. Anderson, 'A time of darkness, a time of light', p. 222.

REFERENCES

Allard, E. (ed.) *Door Duisternis Tot Licht: Gedachten over en voor het Javaanse volk van Raden Ajeng Kartini* (Amsterdam: Nabritik, 1976).
Anderson, B. 'A time of darkness, a time of light' in B. Anderson (ed.) *Language and Power: Exploring Political Cultures in Indonesia* (Ithaca and London: Cornell University Press, 1991), pp. 241–70.
Chatterjee, P. 'Women and the Nation', in P. Chatterjee, *The Nation and its Fragments: Colonial and Postcolonial Histories* (Princeton, NJ: Princeton University Press, 1993).
— *The Nation and its Fragments: Colonial and Postcolonial Histories* (Princeton, NJ: Princeton University Press, 1993).
Coté J. (ed. and trans.) *Letters from Kartini, Indonesian Feminist, 1900–1904* (Clayton: Hyland House/Monash University, 1992).
— (ed. and trans.) *On Feminism and Nationalism: Kartini's Letters to Stella Zeehandelaar* (Clayton: Monash Asia Institute,1995).
— 'The correspondence of Kartini's sisters, annotations on the Indonesian Nationalist Movement 1905–1925', *Archipel*, 55, 1998, pp. 61–82.
— 'Celebrating women's labour: Raden Ajeng Kartini and the Dutch Women's Exhibition, 1898' in M. Grever and F. Dieteren, (eds), *Een Vaderland voor Vrouwen/A Fatherland for Women* (Amsterdam: IISG/VVG, 2000), pp. 119–35.
— 'Kartini: A personal memoir', *Journal of the Australia–Indonesia Association*, 1994, pp. 16–22.
Geertz, H. 'Introduction', *Letters of a Javanese Princess* (trans A. L. Symmers 1920) (New York: Norton, 1964).
Groeneboer, K. *Weg Naar het Westen: Het Nederlands voor Indië, 1600–1950* (Leiden, KITLV Press, 1993).
Jaquet, F.G.P. *Kartini: Brieven aan Rosa Abdendanon-Mandri en Haar Echtgenoot* (Leiden: KITLV Press, 1987).
Pemberton, J. *On the Subject "Java"* (Ithaca and London: Cornell University Press, 1994).
Poeze, H. *In het Land der Overheersers: Indonesiërs, 1600–1950*, vol. 1 (Dordrecht: Foris Publications, 1986).

Pratt, Mary. L, *Imperial Eyes: Travel Writing and Transculturation* (London: Routledge, 1992).

Raynaud, C. '"Rubbing the paragraph with a soft cloth"? Muted voices and editorial constraints in *Dust Tracks on a Road*' in S. Smith and J. Watson (eds), *De/Colonising the Subject: The Politics of Gender in Women's Autobiography* (Minneapolis: University of Minnesota Press, 1992), pp. 34–64.

Reksonegoro, K. 'The Three Sisters', typescript, translated by Mrs A. King, Satya Wacana Christian University, Salatiga, 1958.

Smith, S. and Watson, J. (eds), *De/Colonising the Subject: The Politics of Gender in Women's Autobiography* (Minneapolis: University of Minnesota Press, 1992).

Taylor, J. 'Kartini in her historical context', *Bijdragen*, vol. 145, pp. 295–307.

— 'Once More Kartini,' in L. Sears (ed.), *Autonomous Histories, Particular Truths: Essays in honour of John Smail* (Madison: University of Wisconsin-Madison, 1993).

Tjitrosomo, A. S. 'Dr Sosro Kartono, Sebagai sarjana, nasionalis, patriot, pelopor, pantjasila dan pengemban amanat penderitaan rakjat' (Typescript, KITLV Archive, H.897, 1967

Vreede-de Steurs, C. 'Kartini: Feiten en Ficties', *Bijdragen*, vol. 121, 1965, pp. 213–44.

Whitlock G. *The Intimate Empire: Reading Women's Autobiography* (London and New York: Cassell, 2000).

10

New Frontiers in the History of Education: Oral Histories and History Teaching in South Africa

ZIPHORA K. MOICHELA

In a call to action in education, the minister, Professor K. Asmal, refers to rampant inequality in South Africa:

> Firstly, there is rampant inequality of access to educational opportunities of a satisfactory standard. In particular, poor people in all communities, of whom the over-whelming majority are rural Africans, continue to attend decrepit schools, too often without water or sanitation, electricity or telephone, library, workshop or laboratory. Their teachers may never see their supervisors from one year to the next. Their parents remain illiterate, poor and powerless. They are unable to give practical and intellectual support to the educational aspirations of their children. For such children of a democratic South Africa, the promise of the Bill of Rights remains a distant dream. Without a solid foundation of learning, their chances of education and economic success in later years are dim, so poverty reproduces itself.[1]

I am now a woman academic but this is the background that I came from. As a girl, I had admired stories from my mother, relatives and elderly women. The MEd course I followed in 1995 included work on primary sources and provided me with skills as an oral historian. The oral history stories I have begun to collect demonstrate that history textbooks in South Africa are full of silences and large hidden gaps. They present the past from one particular view, which is essentially Eurocentric and white-dominated.

The arrival and settlement of Jan van Riebeeck in the Cape in 1652 is generally seen as the moment when South African history begins. This explains why South African history could have textbooks with titles such as *Van Riebeeck to Vorster 1652–1970s*. Such titles were and still are commonly found in textbooks that history students and teachers use daily. By removing the indigenous people from the landscape, this view keeps alive the myth that South Africa was 'discovered' by the Dutch and therefore the land belongs rightfully to the Afrikaner, the descendants of the Dutch 'discoverers'. Piet Retief and Simon van der Stel were the heroes that students had to learn about and the events which influenced history were those like the arrival of Jan van Riebeeck or the Great Trek. Africans were seen as playing no real role in history and so they were excluded from the historical narratives. When they were included, they were often shown as inferior, or as the villains, as exemplified by the portrayal of Dingane in most history textbooks. In textbooks of this type, history has served the political aim of supporting the ideas of white supremacy and Afrikaner nationalism. My aim as a historical researcher is to use 'words' of mouth – a potentially powerful historical tool for reshaping the nature of South African history[2] – to redress imbalances in history education in South African schools, a task that requires a bold stance.

In the first part of this chapter I tell the story of my oral history research with the semi-rural people of 'Maamuse'/Schweizer-Reneke. I focus particularly on the stories of three women which encouraged me to embark on this field of research. In South Africa, women are differentiated on the basis of race and class: white women, black women and coloured women (Afrikaans-speaking non-white women, Asiatics and others), with a sub-classification of the so-called women of colour – namely, black women, coloured women and other than white women. The chapter is limited to women of colour and, specifically, black women in the semi-rural area of North West Province known as 'Maamuse/Schweizer-Reneke.

In the second part of the chapter, I recount conversations from a history teachers' conference to illustrate my work with teachers based on my research with the three women of 'Maamuse'/Schweizer-Reneke. The ending of the ideological domination exercised for many years in South Africa by proponents of apartheid history allows us to start thinking of new ways to approach history in South Africa and to begin devising new ways of getting pupils to think about history. For teachers in South Africa there is the challenge of finding new material and new ways of teaching history – ways which enable them to respond to the silences of the textbooks by demonstrating that history is not simply about learning what happened in the past but also about an investigative process, through which we learn how we know about the past. In my work with teachers, I aim to demonstrate the possibilities of using oral testimonies as a viable means of alternative history teaching, one with the potential to illustrate that there are always a number of different versions of the past, and one in which women can make an important contribution. Such approaches can utilise the silences in the textbooks to reveal to students the process of writing history. They enable students to analyse what sources historians have used, what evidence has been left out and why, and the historian's bias or point of view. Questioning how this has given us a particular view of the past is all part of developing critical thinking in students.

STORIES FROM RURAL 'MAAMUSE'/SCHWEIZER-RENEKE

In collecting oral histories, I experienced difficulties in securing appointments with men of the 'ba Phuthatswana', 'Tlhaping' tribe of King Sam Mankuroane in Pudumoe, I had to go through a number of formalities that preceded the interviews. The meeting was with a group of the tribal men at the king's court known as 'Kgotla'. I was instructed to wear a headpiece 'Tuku' since it is customary in certain African cultures for a woman to cover her head as a sign of respect. In addition, I was presented with a woman interpreter chosen by the 'Lekgotla'. I had then to struggle to get the men to talk and found it difficult to access the hidden explanations in their stories. As a woman and also a woman who had not been to a tribal initiation school, I was in an unfavourable position. Even had I been a man, I would not have gained access to the men's secrets because I was a member of a different tribe. I became frustrated with this sort of encounter. In contrast, the women made themselves available for interviews and were more willing to talk, despite the fact that they might have been sweeping or cooking.

The stories the men and the women told were different.

Men's stories

I had earlier interviewed one of the King's chief advisers by the name of 'ntate' (father) Bantobetse.[3] I was puzzled when I met the Kgotla as, first of all, I was requested to relate all what ntate Bantobetse had told me, his version of the history relating to the Tlhaping and the Korana of 'Maamuse'/Schweizer-Reneke and surrounding areas up to Pudimoe. In ntate Bantobetse's oral information, he had pointed out that the Korana were becoming a problem to the Tlhaping and they had to be dealt with. How they were dealt with was subject to question. Fortunately, according to the Kgotla, ntate Bantobetse had related the story like a 'man'. The explanation of the Kgotla was that there are things that are secrets known only to men which can only be explained to those men that have gone through the rituals or the tribal 'initiation' school. In addition, the issue of dealing with the Korana was explained as a ritual performance of stuffing a live goat and sending it to wander in the direction of the Koranas.[4]

227

Women's stories

Ou Dinah related the historical background of 'Maamuse'/Schweizer-Reneke by telling the story of the interactions of the Korana with the Tlhaping around the 1850s. According to Ou Dinah the arrival of the colonists, the Boers in particular, bedevilled the relationship between the (ba)Tlhaping and the Korana, who had previously been on good terms. She went on to say that the Korana took advantage of their ability to speak both (se)Tlhaping and Afrikaans to pose as middlemen in cases of exchange of commodities like sheep, goats, cattle and diamonds. The Korana complicated matters by being double-dealers, that is, they posed as the (ba)Tlhaping's allies while at the same time conniving with the Boers in robbing the (ba)Tlhaping of their land, stock and diamonds. Once the (ba)Tlhaping realised the double standards of the Korana they cast a spell on the Korana by dealing with them as related by ntate Bantobetse and the 'Lekgotla'. Her explanation of the dealing part of the Tlhaping-Kora's affair was that the stuffing of a live goat with deadly 'muti' was for ritual purposes. The poisonous herb would severely irritate the goat, which would run wild as a result of the pain and eventually die as a result of loss of blood. The goat would be spitting blood and in the process a selected tribal man would repeat the words 'bakgothu ha ba swe, ba laege' (let Kora die and learn a lesson, that will serve them right). At that particular moment the Kora would be massacred by the white people or whoever they were battling with.

The visible artefacts around the Kora settlement include rock carvings near the Wentzeldam River near Schweizer-Reneke and remnants of 'dibi' which are collected by women and children for fire consumption. According to Mrs Matloapane, the availability of 'dibi' (dry cow dung) is an indication of the number of cattle the Kora possessed. She said: 'They were well-to-do all because of the diamonds found around the farm "Rietput" near the Hartz River in Schweizer-Reneke. There is also a grave site in a circular pattern whereby one can figure out where adults and children were buried.' The stories of Mrs Matloapane (Ou Dinah), Mrs Lihihi and Ms Makhobosi cover the development of the town Schweizer-Reneke between 1881–85, 1899–1902 and also include the Kora–Boer wars, the Tlhaping–Kora wars and the Anglo–Boer war.[5]

Written stories

For much of the eighteenth and nineteenth centuries, the flood plains between the Vaal and Hart rivers was largely the preserve of bands of nomadic and semi-nomadic San and Korana. More settled Tswana speakers concentrated to the south and west of the grassland and acacia bush largely as hunting preserve or as a supplementary grazing for their cattle.[6]

The difference between Ou Dinah's story and ntate Bantobetse and the Kgotla was in her explanation of the dealing part of the Tlhaping-Kora's affair. Her explanation alleviated my frustration. I now understood and could make sense of what the Tlhaping men meant by dealing with the Korana. The story of Ou Dinah in particular gave me valuable information with regard to the interpretation of the local history of 'Maamuse'/Schweizer-Reneke, especially when she pointed out that the Korana were double-dealers since they were able to speak Afrikaans and Setswana/Tlhaping, so that they became natural middlemen between the

Tlhaping and the Korana in incidents of war, the exchange of commodities and bartering between the Tlhaping and the colonists. It seems that the Korana benefited from the booties of the Tswana-Tlhaping and were rewarded with cattle, sheep and goats when they aligned themselves with the Boers or English against the Tswana/Tlhaping.

Written accounts give no explanation as to how the nomadic Koranas managed to acquire so many cattle and such wealth. This is a missing link in the accounts of the area which, were it not for the versions presented by Ou Dinah and Mme Seiphetlo, would remain hidden. This missing link demonstrates that scholars and students and teachers of history should be cautious in reading historical accounts and not take anything at face value. They should learn to identify silences and question their existence, asking: Who writes history? Why are they writing it this way?[7]

Story-telling has come to be valued as a way of preserving identities lest they be lost as a result of current social upheavals, diasporic trends, emigration and global relocations.[8] The oral testimonies of Ou (old) Dinah, 'Mme' (mother) Seiphetlo and Mme Phutologo demonstrate that the rich insights offered by the voices and life stories of these women can inform scholarly research and expand our understanding of both the shared experiences of gender (as well as the profound differences amongst women). They also demonstrate the possibility of using oral testimonies as alternative historical tools to challenge the monopoly of the printed word and to create an opportunity for dialogue with ordinary people by giving them the chance to produce 'official' historical knowledge.

The history curriculum in South Africa has been reconceptualised as a curriculum that aims to take the diverse cultures, races, ethnicities, sexes, political movements and classes into consideration and one that should deal with the political, social, economic, cultural and environmental dimensions of human experience. The teaching method for history is intended to be democratic through the mode of classroom discourse and the experiences of students in the classroom.[9] In developing a theme on the Anglo–Boer war (1881–1902), and its relevance to the semi-rural area of 'Maamuse'/Schweizer-Reneke, I used the oral history research I had conducted. This formed the basis for Chapter 1 of *Teachers Transform History* (1977), a book which encourages students to engage with their own history, a history characterised by excitement, creativity and a sense of challenge.[10] As my story in the second part of the chapter demonstrates, introducing this approach to teachers also provided me with a challenge.

SOUTH AFRICAN TEACHERS AND THE CHALLENGE OF ORAL HISTORY

It was the annual History Teachers' Conference and Ziporah Moichela was nervous. She had attended the conference regularly, but usually as an observer. This year, however, she was to be a participant, presenting a paper on some research that she had done, and the sinking feeling in her stomach would not go away. At tea, just before her presentation, she had joined in a discussion with some history teachers from all over the country. They were angry and dissatisfied, not a very receptive audience, Ziporah thought. They had discussed a number of issues.

'It's the "new" South Africa, but nothing's changed,' exclaimed Jane Ntsane, a history teacher from Atteridgeville. 'There are still no new textbooks. What are we meant to use to teach this "new" history?'

'Yes,' agreed Moses Tabane from the Northern Province. 'There's an interim syllabus, but no interim textbook.'

'And even when we have to make do with the old textbooks, there are not enough to go around. I have about one textbook to every five students,' said a young teacher from a small village in the Free State.

'But teaching from a textbook is a major problem anyway,' commented Zach Mashilo. 'The textbook is one-sided, and doesn't show how complex history really is. We need to teach students about historical investigation and about different interpretations and explanations of events. We should throw the textbooks away,' he finished with a flourish.

Mrs Simango scoffed: 'Oh yes, and then where would you get your facts from? What exactly would you teach these children?'

Well, like the last speaker said, we could read up on issues, we could draw up interesting worksheets which challenge students to think differently about history,' Zach responded.

'Hmmph! It's all very well for these universities to talk about creative ideas, but they don't have to face our problems,' said Mrs Simango. 'We have a syllabus to cover. We have to teach all those facts to the children so that they can pass the exam. And we have to teach these children in very bad conditions – too many in one class, no books, not enough desks . . .'

From there the conversation became like a competition, with each teacher claiming to work in the very worst conditions.

Starting her presentation, Ziporah now faced these same teachers from the front of the hall.

'I, too, face the same problems as many of you. I teach Standard 7/Grade 9 History in a school which used to fall under the Department of Education and Training (DET). Resources are scarce. My fellow teachers are nervous about trying different methods even though many of the insensitive inspectors who terrorised them have retired. My school does not even have a proper school library where students and teachers can do extra research. The "library" is just a collection of novels that some teachers have brought from their homes. But I love history and I love teaching history. I did not want to be defeated by the conditions that I work under.'

'That's all very well for you to say, but what are we meant to do?' demanded Jane Ntsane.

'I think there are things we can do as teachers. That's what I want to talk about today. When I was teaching the "Anglo–Boer" War to my students, I became very aware of the silences in the textbooks.'

'Silences? What does that mean?' asked Moses.

'I mean the history that is not written in the textbook, the history that is hidden from us. Our history, the history of African people, is not there,' said Ziporah angrily. 'Where are the African people in the "Anglo–Boer War?" Was this a war between the Boers and British? This didn't fit in with the stories that I had heard when I was growing up. My grandmother used to tell me about my grandfather who had been forced to fight in the War. He was forced to enter the army. And then when he was in Pietersburg, his unit was defeated and my grandfather was taken to Bulawayo as a war captive. But in the school textbook, only the Boers' suffering was mentioned. I began to wonder how history could become so distorted.

'I grew up in "Maamuse"/Schweizer-Reneke, a small town in the far western Transvaal. On 7 August 1993, I remember hearing Eugene Terreblanche, the leader of the Afrikaner Weerstandsbeweging (AWB), making a speech on television. He and the AWB had just been given the freedom of the white section of Schweizer-Reneke. Terreblanche, addressing a full military parade of the AWB, claimed: "This land is ours by right of conquest!"'.

The audience muttered and looked angry.

'Yes, and then he went on to say, referring to Schweizer-Reneke: "This is where we ended and the third Boer War, another South African war, will start here again."'

'This got me thinking: was Schweizer-Reneke just the Boers' land, as Terreblanche had implied? There seemed to be more silences on the subject of **all** the people of "Maamusa"/Schweizer-Reneke. So I started doing some research on the matter. I began by reading what I could on the subject. Of course, the history of the pre-colonial settlement of the Tswana/Tlhaping and Kora/Korana in the area had received little or no attention in History textbooks!'

The audience nodded in agreement. The idea of silences was becoming clear to them.

'Two Afrikaans historians had recorded the history of Schweizer-Reneke, namely H. P. Maree and M. M. B. Liebenberg. These histories of Schweizer-Reneke provided a very white, Eurocentric view of events. In my view, they were only concerned with one section of the community of Schweizer-Reneke – the white population.'

'Well that's just typical!' exclaimed Jane angrily. 'I suppose these historians just forgot who ploughed their land, washed their clothes, cooked their meals and looked after their children!'

Ziporah smiled. 'No, they don't completely ignore the African inhabitants, but they use European standards to judge them. For example, Maree grades the Kora's level of intelligence according to his own Western ideas of intelligence. He suggests that the Kora's level of intelligence is higher than that of the Bushmen because:

They had the knowledge of trading with domestic animals, they could train their cattle to communicate with the supernatural powers, they could utilise their cattle for transporting their luggage when they were moving from one place to another. They were not barbaric, they had astronomical knowledge though it was full of superstitious belief...They did not live in huts but in four-squared houses of bricks, an indication that these houses were built by whites.

I think it becomes clear that when writing the local history of

'Maamusa'/Schweizer-Reneke, Maree and Liebenberg were concerned with the concept that "all that is white in form is best".'

'I imagine that this could explain why the history of the local inhabitants of the interior, like the Tswana, Sotho, Nguni, Venda and Tsonga, has received so little attention in the school history books,' said Zach.

Jane nodded. 'It's as if it's only 'real' history if it's white history. We have grown up with the idea that Africans have no history. The only time Africans enter the textbooks is when they interact with whites.'

'Yes, that does seem to be the case,' agreed Ziporah.

'Because Africans are not presented accurately in books, and history textbooks for that matter, it becomes important not to accept anything which is written as being the truth, as being what actually happened. You have to question it,' said Ziporah forcefully.

'But how do we question it?' asked Moses. 'Is it just a matter of not agreeing with it and therefore saying it's wrong? Where do we get the information from?'

'Yes, that can be a problem. Often we don't have the resources available. But perhaps a greater problem is that the history of the African people has not always been written down and so many historians have come to accept that history is only that which has been recorded in written form, but that's a narrow view. I believe that oral history can be useful to connect some of the information, to fill in the gaps and silences,' answered Ziporah.

'Oral history?' sneered Mrs Simango. 'That's not "real" history! Where are the facts? It's just about some old people's memories, it's just useless.'

Ziporah disagreed. 'I don't think that oral history is useless. Oral history gives us the voice of people whose stories were not written down. These perspectives can help us deal with the racist, sexist and other biases that are found in history.' 'Let me give you an example from my research on 'Maamusa'/Schweizer-Reneke, said Ziporah. In the official documents relating to the proclamation of the town, "Maamusa" is referred to as "Mamusa, die voorige Stad van Massouw". As a result, in all official accounts of the area, including the histories written by Maree and Liebenberg, "Maamusa" is referred to as "Mamusa".'

'Is the fact that the place is misspelled really an important issue?' asked a white teacher sitting in the audience.

'Yes, I think it is,' answer ed Ziporah. 'This is not just a spelling mistake. It has altered the *meaning* of the place. Maree also did not think there was anything wrong in naming a place "Mamusa". As a white historian, the name of the place and its meaning, was of little concern to him. According to Maree, he believes that the name 'Mamusa' comes from the sound made by the wind when blowing through the reeds–Maa–Moe–Saa! When pronounced quickly, it sounds like "Mamusa".'

'But when I interviewed a resident of "Maamusa", a Mr Michael Seiphemo, he had another story to tell. He said that the name "Maamusa" originated from the Tswana concept of *Ma* – mother – *amusa* – breastfeeds – who breastfeeds milk to her children. This naming implies that the Tswana/Tlhaping of "Maamusa" possessed abundant cattle milk to "breastfeed" the local community. Such a naming of the place suggests something about the Tswana/Tlhaping living in this community and how they regarded themselves. It tells us that they were a wealthy community – cattle being an important source of wealth. It also suggests that the original land belonged to the Tswana/Tlhaping. This is in itself interesting. When the trekkers arrived in the area, they chose to conduct their transactions with the Kora, ignoring the other local inhabitants. The Kora were made to pose as "landlords" over the affairs of the local tribes in this area. But the land belonged to the Tswana/Tlhaping.'

'But is the whole question of names and naming places, really important?' asked Moses.

'Yes, I believe it is,' answered Ziporah. 'Once you name something, you create a boundary around it. You define the place, person or event in your own terms. Thus it was convenient for the Boers to call "Maamusa" by a different name from the original. By doing this they were in a sense denying who the rightful owners of the land were and asserting their right to deal with the Tswana/Tlhaping.'

'During the "Anglo–Boer" War, Schweizer-Reneke was used as a battle forefront and communication centre by the Transvaal forces against the British forces. The local history accounts of the war in "Maamusa"/Schweizer-Reneke record only the plight of the Boers as they fought against the British. The Boer women and children from the area were confined in concentration camps and suffered terribly. Much has been made of the suffering of the Boers in the Anglo–Boer War in our history textbooks. But what of the Africans of "Maamusa"/Schweizer-Reneke? For example, what about the life of Sekwala Maine, who served as a wagon driver during the war? He suffered great losses. He lost his sheep, goats and ploughs and his family was driven out of the area by the British forces. Are his accounts of less importance than those of the white community who have been given wider coverage in South African school textbooks? If the history of people like Sekwala Maine had not been uncovered by the historian Charles van Onselen through the use of oral interviews, we would remain under the impression that the Anglo–Boer War involved only the British and the Boers. Perhaps it would be more appropriate to name this conflict between 1899 and 1902, the *South African War*. This would provide a far better idea of the War, implying that all South Africans, black and white, were involved or affected.'

'Mmm, I can see the value of oral history,' exclaimed Zach. 'But tell us, how did you conduct these interviews? Who did you speak to and how did you know what questions to ask?'

'It wasn't always as easy as I expected,' answered Ziporah. 'The very first person that I interviewed was a woman, Mrs Matloapane, who had been born in "Maamusa" in 1918. I thought that she would enjoy being asked about her past and would speak quite openly to me. I was wrong.'

'Why? What happened?' asked Jane.

'Well, she was incredibly suspicious of me. She said: "Why do you want this information. Do you want to put me in jail?" It was important to gain her trust before she would speak to me openly. I had to spend quite a long time reassuring her. Eventually I had to buy sweets to encourage her to talk to me. With the men it was worse. I had to take along brandy to loosen their tongues. Doing oral interviews turned out to be quite an expensive affair,' Ziporah laughed.

'But Mrs Matloapane is quite old. Surely you can't trust her memory of things?' asked Mrs Simango.

'I even interviewed a woman who was 94 years of age. And yes, memory can be a problem. But strangely enough, these old people had strong memories of the long age past; it was things that happened last week or yesterday that they seemed to struggle with. But it is important when conducting oral interviews to check the information gained from the interview, either from accounts in books or other informed people.'

'Ziporah, this has all been very interesting and exciting, but what are we meant to do with it? How are we meant to use your idea in our school teaching and the school syllabus?' asked Jane.

'Yes, this all seems a bit too personal. Is this really "history"?' asked Mrs Simango.

'I believe that there is a place for it,' answered Ziporah. 'Firstly, I believe that we should encourage our students to use oral history. By doing this, we can free them and ourselves from the tyranny of the textbook.'

'But in what context could we do this? And how do we justify this as "history?"' asked Zach.

'We could encourage our students to conduct a local study of their own community. In this way, students could uncover the hidden history of their parents and grandparents.'

'I still can't see how this is "history?"', complained Mrs Simango.

'Of course it is. In fact, through studying a local community, the students will become aware of the investigative approach in history. They will learn to be historians. They will have to collect evidence themselves, and choose and select evidence; they will have to justify their conclusions with reference to the evidence they have gathered. In this way they will learn how historians work. Also, by conducting a local study, you show students the possibility of uncovering some of the hidden history of this country.'

'But what about the syllabus?' asked Mrs Simango. 'How can we just abandon the syllabus and get our pupils to do local studies?'

'I think there are ways of doing this,' answered Ziporah firmly. 'Firstly, the new interim syllabus does not lay down exactly what we have to teach. There are spaces for us to be creative with the syllabus. And it's not as if the syllabus does not allow for any kind of local study at all. Look at the Standard 2/Grade 4 syllabus.'

'That's right,' said Moses. 'The Standard 2 syllabus allows pupils to do local studies of the family and so on.'

'Yes, but by placing this kind of activity in Standard 2, it implies that it is an activity for small children – you know, baby stuff!' exclaimed Zach.

'And of course, it is not only for small children!' exclaimed Ziporah. 'The study of local history is what historians do all the time. It is through collecting various local studies that historians can identify general trends and particular differences according to different localities. That is the stuff that history is made of! I believe that some form of local study should be included in every year of study at school.'

'I agree,' said Jane Ntsane. 'After all, it is local stories and events that make history interesting.'

'This may well be true,' said Mrs Simango, returning to her familiar theme, 'but I can't replace the syllabus with local history studies. My head of department just wouldn't hear of it.'

'I don't think the idea is to replace the syllabus with local studies. It is to enrich and supplement the syllabus with a local study here and there. In this way, we would make history more interesting as well as teaching our pupils to work as historians.'

Ziporah glanced at her watch. Her session was over. As the teachers filed out to tea, she could hear many of them discussing vigorously the ideas that had been raised in her talk.

CONCLUSION

The oral histories from 'Maamuse'/Schweizer-Reneke illustrate the potential that finding ways for rural people to reconstruct their local histories, their fragmented and distorted pasts, holds for enabling them to see themselves as partners in the construction of knowledge rather than as subjects of alien knowledge. In particular, the three women's stories demonstrate the rich and powerful storehouse of South Africa's past. The oral histories show how different individuals, and different groups will very often have different stories to tell about the past, and ones which speak to and against the silences of the written record, and counteract the view that only the written word can be regarded as an authentic source of information.

In the Human Research Science Council's report on the reconceptualisation of the curriculum, Kapp asserts that the approach to the past should be inclusive and democratic: it should explore the experiences of ordinary men and women as well as the experience of leaders and heroes and should deal with the political, social, economic, cultural and environmental dimensions of human experience.[11] Oral testimonies like those of 'Maamuse'/Schweizer-Reneke have the potential to impinge on the teaching methods for history in the way that Kapp outlines. As the History Teacher's Conference illustrates, this is a challenging task.

ENDNOTES

1. K. Asmal, Minister of Education, on Tuesday, July 1999, *Call to Action Mobilising Citizens to Build a South African Education and Training System for the 21st Century*, pp. 2–15.
2. A. Lecorddeur, 'The restructuring of South African history', *South African Historical Journal*, 17, November 1985, pp. 1–8.
3. Oral interview with 'ntate' Bantobetse Lehele, 26 August 1995.
4. Tribal court men on 27 July 1995.
5. Oral interviews with Mrs R. S. Matloapane, 15 July 1993 and August 1995; Mrs D. Lehihi, 21 July 1993 and August 1995; Mrs P. Makhobosi, 18 July 1995; Mrs M. Seiphemo, 20 July 1993. I revisited the site in 1995 when I started collecting data for the research on which this paper is based.
6. Van Onselen's summary of written accounts. C. van Onselen, 'Race and class in South African countryside: rural cultural osmosis and social relations in the sharecropping economy of the South-Western Transvaal, 1900–1950', *American Historical Review*, 95, 1, p. 103.
7. A. Holbrook, R. Barker and T. Truelove, ' Historical explorations of "Other" education' in *Old Boundaries and New Frontiers in Histories of Education, Proceedings of the ANZHES Conference, University of Newcastle, Australia, 1997*, pp. 56–67; Lecorddeur, 'Restructuring' pp. 1–8.

8. C. Castoriadis (ed. and trans. D. A. Curtis), *Word in Fragments: Writing on Politics, Society and Psychoanalysis, and the Imagination* (Stanford: Stanford University Press), pp. 36–7.
9. P, Kapp, *Ondersoek na die Onderwys van Geskiedenis in Sekondere Skole in Suid Afrika.* HSRC, 15 October 1990 (GRN).
10. R. Siebörger, *New History Textbooks for South Africa: Textbooks and the History Curriculum* (Swaziland: Macmillian Boleswa Manzini), p. 3.
11. Kapp, *Ondersoek.*

REFERENCES

Asmal, K. *Call to Action: Mobilizing Citizens to Build a South African Education and Training System for the 21st Century* (Pretoria: In Tirisano/Working Together, Department of Education, 1999).
Castoriadis, C. (ed. and trans. D. A. Curtis), *Word in Fragments: Writing on Politics, Society and Psychoanalysis, and the Imagination* (Stanford: Stanford University Press, 1997).
Holbrook, A. Barker and Truelove, T., 'Historical explorations of "Other" education', *Old Boundaries and New Frontiers in Histories of Education, Proceedings of the ANZHES Conference, University of Newcastle, Australia, 1997.*
Kapp, P. *Ondersoek na die Onderwys van Geskiedenis in Sekondere Skole in Suid Afrika.* HSRC, 15 October 1990 (GRN).
Lecorddeur, A. 'The restructuring of South African history', *South African Historical Journal,* 17, November (1985), pp. 1–8.
Onselen, C. van, 'Race and class in South African countryside: rural cultural osmosis and social relations in the sharecropping economy of the South-Western Transvaal, 1900–1950', *American Historical Review,* 95, 1 (1991), pp. 99–123.
Siebörger, R. *New History Textbooks for South Africa: Textbooks and the History Curriculum* (Swaziland: Macmillian Boleswa Manzini).

Bibliography

'A SCHOOLMASTER WHO IS ACTUALLY INTERESTED IN HIS WORK', letter, *The New Schoolsmaster (TNS)*, May (1921), p. 15.

Abrams, L. and Hunt, K. 'Borders and frontiers in women's history', *Women's History Review*, 9, 2 (2000), pp. 191–200.

Adolph Hitler. Bilder aus dem Leben der Führers (Hamburg/Bahrenfeld: Cigaretten-Bilderdienst, 1936).

Albisetti, J. C. 'Un-learned lessons from the New World? English views of American coeducation and women's colleges, c.1865–1910', in J. Goodman and J. Martin (eds), *Breaking Boundaries: Gender Politics and the Experience of Education, History of Education Special Edition*, 29, 5 (2000), pp. 473–90.

— *Schooling German Girls and Women. Secondary and Higher Education in the Nineteenth Century* (Princeton, NJ: Princeton University Press, 1988).

Allard, E. (ed.), *Door Duisternis Tot Licht: Gedachten over en voor het Javaanse volk van Raden Ajeng*, (Amsterdam: Nabrink, 1976).

Allebé, G. A. N. *De Ontwikkeling van het Kind naar Ligchaam en Geest. Eene Handleiding voor Moeders bij de Eerste Opvoeding* (Amsterdam: Mosmans, 1845).

Altman, D. 'On global queering', *Australian Humanities Review*, July (1996), http://www.lamp.ac.uk/ahr/archive/Issue-July-1996/altman. html, downloaded 18 January 2001.

Anderson, B. 'A time of darkness, a time of light' in B. Anderson (ed.) *Language and Power: Exploring Political Cultures in Indonesia* (Ithaca/London: Cornell University Press, 1991), pp. 241–70.

Annable, R. *Biographical Register: The Women's College within the University of Sydney, vol. 1 1892–1939* (Sydney: Council of the Women's College, 1995).

Anon., 'Conference report: first public session', *TNS*, May (1936), pp. 25–30.

— 'Judith Butler', http://www.theory.organisation.uk/ctr-butl.html, downloaded 18 January 2001.

— 'Napoleon and Teaching', *TNS*, July (1921), p. 15.

— 'On Theorising', *TNS*, October (1921), pp. 13–14.

— 'Pioneering for Peace', *TNS*, June (1931), p. 28.

— 'The Thirteenth Annual Conference at Coventry', *TNS*, May (1938), pp. 1–16.

— *In Grateful Remembrance AW Headmistress, supplement to Wycombe Abbey School Gazette July 1967* (Sussex: Dolphin Press, 1967)

Anstruther, I. *Oscar Browning, a Biography* (London: John Murray, 1983).

Anzaldua, G. *Borderlands/L Frontera: The New Mestiza* (San Fransciso, CA: Spinsters/Aunt Lute, 1987).

Apple, R. D. 'Constructing mothers: scientific motherhood in the nineteenth and twentieth centuries', *Social History of Medicine*, 8 (1995), pp. 161–78.

Association of Head Mistresses, Records 1899–1914 (Modern Records Centre, Warwick, Mss 188).

Asmal, K. *Call to Action Mobilizing Citizens to Build a South African Education and Training System for the 21st Century* (Pretoria: In Tirisano/Working Together, Department of Education, 1999).

Badinter, E. *L'amour en Plus. Histoire de L'amour Maternel* (XVIIe–XXe siècle) (Paris: Flammarion, 1980).

Bailey, M. 'A boys' school in Germany', *TNS*, June (1935), pp. 22–3.

Bain, P. *St. Swithun's. A Centenary History* (Chichester: Phillimore, 1984).

Baird, J. W. *To Die for Germany: Heroes in the Nazi Pantheon* (Bloomington: Indiana University Press, 1990).

Bakker, N. *Kind en Karakter. Nederlandse Pedagogen over Opvoeding in het Gezin, 1845–1925* (Amsterdam: Het Spinhuis, 1995).

— 'Opvoeden met de harde hand? Een historisch-kritische beschouwing van de neo-calvinistische opvoedingsmentaliteit 1880-1930', in G. Biesta, B. Levering and I. Weijers (eds), *Thema's uit de wijsgerige en historische pedagogiek* (Utrecht: SWP, 1998), pp. 79–85.

— 'Child-rearing literature and the reception of individual psychology in the Netherlands, 1930–1950: the case of a Calvinist pedagogue', *Paedagogica Historica. International Journal of the History of Education*, Special Series III (1998), pp. 583–602.

— 'Health and the medicalization of advice to parents in the Netherlands, ca. 1890-1950', in M. Gijswijt and H. Marland (eds), *Child Health and National Fitness in the Twentieth Century* (Amsterdam/Atlanta: Rodopi,

2001, forthcoming).

Barker, R. *Conscience, Government and War* (London: Routledge, 1982).

Barnard, N. 'Unions Unveil Wishlist', *Times Educational Supplement*, 18 August, (2000), p. 2.

Barry, K. *Susan B. Anthony: A Biography of a Singular Feminist* (New York: New York University Press, 1988).

Bavinck, H. *Bijbelsche en Religieuze Psychologie* (Kampen: Kok, 1920).

— *Het Christelijk Huisgezin* (Kampen: Kok, 1908).

Becker, A. 'The Avant-Garde, Madness and the Great War', *Journal of Contemporary History*, 35, 1 (2000), pp. 71–84.

Bellamy, J. and Saville, J. (eds), *The Dictionary of Labour Biography*, 6 (London: Macmillan, 1982).

Ben-Ghiar, R. 'Italian Fascism and the Aesthetics of the "Third Way"', *Journal of Contemporary History*, 31, 2 (1996), pp. 293–316.

Berry, N. O. *War and the Red Cross: The Unspoken Mission* (New York: St Martins Press, 1997).

Betts, R. S. 'The National Union of Teachers, the Educational Newspaper Company and the *Schoolmaster*, 1871–1909', *Journal of Educational Administration and History*, 2, 1 (1993), pp. 33–40.

— '"A New Type of Elementary Teacher": George Collins 1839–1891', *History of Education*, 27, 1 (1998), pp. 15–27.

— *Dr Macnamara 1861–1931* (Liverpool: Liverpool University Press, 1999).

Bhabha, H. 'The Third Space: interview with Homi Bhabha', in J. Rutherford (ed.), *Identity, Community, Culture, Difference* (London: Lawrence and Wishart, 1990), pp. 207–21.

Bilder deutscher Geschichte Reemtsma No. 12 (Hamburg-Bahrenfeld: Cigaretten-Bilderdienst, 1936).

Blair, M., Holland, J. and Sheldon, S. (eds), *Identity and Diversity – Gender and the Experience of Education: A Reader* (Clevedon: Multilingual Matters/The Open University Press, 1995).

Bokel, F. '"Great Days" in Germany: Third Reich Celebrities as Mediators between Government and People', Unpublished PhD thesis, University of Texas, Austin, 1995.

Booth, M. letter, *TNS*, January, (1939), p. 12.

Bosanquet, N. 'From Bermondsey to Canary Wharf: the social context of change in industrial relations, 1800–2000', *British Journal of Industrial Relations*, 31, 2 (1992), pp. 237–53.

Bourke, J. *Dismembering the Male: Men's Bodies, Britain and the Great War* (London: Reaktion Books, 1996).

— *An Intimate History of Killing: Face-to-Face Killing in Twentieth-*

Century Warfare (London: Granta Books, 1999).

Bourne, J. 'The British working man in arms', in H. Cecil and P. H. Liddle (eds), *Facing Armageddon: The First World War Experienced* (London: Leo Cooper, 1996), pp. 336–52.

Bowen, J. *A History of Western Education*, vol. III, (London: Methuen, 1980), p. 481.

Bowerman, E. *Stands There a School: Memories of Dame Frances Dove* (Sussex: Dolphin Press, nd).

Bradley, H. *Men's Work, Women's Work: A Sociological History of the Sexual Division of Labour in Employment* (Cambridge: Polity Press, 1989).

Brah, A. *Cartographies of Diaspora: Contesting Identities* (London: Routledge, 1996).

Brewer, J. D. 'The British Union of Fascists: some tentative conclusions on its membership', in S. Ugelvik Larsen, B. Hagtvet and J. P. Myklebust (eds), *Who Were the Fascists? Social Roots of European Fascism* (Bergen: Universitetsforlagen, 1980), pp. 542–56.

Briggs, A. and Macartney, A. *Toynbee Hall: The First Hundred Years* (London: Routledge and Kegan Paul, 1984).

Britzman, D. P. *Lost Subjects, Contested Objects* (Albany, NY: State University of New York Press, 1998).

Brown, W. J. 'Open-air recovery schools'. Reprinted from *The Millgate*, in *Comradeship and Wheatsheaf*, December 1913.

Browning, O. 'On Science Teaching in Schools,' *The Chemical News*, v. 17 (1868), pp. 243–4. British Library Science Division (P)J00-E(9).

— *Introduction to the History of Educational Theories* (London: K. Paul, Trench and Company, 1881).

— 'Arnold and Arnoldism' *Education*, 1, (1890), pp. 309–10. British Library Manuscripts, p. p. 1187.id.

— *Memories of Sixty Years at Eton, Cambridge and Elsewhere* (London: John Lane, The Bodley Head, 1910; New York: John Lane Company, 1910).

— Unpublished Letter, 1918, Berg Collection, New York City Public Library, Main Branch.

— 'The Importance of the Training of Teachers', (1906), pp. 1–15. Cam.d.906.13 Cambridge University Library, England.

Bruce, S. *No Pope of Rome: Militant Protestantism in Modern Scotland* (Edinburgh: Mainstream, 1985).

Bulhof, I. N. 'The Netherlands', in T. F. Glick (ed.), *A Comparative Analysis of the Reception of Darwinism* (Austin, TX: University of Texas, 1974).

Bullock, A. and Trombley, S. (eds), *The New Fontana Dictionary of Modern Thought* (London: Collins, 1999).

Burstall, S. *Retrospect and Prospect: Sixty Years of Women's Education* (London: Longman's Green and Co, 1933).

Burton, A. *Burdens of History. British Feminists, Indian Women and Imperial Culture 1865–1915* (Chapel Hill, NC: University of North Carolina Press, 1994).

Bush, J. *Edwardian Ladies and Imperial Power* (Leicester: Leicester University Press, 2000).

Butler, J. *Gender Trouble: Feminism and the Subversion of Identity* (New York: Routledge, 1990).

Butler, J. T. and McMorran, H. L. *Girton College Register, 1869–1946* (Cambridge: privately printed for Girton College, 1948).

Calcar, E. van *Onze ontwikkeling of de magt der eerste indrukken* (Amsterdam: Van Gelder, 1861–2), 6 vols.

— *Het Jonge Leven. Hoe het te Kweeken en te Beschermen. Een Boek voor Ouders en Opvoeders* ('s-Gravenhage: IJkema, 1905).

Calder, A. 'Miss Brodie and the Kaledonian Klan' in A. Calder (ed.), *Revolving Culture: Notes from the Scottish Republic* (London: I. B. Taurus, 1994), pp. 152–5

Card, T. *Eton Renewed, A History from 1860 to the Present Day* (London: John Murray Ltd, 1994).

Casey, K. *I Answer with my Life: Life Histories of Women Teachers Working for Social Change* (London: Routledge, 1993).

Castoriadis, C. (ed. and trans. D. A. Curtis), *Word in Fragments: Writing on Politics, Society and Psychoanalysis, and the Imagination* (Stanford, CA: Stanford University Press, 1997).

Central Labour College Minutes 1909–1918 (Trades Union Congress library collections, University of North London).

Chatterjee, P. *The Nation and its Fragments: Colonial and Postcolonial Histories*, (Princeton, NJ: Princeton University Press, 1993).

— 'Women and the Nation', in P. Chatterjee, *The Nation and its Fragments: Colonial and Postcolonial Histories* (Princeton, NJ: Princeton University Press, 1993).

Ciolina, E. and Ciolina, E. *Garantirt Aecht. Das Reklamesammelbild als Spiegel der Zeit* (München: Edition Wissen and Literatur, 1987).

Colonial Intelligence League, *Annual Reports*, 1910–1914 (National Library of Women).

— County Organisation Sub-Committee, Minutes (no year)

— Minutes, 1910–1914.

Cook, C. 'A Fascist memory: Oswald Mosley and the myth of the airman', *European Review of History*, 4, 2 (1997), pp. 147–61.

Coolsma, C. W. *Jean Paul's Levana* (Groningen/Den Haag: Wolters, 1919).

241

Copelman, D. *London's Women Teachers: Gender, Class and Feminism, 1870–1930*, (London: Routledge, 1996)

Cory, W. J. *Ionica* (London: George Allen, 1891).

—*Hints for Eton Masters* (London: Henry Frowde Oxford University Press Warehouse Amen Corner E. C., 1898); British Library 8304.bbb.4 ff. 1–7.

Coté J. (ed. and trans.), *Letters from Kartini, Indonesian Feminist, 1900–1904*, (Clayton: Hyland House/Monash University, 1992).

— *On Feminism and Nationalism: Kartini's Letters to Stella Zeehandelaar* (Clayton: Monash Asia Institute,1995).

— 'The correspondence of Kartini's sisters, annotations on the Indonesian Nationalist Movement 1905–1925, *Archipel*, 55, 1998, pp. 61–82.

— 'Celebrating women's labour: Raden Ajeng Kartini and the Dutch Women's Exhibition, 1898' in M. Grever and F. Dieteren (eds), *Een Vaderland voor Vrouwen/A Fatherland for Women* (Amsterdam: IISG/VVG, 2000), pp. 119–35.

— 'Kartini: A personal memoir', *Journal of the Australia–Indonesia Association* (1994), pp. 16–22.

Cott, N. *The Bonds of Womanhood. 'Woman's Sphere' in New England, 1780–1835* (New Haven/London: Yale University Press, 1977).

Cotton Factory Times, 1913, 1915, 1916.

Craik, W. W. *The Central Labour College* (London: Lawrence and Wishart, 1964).

Croall, J. *Neill of Summerhill: The Permanent Rebel* (London: Routledge and Kegan Paul, 1983).

Cronin, M. 'The Blueshirt Movement, 1932–5: Ireland's Fascists?', *Journal of Contemporary History*, 30, 2 (1999), pp. 311–32.

Crouzet, F. *The Victorian Economy* (trans. A. Forster) (New York: Columbia University Press, 1982).

Cullen, S. M. 'Political violence: the case of the British Union of Fascists', *Journal of Contemporary History*, 28, 2 (1993), pp. 245–67.

Cunningham, P. 'Innovators, networks and structures towards a prosopography of progressivism', in J. Goodman and J. Martin (eds), *Reforming Lives? Progressivism, Leadership and Educational Change, History of Education*, Special Edition, 30, 5 (2001), pp. 33–52.

Curti, M. and Carstensen, V. *The University of Wisconsin: A History, 1848–1925* (2 vols.) (Madison, WI: University of Wisconsin Press, 1949).

Darke, M. 'The NUT and the Equal Pay Campaign', *Education Review*, 6, 1 (1992), pp. 23–7.

Das deutsche Heer im Manöver: Eine Bildfolge vom Wirken unseres Heeres

(Dresden-A: Cigaretten-Bilderdienst, 1936).

de Grazia, V. *How Fascism Ruled Women: Italy, 1922–1945* (Berkeley, CA: University of California Press, 1992).

De Lauretis, T. (ed.) *Feminist Studies/Critical Studies* (Bloomington, IN: Indiana University Press, 1986).

Demos, J. *Past, Present and Personal. The Family and the Life Course in American History* (Oxford: Oxford University Press, 1986).

Depaepe, M. *Zum Wohl des Kindes? Pädologie, Pädagogische Psychologie und Experimentelle Pädagogik in Europa und den U.S.A., 1890–1940* (Weinheim/Leuven: Deutscher Studien Verlag/Leuven University Press, 1993).

Der Staat der Arbeit und des Friedens: Ein Jahr Regierung Adolf Hitler (Altona/Bahrenfeld: Cigaretten-Bilderdienst, 1934).

Deutsche Arbeit (Hamburg: GEG, 1934).

Deutsche Kulturbilder: Deutsches Leben in 5 Jahrhunderten 1400–1900 (Altona: Cigaretten-Bilderdienst,1936).

Deutsche Uniformen Band 2. Das Zeitalter der deutschen Einigung. Album IV: Die Zeit von 1870 bis 1888 (Dresden: Sturm-Zigaretten, 1933).

Deutschland erwacht. Werden, Kampf und Sieg der NSDAP, Reemtsma Nr. 8, (Hamburg/Bahrenfeld: Cigaretten-Bilderdienst, 1933).

Die deutsche Wehrmacht (Dresden: Cigaretten-Bilderdienst, 1936).

Die Großen der Weltgeschichte (Dresden: Eckstein-Halpaus, 1934).

Die Nachkriegszeit: Historische Bilddokumente 1918–1934 (Dresden: Eckstein-Halpaus,1935).

Die Reichswehr (Dresden: Haus Neuerburg/Waldorff-Astoria/Eckstein-Halpaus, 1933).

Doan, E. N. *The LaFollettes and the Wisconsin Idea* (New York: Rinehart, 1947).

Douma, H. *Opvoeding in het huisgezin* (Loosdrecht: Van Haselen, 1891).

Drenth, A. van and de Haan, F. *The Rise of Caring Power. Elizabeth Fry and Josephine Butler in Britain and the Netherlands* (Amsterdam: Amsterdam University Press, 1999).

Durham, M. *Women and Fascism* (London: Routledge, 1998).

Edwards, E. 'Women principals, 1900–1960: gender and power', *History of Education*, 29, 5 (2000), pp. 405–15.

Edwards, E. *Women in Teacher Training Colleges, 1900–1960: A Culture of Femininity* (London: Routledge, 2001).

Egan, D. '"A cult of their own": syndicalism, and The Miners' Next Step', in A. Campbell, N. Fishman, and D. Howell (eds), *Miners, Unions and Politics, 1910–1947* (Aldershot: Scolar Press, 1996), pp. 13–33.

Eisenmann, L. 'Creating a framework for interpreting US women's educational history: lessons from historical lexicography', in J. Martin and J. Goodman (eds), *Reforming Lives? Progressivism, Leadership and Educational Change History of Education*, 30, 5 (2001), pp. 453–70.

Eksteins, M. *Rites of Spring: The Great War and the Birth of the Modern Age* (London: Black Swan, 1990).

Elder, G. H. 'Appearance and education in marriage mobility', *American Sociological Review*, 34 (1969), pp. 519–33.

Erben, M. (ed.) *Biography and Education: A Reader* (London: Falmer, 1998)

Escott, H. F. 'This Education Business in Progressive Japan', *TNS*, July (1934), pp. 17–18.

Ferguson, N. *The Pity of War* (Harmondsworth: Penguin, 1998).

Fieldhouse, R. 'The 1908 Report: antidote to class struggle?' in G. Andrews, H. Kean and J. Thompson (eds), *Ruskin College, Contesting Knowledge, Dissenting Politics* (London: Lawrence and Wishart, 1999), pp. 35–57.

Forster, E. M. *Maurice* (New York: W. W. Norton and Company, 1971).

Fromm E. *The Erich Fromm Reader*, R. Funk (ed.), (New Jersey: Humanities Press, 1994).

Frow, E. and Frow, R. 'The spark of independent working-class education: Lancashire, 1909-1930' in B. Simon (ed.) *The Search for Enlightenment: the Working Class and Adult Education in the Twentieth Century* (London: Lawrence and Wishart, 1990), pp. 71-104.

Gallacher, W. *Revolt on the Clyde* (London: Lawrence and Wishart, 1980).

Gardner, P. 'Reconstructing the Classroom Teacher, 1903–1945', in I. Grosvenor, M. Lawn and K. Rousmaniere (eds), *Silences and Images: The Social History of the Classroom* (New York: Peter Lang, 1999), pp. 123–44.

Gaus, D. 'Bildende Geselligkeit. Untersuchungen geselliger Vergesellschaftung am Beispiel der Berliner Salons um 1800', *Jahrbuch für Historische Bildungsforschung*, 4 (1998), pp. 165–208.

Geertz, H. 'Introduction', *Letters of a Javanese Princess* (trans. A. L. Symmers 1920), (New York: Norton, 1964).

'Getting Gray', letter, *TNS*, May (1921), p.14.

Gilbert R. and Gilbert, P. *Masculinity Goes to School* (London: Routledge, 1998).

Giles, G. J. 'Die erzieherische Rolle von Sammelbildern in politischen Umbruchszeiten', in D. Papenfuß and W. Schieder (eds), *Deutsche Umbrüche im 20. Jahrhundert* (Köln/Weimar/Wien: Böhlau, 2000), pp. 241–65.

— 'Popular education and the new media: the cigarette card in Germany', in M. Depaepe and B. Henkens (eds), *The Challenge of the Visual in the History of Education*. Paedagogica Historica, Supplementary Series,

Volume VI (Gent: Paedagogica Historica, 2000), pp. 449–69.

Gilmour, D. *Curzon* (London: John Murray Ltd, 1995).

Gilroy, P. 'Route Work: the Black Atlantic and the politics of exile', in I. Chambers and L. Curtin (eds), *The Post-Colonial Question: Common Skies, Divided Horizons* (London: Routledge, 1996), pp. 17–29.

Gleadle, K. and Richardson, S. (eds), *Women in British Politics, 1760–1918: the Power of the Petticoat* (London: Macmillan, 2000).

Glover D. and Kaplan, C. *Genders* (London: Routledge, 2000).

Glover, J. *Humanity: A Moral History of the Twentieth Century* (London: Jonathan Cape, 1999).

Goldman, L. 'Intellectuals and the English working class 1870–1945: the case of adult education', *History of Education*, 29, 4 (1999), pp. 281–300.

Gooch, J. W. *Transplanting Extension: A New Look at the 'Wisconsin Idea'* (Madison, WI: Office of Outreach Development and Extension Liaison, 1995).

Goodman, J. 'Undermining or building up the nation? Elizabeth Hamilton (1758–1816), national identities and an authoritative role for women educationists', in G. McCulloch and R. Lowe (eds), *Education and National Identity, History of Education*, Special Edition, 28, 3 (1998) pp. 279–297.

— and Harrop, S. 'Governing ladies: women governors of middle-class girls' schools, 1870–1925', in J. Goodman and S. Harrop (eds), *Women, Educational Policy-Making and Administration in England: Authoritative Women Since 1800* (London: Routledge, 2000), pp. 37–55.

— and — '"Within marked boundaries": women and the making of educational policy since 1800', in J. Goodman and S. Harrop (eds), *Women, Educational Policy-Making and Administration in England: Authoritative Women Since 1800* (London: Routledge, 2000), pp. 1–13.

— and Martin, J. (eds) *Breaking Boundaries: Gender Politics and the Experience of Education, History of Education*, 29, 5 (2000).

Gordon, L. D. *Gender and Higher Education in the Progressive Era* (New Haven/London: Yale University Press, 1990).

Grant , J. *Raising Baby by the Book: The Education of American Mothers* (New Haven/London: Yale University Press, 1998).

Graves, P. *Labour Women. Women in British Working-Class Politics, 1918–1939* (Cambridge: Cambridge University Press, 1996).

Greven, P. *The Protestant Temperament. Patterns of Child-rearing, Religious Experience, and the Self in Early America* (New York: Knopf, 1977).

— *Spare the Child. The Religious Roots of Punishment and the Psychological Impact of Physical Abuse* (New York: Vintage Books, 1992).

Grewal, I. *Home and Harem: Nation, Gender Empire and the Cultures of Travel* (Leicester: Leicester University Press, 1996).

Griffin, R. *The Nature of Fascism* (London: Routledge, 1994).

Griffiths, R. *Fellow Travellers of the Right: British Enthusiasts for Nazi Germany, 1933–1939* (London: Constable, 1980).

Griggs, C. 'The National Union of Teachers in the Eastbourne area 1874–1916: a tale of tact and pragmatism', *History of Education*, 20, 4 (1991) pp. 235–340.

Griggs, C. *The Trades Union Congress and the Struggle for Education 1968–1925* (Lewes: Falmer Press, 1983).

Grimshaw, M. E. *Newnham College Register, 1871–1971* (Cambridge, privately printed for Newnham College, 1979).

Groeneboer, K. *Weg Naar het Westen: Het Nederlands voor Indë, 1600–1950* (Leiden: KITLV Press, 1993).

Groenendijk, L. F. *De Nadere Reformatie van het Gezin. De Visie van Petrus Wittewrongel op de Christelijke Huishouding* (Dordrecht: Van den Tol, 1984).

Grosvenor, I. '"There's no place like home": education and the making of national identity', *History of Education*, 28, 3 (1998), pp. 237–50.

Grundy, T. *Memoir of a Fascist Childhood: A Boy in Mosley's Britain* (London: Heinemann, 1998).

Gunning J. H. Wzn., 'De rechten van het kind', *Het Kind*, 6 (1905), pp. 66–8, 73–5, 81–3, 91–3, 101–2.

— 'Iets over godsdienstonderwijs', *Het Kind*, 5 (1904), pp. 58–9.

Hall, C. 'Histories, empires and the post-colonial moment', in I. Chambers and L. Curti (eds), *The Post-Colonial Question: Common Skies, Divided Horizons* (London: Routledge, 1996), pp. 65–77.

— 'Missionary stories: gender and ethnicity in England in the 1830s and 1840s', in C. Hall, *White Male and Middle Class: Explorations in Feminism and History* (London: Polity, 1996), pp. 205–51.

— 'Introduction: thinking the postcolonial, thinking the empire', in C. Hall, (ed.) *Cultures of Empire: Colonizers in Britain and the Empire in the Nineteenth and Twentieth Centuries. A Reader* (Manchester: Manchester University Press, 2000), pp. 1–33.

— 'The rule of difference: gender, class and empire in the making of the 1832 Reform Act', in I. Blom, K. Hagerman and C. Hall (eds), *Gendered Nations: Nationalisms and Gender Order in the Long Nineteenth Century* (Oxford: Berg, 2000), pp. 107–36.

Hall, L. A. 'Impotent ghosts from no man's land: flappers' boyfriends, or crypto-patriarchs? Men, sex and social change in 1920s Britain', *Social History*, 21, 1 (1996), pp. 54–70.

Hall, S. 'Cultural identity and diaspora', in J. Rutherford (ed.), *Identity, Community, Culture, Difference* (London: Lawrence and Wishart).

— 'New ethnicities', in J. Donald and A. Rattansi (eds), *'Race, Culture and Difference* (Milton Keynes: Open University Press, 1992), pp. 252–9.

Hamilton, I. W. 'Education for revolution. The Plebs League and Labour College Movement 1908–1921, Unpublished MA thesis, University of Warwick.

Hannam, J. and Hunt, K. 'Gendering the stories of socialism: an essay in historical criticism' in M. Walsh (ed.), *Working Out Gender. Perspectives from Labour History* (Aldershot: Ashgate, 2000), pp. 102–118.

Hardyment, C. *Dream Babies. Child Care from Locke to Spock* (Oxford: Oxford University Press, 1984).

Harris, J. 'Political thought and the welfare state 1870–1940: an intellectual framework for British educational thought and practice', *Past and Present*, 135 (1992), pp. 116–41.

Hausen, K. 'Die Polarisierung der "Geschlechtskaraktere". Eine Spiegelung der Dissoziation von Erwerbs- und Familienleben', in W. Conze (ed.), *Sozialgeschichte der Familie in der Neuzeit Europas* (Stuttgart: Klett, 1976), pp. 363–93.

Hendrick, H. *Images of Youth: Age, Class and the Male Youth Problem, 1880–1920* (Oxford: Clarendon, 1990).

Herbart, J. F. *The Science of Education* (Preface by Oscar Browning) (Boston, MA: D. C. Heath and Co., Publishers, 1900).

Herzstein, R. E. *When Nazi Dreams Come True* (London: Abacus, 1982).

Heward, C. *Making a Man of Him: Parents and their Sons' Education at an English Public School, 1929–1950* (London: Routledge, 1988).

Heymans, G. *Psychologie der Vrouwen* (Amsterdam: Maatschappij voor Goede en Goedkoope Lectuur, 1911) orig. edited in German in 1910.

Hickman, M. 'Constructing the nation, segregating the Irish: the education of Irish Catholics in nineteenth-century Britain', *Aspects of Education*, 54 (1997), pp. 33–54

— *Religion, Class and Identity: the State, the Catholic Church and the Education of the Irish in Britain* (Aldershot: Avebury, 1995)

Hickson, A. *The Poisoned Bowl. Sex Repression and the Public School System* (London: Constable and Company Limited, 1995).

Higonnet, M. R., Jenson, J., Michel, S. and Collins Weitz, M. (eds), *Behind the Lines: Gender and the Two World Wars* (New Haven/London: Yale University Press, 1987).

'HM', 'Conference Viewed by the New Member', *The New Schoolmaster*, May, (1924), pp. 28–30.

Holbrook, A., Barker, R. and Truelove, T. 'Historical explorations of "Other" education', in *Old Boundaries and New Frontiers in Histories of Education, Proceedings of the ANZHES Conference*, University of Newcastle, Australia, 1997.

Holden, K. 'Formations of discipline and manliness: culture, politics and 1930s women's writing', *Journal of Gender Studies*, 8, 2 (1999), pp. 141–57.

Hollis, C. *Eton, A History* (London: Hollis and Carter, 1960).

Horowitz, H. L. *Alma Mater: Design and Experience in the Women's Colleges from their Nineteenth-Century Beginnings to the 1930s* (Amherst, MA: University of Massachusetts Press, 1993).

Howson, J. 'Men Fail to Get Places', *Times Educational Supplement*, 22 September (2000), p. 23.

Humphries, S. and Gordon, P. *A Man's World: from Boyhood to Manhood 1900–1960* (London: BBC Books, 1996).

— and —*Forbidden Britain: Our Secret Past 1900–1960* (London: BBC Books, 1994)

Hunt, F. *Gender and Policy in English Education, 1902–1944* (London: Harvester Wheatsheaf, 1991).

Jackson, L. A. *Child Sexual Abuse in Victorian England* (London: Routledge, 2000).

Jagose, A. 'Queer theory', *Australian Humanities Review*, December 1996, http://www.lamp.ac.uk/ahr/archive/Issue-Dec-1996/jagose. html, downloaded 18 January 2001.

Jansz, U. *Denken over Sekse. De Eerste Feministische Golf* (Amsterdam: Sara/Van Gennep, 1990).

Jaquet, F. G. P. *Kartini: Brieven aan Rosa Abdendanon – Mandri en Haar Echtgenoot* (Leiden: KITLV Press, 1987).

Jenkyns, R. *The Victorians and Ancient Greece* (Cambridge, MA: Harvard University Press, 1980).

Jennings, B. *Knowledge is Power. A Short History of the W.E.A. 1903–78* (Hull: University of Hull Department of Adult Education, Newland Papers Number One, 1979).

Johnson, M. *Failing School, Failing City: The Reality of Inner City Education* (Charlbury: Jon Carpenter, 1999).

Johnson, R. '"Really useful knowledge": radical education and working-class culture, 1790–1848' in R. Dale, G. Esland, Ferguson and N. MacDonald (eds), *Politics, Patriarchy and Practice* (Lewes: Falmer Press, 1981), pp. 3–19.

— *The State and the Politics of Education*, Unit 1 E353, Society, Education and the State (Milton Keynes: Open University Press, 1981).

Johnson V. and Jensen, H. *A History of Diocesan High School for Girls*

Auckland 1903–1953 (Auckland: Whitcombe and Tombs Ltd., 1953).

Jonge, J. A. de *De Industrialisatie van Nederland tussen 1850 en 1914* (Nijmegen: SUN, 1976).

Justice, 1904, 1909.

Kamenetsky, C. *Children's Literature in Hitler's Germany: The Cultural Policy of National Socialism* (Athens, OH/London: Ohio University Press, 1984).

Kampf um's Dritte Reich: Eine historische Bilderfolge (Altona/Bahrenfeld: Cigaretten-Bilderdienst, 1933).

Kaplan C. and Grewal I. 'Transnational feminist cultural studies: beyond the marxism/poststructuralism/feminism divides', *positions*, Fall (1994), pp. 430–45.

Kapp, P. *Ondersoek na die Onderwys van Geskiedenis in Sekondere Skole in Suid Afrika*, HSRC, 15 October 1990 (GRN).

Kean, H. *Challenging the State?* (Lewes: Falmer Press, 1990).

— and Oram, A. '"Men must be educated and women must do it": The National Federation (later Union) of Women Teachers and contemporary feminism, 1910–1930', *Gender and Education*, 2, 2 (1990), pp. 147–67.

Kelly, L., Burton, S. and Regan, L. 'Researching women's lives or studying women's oppression? Reflections on what constitutes feminist research', in M. Maynard and J. Purvis (eds), *Researching Women's Lives from a Feminist Perspective* (London: Taylor and Francis, 1994), pp. 27–48.

Kenney, R. 'Education for the workers', *New Age*, 26 March 1914.

Kerber, L. K. 'The Republican mother: women and the enlightenment: an American perspective,' *American Quarterly* 28 (1976), pp. 187–205.

— *No Constitutional Right to be Ladies: Women and the Obligations of Citizenship* (New York: Hill and Wang, 1998).

Khan, Y. 'Schooling Japan's imperial subjects in the early Shôwa period', *History of Education*, 29, 2 (2000), pp. 213–23.

Kind, Het. Veertiendaagsch Blad voor Ouders en Opvoeders, 3 (1902)–27 (1926), first printed under the title *Maatschappelijk Werk, Afdeeling B* 1 (1900) – 2 (1901).

King, S. 'Feminists in teaching: the National Union of Women Teachers, 1920–1945', in M. Lawn and G. Grace (eds), *Teachers: The Culture and Politics of Work* (Lewes: Falmer Press, 1987).

Koch, H. W. *The Hitler Youth: Origins and Development 1922–1945* (New York: Barnes and Noble, 1996).

Kooistra, I. *Zedelijke Opvoeding* (Groningen: Wolters, 1894).

— *Opvoeder en kind. Paedagogische Voordrachten en Schetsen* (Amsterdam: Van Kampen, 1916).

— *Onze Groote Kinderen* (Amsterdam: Van Kampen, 1918–19), 2 vols.

249

Kosambi, M. 'A window in the prison house: women's education and the politics of social reform in nineteenth-century Western India', *History of Education*, 29, 5 (2000), pp. 429–43.

Kruithof, B. 'Continuïteit in opvoedingsadviezen in protestants Nederland van de 17e tot de 19e eeuw', *Amsterdams Sociologisch Tijdschrift*, 9 (1982), pp. 476–92.

Kuyper, A. *Antirevolutionair óók in uw huisgezin* (Amsterdam: Kruyt, 1880).

LaRossa, R. *The Modernization of Fatherhood. A Social and Political History* (Chicago/London: University of Chicago Press, 1997).

Lecorddeur, A. 'The restructuring of South African history', *South African Historical Journal*, 17, November 1985, pp. 1–8.

Ledger, S. and McCracken, S. (eds), *Cultural Politics at the Fin-de-Siècle* (Cambridge: Cambridge University Press, 1995).

Lewis, D. S. *Illusions of Grandeur: Mosley, Fascism and British Society, 1931–1981* (Manchester: Manchester University Press, 1987).

Lijphart, A. *The Politics of Accommodation. Pluralism and Democracy in the Netherlands* (Berkeley, CA: University of California Press, 1968).

Limond, D. '"Only Talk in the Staffroom": "subversive" teaching in a Scottish School, 1939–1940', *History of Education*, 29, 3 (2000), pp. 239–52.

Lister, R. *Citizenship: Feminist Perspectives* (New York: New York University Press, 1997).

Littlewood, M. 'Makers of men', *Trouble and Strife*, 5 (1985), pp. 23–9.

Livingstone, G. 'Teachers' professional organisations', in T. G. K. Bryce and W. M. Humes (eds), *Scottish Education* (Edinburgh: Edinburgh University Press, 1999), pp. 978–82.

London Trades Council, Minute Books 1899–1928 (Trades Union Congress library collections, University of North London).

Macey, D. 'Michel Foucault: J'Accuse', *New Formations*, 25 (1995), pp. 5–13.

Macintyre, S. *A Proletarian Science. Marxism in Britain, 1917–1933* (London: Lawrence and Wishart, 1980).

Mackenzie, F. C. *William Cory, a Biography* (London: Constable, 1950).

MacKinnon, A. *Love and Freedom: Professional Women and the Reshaping of Personal Life* (Cambridge: Cambridge University Press, 1997).

MacKinnon, A. and Morris Matthews, K. 'Colonized and colonizers: early Australian graduate women at home and abroad', Unpublished paper, ISCHE Conference, Education and Ethnicity, Sydney, 1999.

Magnus L. *The Jubilee Book of the GPDST 1873–1923* (Cambridge: Cambridge University Press, 1923).

Mahood, L. *Policing Gender, Class and Family: Britain 1850–1940* (London: UCL Press, 1995).

Manen, M. van, *Researching Lived Experience: Human Science for an Action Sensitive Pedagogy* (Albany, NY: The State University of New York Press, 1990).

Mangan, J. A. *The Games Ethic and Imperialism – Aspects of the Diffusion of an Idea* (Harmondsworth: Viking, 1985).

— and Walvin, J. *Manliness and Morality – Middle Class Masculinity in Britain and America 1800–1940* (Manchester: Manchester University Press, 1987).

— (ed.) *The Cultural Bond: Sport, Empire and Society* (London: Frank Cass, 1992).

Mani, L. *Contentious Traditions: the Debate on Sati in Colonial India* (Berkeley, CA: University of California Press, 1998).

Männer und Ereignisse unserer Zeit (Dresden: Bilderstelle Lohse, 1934).

Mansbridge, A. *An Adventure in Working-Class Education* (London: Longmans, Green and Co., 1920).

— *The Trodden Road* (London: J. M. Dent, 1940).

'To "Dear Sir"', 20 April 1910.

Mansell, W. 'More Male Teachers Needed to Help Boys', *Times Educational Supplement*, 1 September (2000), p. 9.

Marcus, J. Book Review of *Oscar Browning: A Biography* by Ian Anstruther. *Victorian Studies*. 28, 3 (Spring 1985), pp. 556–8.

— 'Taking the bull by the udders: sexual difference in Virginia Woolf: a conspiracy theory', in J. Marcus (ed.), *Virginia Woolf and the Languages of Patriarchy* (Bloomington/Indianapolis, IN: Indiana University Press, 1987), pp. 136–62.

Marcus, L. *Auto/biographical Discourses: Theory, Criticism and Practice* (Manchester: Manchester University Press, 1994).

Martin, J. *Women and the Politics of Schooling in Victorian and Edwardian England* (London: Leicester University Press, 1999).

— 'An "Awful Woman?" The life and work of Mrs Bridges Adams, 1855–1939', *Women's History Review*, 8, 1 (1999), pp. 139–61.

— '"Women not wanted" the fight to secure political representation on Local Education Authorities, 1870–1907', in J. Goodman and S. Harrop (eds), *Women, Educational Policy-Making and Administration in England: Authoritative Women Since 1800* (London: Routledge, 2000), pp. 78–96.

— '"Working for the people"? Mrs Bridges Adams and the London School Board, 1897-1904', *History of Education*, 29, 1 (2000), pp. 49–62.

Maynard, M. and Purvis, J. (eds), *New Frontiers in Women's Studies: Knowledge, Identity and Nationalism*, (London: UCL Press, 1996).

Mayall, L. A. E. Nym, Levine, P. and Fletcher, E. C. 'Introduction', in E. C. Fletcher, L. A. E. Nym Mayall and P. Levine (eds), *Women's Suffrage in the British Empire: Citizenship, Nation and Race* (London: Routledge, 2000).

McCann, W. P. 'Trade unionist, co-operative and socialist organisations in relation to popular education, 1870-1902', Unpublished PhD thesis, University of Manchester, 1960.

Meacham, S. *Toynbee Hall and Social Reform 1880–1914* (London: Yale University Press, 1987).

Mertz, T. J. '"A Peculiar Public Matter": school politics, policy and Wisconsin women, 1885-1921.' Paper presented at the History of Education Society Annual Conference, Chicago, October 1998.

Messner, M. A. *Politics of Masculinities: Men in Movements* (Thousand Oaks: Sage, 1997).

Mill, J. S. 'Inaugural Address at St. Andrews,' in Cavenaugh, F. A. (ed.), *James and John Stuart Mill on Education* (London: Cambridge University Press, 1931).

Miller, S. B. *In the Company of Educated Women* (New Haven, CN/London: Yale University Press).

Mitchell, J. L. *The 13th Disciple* (Edinburgh: B and W Publishing, 1995/1931).

Mollenhoff, D. *Madison: A History of the Formative Years* (Dubuque, IA: Kendall/Hunt Publishing Company, 1982).

Morgan, D. H. J. 'Theater of war: combat, the military, and masculinities', in H. Brod and M. Kaufman (eds), *Theorizing Masculinities* (Thousand Oaks: Sage, 1994), pp. 165–82.

Morris Matthews, K. 'For and About Women: women's studies in New Zealand Universities, 1973-1990', Unpublished PhD thesis, University of Waikato, 1993.

— and Jenkins, K. 'Whose country is it anyway? The construction of a new identity through schooling for Maori in Aotearoa/New Zealand', *History of Education*, 28, 3, (1999), pp. 339–50.

Morris, C. *King's College, A Short History* (Cambridge: Printed for King's College, 1989)

Morton, B. *Action 1919–1969: A Record of the Growth of the National Association of Schoolmasters* (Hemel Hempstead: NAS, 1969).

Mosse, E. L. *Fallen Soldiers: Reshaping the Memory of the World Wars* (Oxford: Oxford University Press, 1990).

Mosse, G. L. *The Image of Man: The Creation of Modern Masculinity* (New York: Oxford University Press, 1996).

Mulder, E. *Beginsel en Beroep. Pedagogiek aan de Universiteit in Nederland*

1900–1940 (Amsterdam: University of Amsterdam, 1989).

— 'Patterns, principles, and profession: the early decades of educational science in the Netherlands', *Paedagogica Historica. International Journal of the History of Education*, Special Series III (1998), pp. 231–46.

Munro, P. *Subject to Fiction: Women Teachers' Life History Narratives and the Cultural Politics of Resistance* (Milton Keynes: Open University Press, 1999).

Mussolini, B. 'Trincerocrazia', *Il Popolo d'Italia*, 15 December, (1917)', in R. Griffin (ed.), *Oxford Readers: Fascism* (Oxford: Oxford University Press, 1995), document 5, pp. 28–9.

Myers, C. D. '"Give her the apple and see what comes of it": University Coeducation in Britain and America, c. 1860–1940' Unpublished PhD Thesis, University of Strathclyde, 1999.

National Association of Schoolmasters First Annual Report and Yearbook, (1920) Modern Records Centre, University of Warwick, MSS.38A/4/3/(1).

Newsome, D. *On the Edge of Paradise: A. C. Benson, the Diarist* (Chicago, IL: University of Chicago Press, 1980).

Northey, H. *Auckland Girls' Grammar School: the First Hundred Years 1888–1988* (Auckland: Auckland Grammar School Old Girls' Association).

O'Connell, M. *The Oxford Conspirators; A History of the Oxford Movement 1833–1845* (New York: Macmillan, 1969).

O'Dell, F. *Socialisation through Children's Literature: The Soviet Example* (Cambridge: Cambridge University Press, 1978).

Ollard, R. *An English Education, A Perspective of Eton* (London: Collins, 1982).

Onselen, C. van 'Race and class in South African : rural cultural osmosis and social relations in the sharecropping economy of the South-Western Transvaal, 1900–1950', *American Historical Review*, 95, 1 (1991), pp. 99–123.

Oram, A. '"Men must be educated and women must do it": The National Federation (later Union) of Women Teachers and contemporary feminism, 1910–1930', *Gender and Education*, 2, 2 (1990), pp. 147–67.

— 'Inequalities in the teaching profession: the effect on teachers and pupils, 1910–1939', in F. Hunt (ed.), *Lessons for Life: The Schooling of Girls and Women, 1850–1950* (Oxford: Basil Blackwell, 1987), pp. 101–23.

— *Women Teachers and Feminist Politics, 1900–1939* (Manchester: Manchester University Press, 1996).

— '"To Cook Dinners With Love in Them"?: Sexuality, marital status and women teachers in England and Wales, 1920–1939', in K. Weiler and S. Middleton (eds), *Telling Women's Lives: Narrative Inquiries in the History of Women's Education* (Milton Keynes: Open University Press, 1999), pp. 96–112.

Orlow, D. 'A difficult relationship of unequal relatives: the Dutch NSB and Nazi Germany, 1933–1940', *European History Quarterly*, 29, 3 (1999), pp. 349–80.

Ozment, S. *When Fathers Ruled. Family Life in Reformation Europe* (Cambridge, MA/London: Harvard University Press, 1983).

— *The Bürgemeister's Daughter. Scandal in a Sixteenth-century German Town* (New York: St Martin's Press, 1996).

Pan-Anglican Congress of 1908, *Report of the Women's Meetings* (London, 1908).

Parteitag der N.S.D.A.P. Nürnberg 1933 (Dresden: Lande, 1933).

Partington, G. *Women Teachers in the 20th Century in England and Wales* (Windsor: NFER, 1976).

Pearlman, M. 'To make the university safe for morality: higher education, football and military training from the 1890s through the 1920s', *Canadian Review of American Studies* 12, 1 Spring (1981), pp. 37–56.

Pemberton, J. *On the subject "Java"*, (Ithaca/London: Cornell University Press, 1994).

Perl, S. and Wilson, N. *Through Teachers' Eyes: Portraits of Writing Teachers* (Portsmouth, NH: Heinemann, 1986).

Peukert, D. *Inside Nazi Germany: Conformity, Opposition, and Racism in Everyday Life* (New Haven, CT: Yale University Press, 1987).

Pierotti, A. M. *The Story of the National Union of Women Teachers* (Southend-on-Sea: NUWT, 1963).

Poeze, H. *In het Land der Overheersers: Indonesiërs, 1600–1950*, vol. 1 (Dordrecht: Foris Publications, 1986).

Pratt, M. L. *Imperial Eyes: Travel Writing and Transculturation* (London: Routledge, 1992).

Prentice, A. 'Laying siege to the history professoriate', in B. Boutilier and A. Prentice (eds), *Creating Historical Memory: English Canadian Women and the Work of History* (Toronto: University of Toronto Press, 2000), pp. 197–232.

Price M. and Glenday, N. *Reluctant Revolutionaries: a Century of Headmistresses 1874–1974* (Bath: Pitman, 1974).

Pumphrey, G. H. 'An Elementary School in Germany', *TNS*, December (1938), pp. 11–12.

Pyre, J. F. A. *Wisconsin* (New York: Oxford University Press, 1920).

Rabinow, P. 'Introduction', in M. Foucault, *The Foucault Reader: An*

Introduction to Foucault's Thought, P. Rabinow (ed.) (Harmondsworth: Penguin, 1991), pp. 1–29.

Ralston Saul, J. *The Unconscious Civilization* (Harmondsworth: Penguin, 1997).

Raubstaat England, Reemtsma No. 16 (Hamburg/Bahrenfeld: Cigaretten-Bilderdienst, 1941).

Rawnsley, S. 'The membership of the British Union of Fascists', in K. Lunn and R. Thurlow (eds), *British Fascism* (London: Croom Helm, 1980), pp. 150–65.

Raynaud, C. ' "Rubbing the paragraph with a soft cloth"? Muted voices and editorial constraints in *Dust Tracks on a Road*', in S. Smith and J. Watson (eds), *De/Colonising the Subject: The Politics of Gender in Women's Autobiography* (Minneapolis, MN: University of Minnesota Press, 1992), pp. 34–64.

Reksonegoro, K. 'The Three Sisters', typescript, trans. by Mrs A. King, Satya Wacana Christian University, Salatiga, 1958.

Renton, D. *Fascism: Theory and Practice* (London: Pluto, 1999).

— 'Was Fascism an Ideology? British Fascism Reconsidered', *Race and Class*, 41, 3 (2000), pp. 72–84.

Richter, J. P. *Levana. Wenken voor de Opvoeding van Kinderen voor Ouders en Jonggehuwden* (Amsterdam: Portielje, 1844).

— *Levana oder Erziehlehre*. Besorgt von K. G. Fischer (Paderborn: Schöningh, 1963).

Riley, D. *Am I That Name? Feminism and the Category of 'Women' in History* (London: Macmillan, 1988).

Ripley, B. J. and McHugh, J. *John Maclean* (Manchester: Manchester University Press, 1989).

Ritter, P. H. *Paedagogische Fragmenten* (Utrecht: Beijers, 1888, 2nd edn).

Robinson, W. 'Women and teacher training: women and pupil-teacher centres, 1880–1914', in J. Goodman and S. Harrop (eds), *Women, Educational Policy-Making and Administration in England: Authoritative Women Since 1800* (London: Routledge, 2000), pp. 99–115.

Rohrbach, R. '... *bis zum letzten Atemzuge* ...': *Propaganda in der NS-Zeit. Texte und Materialien zur Ausstellung des Museumsverbundes Südniedersachsen* (Göttingen: Museumsverbund Südniedersachsen, 1995).

Rooy, P. de *Darwin en de Strijd langs vaste Lijnen* (Nijmegen: SUN, 1987).

Roper, J. and Tosh, J. (eds) *Manful Assertions: Masculinities in Britain Since 1800* (London: Routledge, 1991).

Ross A. and Thomson, D. 'The vanishing male maths teacher', *Times*

Educational Supplement, 12 November (1999), p. 24.

Ross, I. *Little Grey Partridge: First World War Diary of Isobel Ross Who Served With the Scottish Women's Hospitals Unit in Serbia*, J. Dixon (ed.), (Aberdeen: Aberdeen University Press, 1988).

Roulston K. and Mills, M. 'Male Teachers in feminised teaching areas: marching to the beat of the Men's Movement drums?', *Oxford Review of Education*, 26, 2 (2000), pp. 221–37.

Rubin, G. 'The traffic in women: notes on the "political economy" of sex', in R. R. Reiter (ed.), *Towards an Anthropology of Women* (New York: Monthly Review Press, 1975), pp. 157–210.

Rubin, G. 'Thinking sex: notes for a radical theory of the politics of sexuality', in H. Abelove, M. A. Barale and D. Halperin, (eds), *The Lesbian and Gay Studies Reader* (New York: Routledge, 1993), pp. 3–44.

Ruhmesblätter Deutscher Geschichte (Dresden: Eckstein-Halpaus, 1934).

Sanderson, M. *The Universities and British Industry 1850–1970* (London: Routledge and Kegan Paul, 1972).

Savage, M., Barlow, J., Dickens. P. and Fielding, T. *Property, Bureaucracy and Culture: Middle-Class Formation in Contemporary Britain* (London: Routledge, 1992).

Schrag, F. 'Why Foucault Now?', *Journal of Curriculum Studies*, 31, 4 (1999), pp. 375–83.

Scott, J. W. *Gender and the Politics of History* (New York: Columbia University Press, 1988).

— 'Experience', in Scott, J. W. (ed.), *Feminist Theorise the Political* (London: Routledge, 1992).

Shor, I. *When Students Have Power: Negotiating Authority in a Critical Pedagogy* (London: The University of Chicago Press, 1996).

Showalter, E. *Daughters of Decadence: Women Writers of the Fin-de-Siècle* (London: Virago, 1993).

Siebörger, R. *New History Textbooks for South Africa: Textbooks and the History Curriculum* (Swaziland: Macmillian Boleswa Manzini).

Simon, B. 'The struggle for hegemony, 1920–1926' in B. Simon (ed.), *The Search for Enlightenment: the Working Class and Adult Education in the Twentieth Century* (London: Lawrence and Wishart, 1990), pp. 15–70.

Simpson, W. B. *In the Highest Degree Odious: Detention Without Trial in Wartime Britain* (Oxford: Oxford University Press, 1994).

Smart, B. *Postmodernity* (London: Routledge, 1993).

Smith, H. L. 'British feminism and the Equal Pay issue in the 1930s', *Women's History Review*, 5, 1 (1996), pp. 97–110.

Smith, S. and Watson, J. (eds), *De/Colonising the Subject: The Politics of Gender in Women's Autobiography* (Minneapolis, MN: University of

Minnesota Press, 1992).

Snell, Lord, *Men, Movements and Myself* (London: J. M. Dent, 1936).

Springhall, J. *Youth, Empire and Society – British Youth Movements 1883–1940* (London: Croom Helm, 1977).

Stanley, L. 'Introduction: on academic borders, territories, tribes and knowledges', in L. Stanley (ed.), *Knowing Feminisms* (London: Sage, 1997).

Steadman, C. *In the Days of Miss Beale: A Study of her Work and Influence* (London: Burrow, 1931).

Stearns, P. N. 'Fatherhood in historical perspective: the role of social change', in F. W. Bozett and S. M. H. Hanson (eds), *Fatherhood and Families in Cultural Context* (New York: Springer, 1991), pp. 28–52.

Steedman, C. *Childhood, Culture and Class in Britain. Margaret McMillan 1860–1931* (London: Virago, 1990).

Sternglass, M. *Time to Know Them: A Longitudinal Study of Writing and Learning at the College Level* (Mahwah, NJ: Lawrence Erlbaum Associates, 1997).

Sternhell, Z. Sznajder M. and Asheri, M. trans. D. Maisel, *The Birth of Fascist Ideology: From Cultural Rebellion to Political Revolution* (Princeton, NJ: Princeton University Press, 1992).

Stocks, M. O. *The WEA: The First Fifty Years* (London: George Allen and Unwin, 1955).

Stoler, A. L. 'Carnal knowledge and imperial power: gender, race and morality in colonial Asia', in J. Wallach Scott (ed.), *Feminism and History* (Oxford: Oxford University Press, 1997), pp. 209–66.

— and Cooper, F. 'Between metropole and colony: rethinking a research agenda', in A. L. Stoler and F. Cooper (eds), *Tensions of Empire: Colonial Cultures in a Bourgeois World* (Berkeley, CA: University of California Press, 1997), pp. 1–58.

Stuurman, S. *Verzuiling, Kapitalisme en Patriarchaat. Aspecten van de Ontwikkeling van de Moderne Staat in Nederland* (Nijmegen: SUN, 1983).

— *Wacht op onze Daden. Het Liberalisme en de Vernieuwing van de Nederlandse Staat* (Amsterdam: Amsterdam University Press, 1992).

Summerfield, P. 'Women and the professional labour market 1900–1950: the case of secondary schoolmistresses', in P. Summerfield (ed.) *Women, Education and the Professions* (Leicester: History of Education Society, Occasional Publication no. 8, 1987), pp. 37–52.

— *Reconstructing Women's Wartime Lives: Discourse and Subjectivity in Oral Histories of the Second World War* (Manchester: Manchester University Press, 1999).

Taylor, J. 'Kartini in her historical context', *Bijdragen*, vol. 145, pp. 295–307.

— 'Once More Kartini,' in L. Sears (ed.), *Autonomous Histories, Particular Truths: Essays in Honour of John Smail* (Madison WI: University of Wisconsin-Madison, 1993).

Thelen, D. P. *The New Citizenship: Origins of Progressivism in Wisconsin, 1885–1900* (Columbia, MO: University of Missouri Press, 1972).

Theobald, M. *Knowing Women: Origins of Women's Education in Nineteenth-Century Australia* (Cambridge: Cambridge University Press, 1996).

Theweliet, K. *Male Fantasies: Women, Floods, Bodies and History*, trans. E. Carter and C. Turner (Cambridge: Polity Press, 1987).

— *Male Fantasies, Male Bodies, Psychoanalyzing the White Terror*, trans. C. Turner, E. Carter and S. Conway (Cambridge: Polity Press, 1989).

Thompson, P. *Socialists, Liberals and Labour, the Struggle for London, 1885–1914* (London: Routledge and Kegan Paul, 1967).

Thorne, W. *My Life's Battles* (London: George Newnes, n.d.).

Tjitrosomo, A. S, 'Dr Sosro Kartono', Sebagai sarjana, nasionalis, patriot, pelopor, pantjasila dan pengemban amanat penderitaan rakjat' (Typescript, KITLV Archive, H.897, 1967 Vreede-de Steurs, Cora, 'Kartini: Feiten en Ficties', *Bijdragen*, 121 (1965), pp 213–44.

Todd, M. *Christian Humanism and the Puritan Social Order* (Cambridge: Cambridge University Press, 1987).

Tolstoy, L. N. *Pedagogical Articles/Linen-Measurer, The Complete Works of Count Tolstoy*, vol iv. (New York: Colonial Press Co., 1904).

Trevor-Roper, H. *Hitler's Table Talk 1941–1944: His Private Conversations* (New York: Enigma, 2000).

Tropp, A. *The School Teachers: The Growth of the Teaching Profession in England and Wales from 1800 to the Present Day* (London: Heinemann, 1957).

Unsere Reichsmarine: Bilder aus dem Leben der Matrosen (Berlin: Caid, 1934).

Vance, M. M. *Charles Richard Van Hise: Scientist Progressive* (Madison, WI: University of Wisconsin Press, 1960).

Vicinus, M. *Independent Women: Work and Community for Single Women 1850–1920* (London: Virago, 1985).

Vickery, A. 'Golden age to separate spheres: a review of the categories and chronology of English women's history, *Historical Journal*, 36, 2 (1993), pp. 384–414.

Vreede-de Steurs, C. 'Kartini: feiten en ficties', *Bijdrapen*, 121 (1965), pp. 213–44.

Vries, P. de *Kuisheid voor Mannen, Vrijheid voor Vrouwen. De Reglementering en Bestrijding van Prostitutie in Nederland, 1850–1911* (Amsterdam: Het Spinhuis, 1997).

Wade, 'The Boy Can't Help It', *Spectator*, 2 September 2000, p. 26.

Walkerdine, V. *Schoolgirl Fictions* (London: Verso, 1990).

Ware, V. 'Defining forces: 'race', gender and memories of empire', in I. Chambers and L. Curti (eds), *The Post-Colonial Question: Common Skies, Divided Horizons* (London: Routledge, 1996), pp. 142–56.

Wasem, E. *Sammeln von Serienbildchen. Entwicklung und Bedeutung eines beliebten Mediums der Reklame und der Alltagskultur* (Landshut: Trausnitz, 1981).

— *Das Serienbild. Medium der Werbung und Alltagskultur* (Dortmund: Harenberg, 1987).

Watts, R. 'Breaking the boundaries of Victorian imperialism or extending a reformed "paternalism"? Mary Carpenter and India', *History of Education*, 19, 5 (2000), pp. 443–56.

Weiler, K. 'Reflections on writing a history of women teachers', in K. Weiler and S. Middleton (eds), *Telling Women's Lives* (Milton Keynes: Open University Press, 1999) pp. 43–59.

— and Middleton, S. (eds) *Telling Women's Lives: Narrative Enquiries in the History of Women's Education* (Milton Keynes: Open University Press, 1999).

Weiner, G. *Feminisms and Education* (Milton Keynes: Open University Press, 1994).

— 'Harriet Martineau and her contemporaries: past studies and methodological questions on historical surveys of women', *History of Education*, 29, 5 (2000), pp. 389–404.

Weis, L. and Fine, M. *Beyond Silenced Voices: Class, Race, and Gender in United States Schools* (Albany, NY: State University of New York Press, 1993).

Wells, H. G. *Travels of a Republic Radical in Search of Hot Water* (Harmondsworth: Penguin, 1939).

West, R. 'The Working Women's College', *The Clarion*, 14 February 1913.

Weltkriegsbilder 1914–1918 (Obercunnersdorf: Reunion, 1933).

Wetherall M. and Griffin, C. 'Feminist psychology and the study of men and masculinity, part 1: assumptions and perspectives', *Feminism and Psychology*, 1, 3 (1992), pp. 361–91.

Whitlock G. *The Intimate Empire: Reading Women's Autobiography* (London/New York: Cassell, 2000).

Wie die Anderen gerüstet sind! . . . trotz vertraglicher Abröstungspflicht (Bremen: Yosma, 1934).

Wie die Ostmark ihre Befreiung erlebte: Adolf Hitler und sein Weg zu Großdeutschland (München: Austria, 1940).

William Johnson Cory 1823–1892 (Cambridge: Rampant Lions Press, 1959).

Willis, R. 'W. B. Hodgson and educational interest groups in Victorian Britain', *History of Education Society Bulletin*, 67 (2001), pp. 41–50.

Winston, R. 'A Pleasing Valediction', *TNS*, January (1922), p. 27.

Witz, A. *Professions and Patriarchy* (London: Routledge, 1992).

Wolff, E. *Proeve over de Opvoeding, aan de Nederlandsche Moeders* (Meppel/Amsterdam: Boom, 1977; orig. 1779).

Wollacott, A. 'Sisters and brothers in arms: family, class, and gendering in World War I Britain', in M. Cooke and A. Wollacott (eds), *Gendering War Talk* (Princeton, NJ: Princeton University Press, 1995), pp. 128–47.

Woolf, V. *A Room of One's Own* (New York: Harcourt Brace Jovanovich Inc., 1929).

Wortham, H. E. *Victorian Eton and Cambridge – Being the Life and Times of Oscar Browning* (London: Constable and Co. Ltd., 1927).

Yeo, S. 'A new life: the religion of socialism in Britain, 1833–1896', *History Workshop*, 4 (1977), pp. 5–56.

Yorkshire Factory Times, 1916.

Young, R. J. G. *Colonial Desire: Hybridity in Theory, Culture and Race* (London: Routledge, 1995).

Young, W. H. 'An Open Letter to the President', *TNS*, December (1932), p. 31.

Zeppelin-Welt Fahrten (Dresden: Greiling, 1993).

Zuill, R. *In Pursuit of Excellence, 1894–1994. The Bermuda High School for Girls* (Toronto: University of Toronto Press, 1995).

Index